# The Political Economy of Institutional Change in the Electricity Supply Industry

To my family, and especially my wife,
without whose faith this book would never have seen the light.

# The Political Economy of Institutional Change in the Electricity Supply Industry

Shifting Currents

Carlos Rufín

*Babson College, Wellesley, Massachusetts, USA*

Foreword by William W. Hogan

**Edward Elgar**

Cheltenham, UK • Northampton, MA, USA

Published by
Edward Elgar Publishing Limited
Glensanda House
Montpellier Parade
Cheltenham
Glos GL50 1UA
UK

Edward Elgar Publishing, Inc.
136 West Street
Suite 202
Northampton
Massachusetts 01060
USA

A catalogue record for this book
is available from the British Library

**Library of Congress Cataloguing in Publication Data**

Rufin, Carlos, 1964–
      The political economy of institutional change in the electricity supply
    industry: shifting currents/Carlos Rufin; foreword by William W. Hogan.
         p. cm.
      Includes bibliographical references and index.
      1. Electric utilities—Economic aspects. 2. Electric utilities—
    Government policy. 3. Structural adjustment (Economic policy). I. Title.
    HD9685.A2R83    2003
    333.793'2—dc21

                                                              2003052825

ISBN 1 84376 203 X

Printed and bound in Great Britain by MPG Books Ltd, Bodmin, Cornwall

# Contents

# Figures and tables

## FIGURES

## TABLES

# Foreword

## William W. Hogan

Institutional change is seldom easy. Transformational institutional change can be even more complicated and marked by unexpected difficulties. The fundamental requirements for success are poorly understood and often underestimated. This is particularly true for the many economic reforms associated with the triumph of capitalism, leading to increased reliance on markets and decreased reliance on governments. Perhaps the most dramatic illustration of recent experience is the continuing saga of the movement from a stultified command-and-control economy in the former Soviet Union, through a complex and extended transition, towards the goal of enjoying a 'normal' economy. In the naïve early days just after Mikhail Gorbachev, many argued that government should simply get out of the way, and the magic of the market would take over. Soon hard lessons piled up about the importance of the rule of law, courts, contracts, financial intermediaries, and even regulation. Those who spoke of a transition period measured in generations now appear prescient. The problem of institutional transformation was not just narrowly economic, it was political economy broadly writ.

Almost in parallel, there have been movements in many countries to transform the electricity supply industry. Motivated by different histories, reinforced by the *zeitgeist* in support of markets, and precipitated by critical innovations in technology, first Chile, then England and Wales, soon Norway, and then many countries from the Americas to the Antipodes made electricity restructuring a major growth industry. Predictably, the requirements for restructuring appeared to many to be relatively straightforward. In the United States, for example, many claimed that introduction of markets had been easy in the natural gas industry, and the same would be true in electricity supply. Basically, government would just have to get out of the way. The details of the specific arrangements needed within the new electricity supply industry seemed not to matter much. The institutional context of the background of culture, government, and economics was hardly considered.

Two years into the new millennium, this optimistic view about simple institutional transformation in electricity supply seemed at least misplaced, and the whole enterprise faced a counter-revolution. The egregious market implosion in California shocked everyone. Pacific Gas and Electric, the largest utility in the United States, declared bankruptcy. Enron, the largest energy trader and most vigorous advocate for electricity markets around the world, disappeared in disgrace less than a year later. The booming electricity trading industry that Enron had championed everywhere suddenly shrank to near extinction under accounting scandals and credit crises. In Brazil, a hydroelectric shortage precipitated a political reaction, and electricity restructuring reversed course. Lesser problems elsewhere sobered most if not all governments and regulators as they realized that institutional transformation in the electricity sector would not be easy, would require much more than just getting out of the way, and might not succeed.

What went wrong? Was greater reliance on markets for electricity a mistake? The jury is still out on the latter question. Some of the reformed electricity markets were working well. Renewed efforts in Europe, the United States, Australia, New Zealand, Mexico, and so on, saw governments working diligently to diagnose the failures and propose reforms of the reforms. Although the final policy outcome remained uncertain, one thing was certain. The policy evaluation would benefit from more and better research to understand what went wrong and what would be needed to achieve success.

The topic of institutional change in the electricity supply industry is one that has received relatively little formal attention, although nearly everyone has armchair theories about the forces that motivate and drive such microeconomic reform. In the case of electricity, the usual problems of balancing gains and losses interact with important technology constraints that impose large externalities. Major serious scholarship has been targeted largely at analysis of the special problems and detailed institutions within the electricity supply industry. These involve important matters such as the specification of trading rules, design of spot market protocols and pricing, or the scope of regulation by government. The literature is building, and a clearer picture is emerging about arcane matters in electricity market design.

But as with the parallel case of the former Soviet system, there has been much less analysis of the larger questions of the economic, political and cultural setting that provides the context for electricity restructuring and may strongly influence what needs to be done or how certain we can be of success. Now comes Carlos Rufin's contribution to this task. This broader research agenda, the political economy of institutional transformation, is the target of the present volume. What drives the use of public versus private property? What explains the choice of mechanisms used to allocate resources? How important is independence of the judiciary, or the power of technocratic elites? Does ideology influence or determine the outcomes? Or is the big story about distributional conflict?

Rufín tackles these problems in the specific case of electricity restructuring, but the book is cast as part of the larger literature on the political economy of institutional change ranging from sector policies to macroeconomic reform. The methodological approach is systematic and eclectic. In the terminology of research design, Rufín provides an example of triangulation. The problem is too complex to yield to any one narrow piece of evidence or analysis. Complementary approaches provide different attacks on the overarching questions, and each provides an important piece of the larger puzzle.

After summarizing the literature to set out both the history and the research questions, Rufín begins the project by presenting an explicit and testable theory of the major influences and their interactions. The model incorporates stylized representations of the behavior of public enterprises, consumer electoral preferences, electoral platform choices of political parties, and side payments by production factors to political parties. The resulting game-theoretic analysis yields predictions of directional effect and relative magnitude.

An attraction of this book is in this systematic development of a theory and then testing of the theory using a variety of empirical approaches. The empirical work is decidedly multidisciplinary and comparative. First there is a 'large N' study across 80 countries. Rufín translates the predictions of his model into measurable proxies that make the predictions operational. He then constructs a large data set, itself a contribution to the research enterprise. This allows tests of the theory using techniques of multivariate statistical analysis. Of course, familiar concerns arise about the internal and external validity of the proxies, and the inherent limitations introduced by the simplifications needed to formalize the ideas using restricted data that can be obtained and compared for many countries.

Awareness of the problems inherent in any such statistical analysis of a cross-country model leads to the complementary 'small N' but in-depth case studies of four countries. Rufín explains the rationale for choosing the examples of electricity restructuring experience to approximate a research design with the maximum differences and controls that can be achieved with only four cases. The four countries are Argentina, Bolivia, Brazil, and Chile. The case studies produce a rich and complex story that extends over connected chapters. The voluminous detail provides some tests and many implications for the larger theory. The usual concern with case studies, that small samples and inadequate controls compromise the validity of the conclusions, recedes given the care of the analysis and the confirming support of the companion statistical work. Collectively, the evidence is convincing. For example, Rufin makes a strong case for his idea that ideology matters.

Not satisfied with a strictly positivist approach of careful research to pose a question, gather data and test a theory, Rufin turns towards policy analysis, or at least prediction, by addressing the case of Mexico. Motivated by a need for greater private foreign direct investment in the electricity supply industry, the Mexican government has been working towards a plan to restructure the industry and remove the government as the guarantor of financing for new generation capacity and related infrastructure. This is an ambitious effort and a daunting challenge given that Mexico's history honors the electricity supply industry with a special constitutional stature. Rufin applies his research to develop insights into the prospects for this nascent reform. His model provides an explanation of the slow progress of Mexican reform and identifies ingredients that would support optimism about the potential for a successful transformation.

This book should be read in Mexico City, and throughout Latin America by anyone interested in these countries. Everyone involved in electricity restructuring in any country would learn from this research and could draw parallels that apply to very different settings. A related audience would be scholars concerned with the broader political economy of institutional transformation, of which this is an important and informative instance. And young scholars could study the use of triangulation to exploit and blend quantitative and qualitative analysis for a rigorous attack on a complex mosaic of problems.

Institutional change is seldom easy. However, research such as this should help in a major way to keep expectations connected to reality and to provide guidance that points to hidden assumptions about the fertility of the field of reform and unintended consequences of planting before the ground is prepared.

# Acknowledgments

Many people have played an important role in my decision to pursue a PhD and have helped along the difficult way of the dissertation. Early on, many friends led with their example: Oliver Attie, Edward Wendt, Ines Ravasini, Alfred Vernis, and not least, Ismael Castiella, who showed me that it was never too late to get on with one's education. Nader Nezam-Mafi has also shown me that a PhD is feasible, and kept my spirits up during hard times. At Harvard, at work, and beyond, I have been fortunate to enjoy the friendship and intellectual stimulation of Pasha Mahmood. Harvard faculty, past and present, have also contributed in no small measure to this endeavor, beginning with Ashutosh Varshney and going on to my dissertation committee members, Richard Caves, Jorge Domínguez and Joseph Kalt. All three of them, and even more my advisor and committee chair, William Hogan, have been extremely gracious in correcting numerous drafts, making important suggestions, and being supportive of my efforts. The Harvard Electricity Policy Group, led by Ashley Brown, very kindly allowed me to partake of its extensive bibliographical resources and research seminars. I benefited financially from the Joseph R. Crump Fellowship awarded by the Center for Business and Government at Harvard University's John F. Kennedy School of Government. The Director of the Center's Environment and Natural Resources Program, Henry Lee, helped with his extensive knowledge and experience with the electricity supply industry. At Babson, Srinivasa Rangan has not only been extremely supportive: his sharp insight and tireless exploration of new ideas and possibilities has greatly helped me improve the quality of the reasoning presented here and extend it in new directions through collaborative ventures; Rajesh Kumar has also brought fresh perspectives to my work, as a co-author in other endeavors and in numerous conversations while he was visiting Babson. Lastly, three persons deserve a special mention: Peter Johnson, who kept alive in me the desire for learning and for a life that reached beyond material rewards; Steve Anderson, whose concern, dedication, and support went far beyond the extraordinary; and my wife Sandra, who patiently put up with this longest of pregnancies.

# 1.  Introduction

The last decade has witnessed the emergence of great interest among all the social sciences in the study of institutions.  More specifically, economists and political scientists like Douglass North have begun to explore the impact of key economic institutions, such as property rights and market exchange, on economic growth and development.  This trend has been paralleled by an unprecedented amount of institutional experimentation and innovation throughout the world.  Privatization and deregulation, including the large-scale changes occurring in the former socialist economies, have dramatically highlighted the role of institutions in fostering investment in human and physical capital.  These changes have also exposed our limited knowledge about the design of such institutions and even more about the forces that shape institutions over time.  Despite an enormous literature on privatization, our understanding of the forces that are shaping institutional changes in infrastructure sectors is still very limited.

This book seeks to shed some light on the process of institutional change by examining two key economic institutions, property rights and competition, in a particular industry (the electricity supply industry, or ESI) where they are embodied in formal rules and organizations, but where new organizational possibilities are rapidly emerging.[1]  By looking at such an industry through a limited set of cases, our understanding of actual institutional dynamics should be enhanced.  In turn, increased knowledge about such processes will allow us to suggest institutional innovations that are both politically sustainable and capable of releasing the economic potential of different countries around the world.

The programs of macroeconomic stabilization undertaken in the aftermath of the financial crises of the 1980s have been followed in developing and industrialized countries alike by a 'second wave' of reforms seeking to promote a more efficient use of economic resources to foster growth and development – in other words, microeconomic reforms.  Far from being sheltered from such reform efforts because of high sunk investment and natural monopoly conditions, infrastructure sectors such as electricity, natural gas, water and sanitation, communications, and transport, have constituted the core of the reform programs; in fact, the ESI has arguably been in many cases the 'flagship' showing the way for change, together with the telecommunications industry.[2]  Along the same lines as the other infrastructure sectors, reforms have profoundly altered the ESI's institutional framework. More specifically, the industry has been restructured in a large number of countries through the deregulation of price and other controls imposed on electric utilities (subsequent to the separation of the industry into segments considered contestable, particularly electricity generation, from those subject to natural monopoly), and the privatization of state-owned electricity companies.

Given the enormous impact of this industry as a key input to economic activity, on domestic and international capital flows, and on the environment, ESI restructuring is important by itself. But in this industry, the institutional framework plays such a crucial role that it provides an excellent setting for analyzing processes of institutional change. The physical and technological characteristics of electricity production, transmission/distribution and use, together with its visibility as the source of a key input in modern industrial economies, pose the key institutional design challenges of the ESI. Electricity generation, transmission and distribution facilities are highly capital-intensive, durable, and immovable. In the cases of transmission and distribution, economies of scale and high sunk costs create conditions of natural monopoly, where a single network of facilities can provide transmission or distribution services more efficiently than duplicative systems. Furthermore, electricity is nonstorable and there are important network externalities in its use, which reinforce the advantages of monopoly and vertical integration over competition and contractual transactions. As a result, the institutional framework of the ESI revolves around two paramount matters: the problem of organizing investment in electricity supply when, once carried out, such investment can be appropriated by others without loss of its economic value; and the problem of limiting the allocative inefficiencies arising from monopoly power. One of the most remarkable features of the wave of reforms in the ESI during the 1990s has been the variety of outcomes of the reform process observed around the world.[3] This study therefore aims to explain these differences and in this way gain a better understanding of the dynamics of institutional change. Since the two key dimensions of the organization of the ESI concern ownership and resource allocation mechanisms, institutional change is analyzed by considering two major questions:

1. What explains the degree of reliance on public versus private property in the reorganization of the ESI in countries where ESI restructuring has taken place?

2. What explains the choice of mechanisms used to allocate resources (competition versus monopoly) in the ESI in countries that have restructured this industry?

Three variables are proposed in this book to answer the two research questions: institutional constraints (mainly judicial independence), ideology, and distributional conflict. To some extent, these factors are suggested by existing and current research on institutional change from various disciplinary perspectives, including research on the specific case of the ESI. However, different disciplines tend to emphasize different factors, leading to incomplete explanations of institutional change. By taking a multidisciplinary perspective, this book overcomes such limitations. In order to understand more precisely the contribution made by the book, we need to understand the current state of the art in greater detail. We therefore turn to this task before describing the organization of the book.

## CURRENT RESEARCH ON INSTITUTIONAL CHANGE

In contrast to the extensive attention devoted in recent years to the political economy of macroeconomic adjustment, relatively little has been written on the 'second wave' of reforms outside the issue of privatization *per se*. This is all the more baffling when we consider that second-wave reforms like deregulation could well have a more important long-term effect than cuts in government spending or foreign debt renegotiation, because second-wave reforms are altering the institutional framework in which economic activity takes place – in other words, the rules of the economic game. Although privatization – a policy with both macro- and microeconomic impacts – has been the subject of countless books and papers, it has generally been treated within the context of macro reform (such as measures to control public sector deficits) rather than the strengthening of property rights. Only in the case of former socialist economies have microeconomic aspects like property rights been the focus of scholarly analyses, but second-wave reforms have affected most non-socialist economies as well. This book helps fill this research gap by examining the reforms of property rights and regulation of economic activity through a variety of analytical lenses – formal modeling, econometrics and case-study comparisons – in the context of the ESI.

The literature relating to the question of institutional change can be divided into several strands that address different issues. A first subset of research is highly theoretical and corresponds to the economic analysis of competition and regulation. A second strand can be grouped under the label of the 'new institutionalism,' and covers a number of contributions from sociology, economics and political science regarding the emergence, role, and transformation of the institutions that govern economic exchange. Finally, there are a growing number of empirical studies of privatization and deregulation both in the electricity sector and in other policy areas.

The economic contribution to the analysis of electricity sector restructuring has a strong normative bent. It concerns mainly the study of conditions under which competitive markets are viable, and the design of regulatory mechanisms. The first topic addressed by economists is the impact of technological change on the range of possible institutional arrangements for the electricity industry, by making competition viable where it was hitherto not the case. Advances in generation technology that have decreased economies of scale are by now well understood and thus do not require further comment. The implications of new technology are, of course, one of the themes of this book, so the reader is referred to the next chapter, where a theoretical model is developed to explore such implications. The second topic, which falls under the label of 'mechanism design', attempts to devise efficient means of attaining policy objectives in the face of strategic behavior by firms, workers, or other counterparts to regulatory and exchange transactions. Within this branch, there are a substantial number of papers dealing specifically with the problem of designing regulatory mechanisms for firms, such as utilities, which enjoy monopoly franchises and superior information about their market or their production costs (Baron 1988; Laffont and Tirole 1993). The highly normative nature of this literature, however, contrasts with the questions addressed in this book, which are eminently positive, concerning the determinants of actual institutional mechanisms.

Another important set of theories fall under the label of the 'new institutionalism', although often their only common characteristic is the interest in the emergence, reproduction, and modification of institutions. Although exact definitions of 'institution' vary among the scholars included here, the meaning of the term in this book follows North (1990: 3–4). Institutions are defined as the formal and informal arrangements setting out the rules of economic and political exchange in a society, such as constitutions and parliamentary rules, norms of business conduct, or private organizations created to address collective action problems.

The importance of the new institutionalist literature lies in its contribution to our understanding of the 'life cycle' of institutions: how they are created, as Ostrom (1990) describes for common-pool resource problems like water use; or maintained, through the re-enactment of explicit or implicit norms of behavior by different actors, as the sociological approach emphasizes; or transformed, as North and others have investigated. The explicit attention of this literature towards these issues has produced a number of case studies and theoretical frameworks for establishing hypotheses about the emergence of new institutions of resource allocation and exchange in the electricity industry.

The neoclassical approach to institutions is best represented by North's earlier work (North and Thomas 1973). In the neoclassical view, institutions are seen as emerging from competition among states or autonomous political entities for power and territory. It is argued that the institutions of the developed countries have historically arisen as the most efficient ones, that is the ones that minimize transaction costs, because lower transaction costs have enabled these countries to improve upon their rivals in international economic and political competition.

The neoclassical perspective on institutions has been shown to be incorrect in portraying political competition as equivalent to economic competition, most famously by North himself in his more recent work (1990), where he carefully examines the persistence of inefficient institutions in the Hispanic world. Competition appears to be a weaker force in political processes than in economic ones, as the former are driven by other factors too, such as identity (for example, cultural, racial, religious, national), organizational capability, ideology, and so forth. The result is that inefficient institutions like the political structures of the Spanish empire survived for long periods despite their condition. Even if competition plays a role in the trajectory of institutions, it may not be a sufficient explanation because the 'competitive' game among various institutions may have multiple equilibria. In such a case, other factors ('history') will play a role in the selection of the actual institutional arrangement that we observe. Institutions may display path dependence (Aoki 2001: 16).

Sociologists, on the other hand, have tended to fall into the opposite extreme of attributing institutions to purely irrational processes, in contrast to the assumption of rational, maximizing rulers of the neoclassical theory of institutions. The best-known sociological formulations of institutional dynamics, in the papers included in Powell and DiMaggio (1991) and in Scott and Meyer (1994), consider institutions as pure myths, devoid of any rational justification for their rules and content, and owing their existence solely to the need for predictability felt by boundedly rational humans in a chaotic world. Although this is clearly an extreme view, symbolic or cultural elements cannot be altogether ignored in explaining institutional dynamics, particularly if human rationality is viewed as bounded.

The theory of repeated noncooperative games has led to the emergence of 'positive political economy' models of institutional outcomes. The consideration of a time dimension, in particular, has notably increased the explanatory power of this type of model (for example, Horn 1995). In a series of papers, Spiller (1993, 1996) has developed specific models of institutional change in the ESI and similar industries such as telecommunications. The major limitation of this approach is that, having originated in reference to the US political system, it is often naïvely extended to other political systems where behavioral patterns are very different. For instance, Spiller's (1996) finding that a constitutional system of separation of powers, and more generally situations of political conflict, make delegation of power to courts and specialized agencies more likely, may be true in a system like that in the US, where repeated interaction of individual legislators among themselves and with the executive create powerful pressures for consensus and compromise.[4] But in a polarized polity, the best strategy may be the opposite of delegation – to try to control as much of the apparatus of government as possible in order to wield its power against political opponents. Another important instance of a problematic extension of US congressional models is the paper by Heller and McCubbins (1996) on the electricity restructuring programs in Chile and Argentina. The focus of the paper on veto points and other constitutional limitations is inappropriate in political systems where constitutional rules do not necessarily reflect a stable political equilibrium, but are still largely open for bargaining.

Uncertainty over the stability of political equilibria brings us, in fact, to a more general strand of positive political economy that, transcending the US framework, examines the effects of uncertainty on policy and institutional outcomes. Uncertainty can be expected to accelerate the delegation of power to courts and specialized agencies because politicians eager to implement certain policies may miss their chance if they wait, either due to the loss of elections or the breakup of coalition governments (or of executive–legislative bargains), as Horn (1995) has pointed out. Since political uncertainty is a much more general characteristic of political systems than the particular conditions examined by the US-centered literature, it offers a more promising and important insight into the nature of institutional change.[5]

Transaction cost economics (for example, Williamson 1985) has also contributed greatly to our understanding of the institutions of market exchange, by pointing attention to the role of asset specificity, bounded rationality and opportunism in the emergence of economic institutions. In recent years, this framework has also been applied to the political sphere as 'transaction cost politics' (Dixit 1996; Epstein and O'Halloran 1999). It is especially applicable to the ESI, in which asset specificity is a key characteristic and opportunistic asset appropriation a major problem. As already mentioned, the perspective followed in this book takes bounded rationality into consideration. It is only natural, then, that transaction cost analysis greatly informs the analysis presented in subsequent chapters. Following the work of Dixit (1996) and Grossman and Helpman (1996 1998), the political transactions involved in the choice of an institutional framework for the ESI are analyzed by means of a formal model in the next chapter. The model thus extends the framework of transaction cost politics to the context of infrastructure sectors.

Empirical studies of restructuring do not abound, in part because of the still nascent experience of electricity sector restructuring throughout the world, but also in part because policy implementation has been relatively neglected as a subject of study. Although there are excellent studies of ESI restructuring by Vickers and Yarrow (1988), Armstrong et al. (1994), and Newbery (1999), they are, like other such studies written from an economic perspective, focused on the results of reforms regarding productive efficiency and welfare, not on the political economy of the reforms. In fact, the political economy of judicial and quasi-judicial institutions, which are a key element of the US regulatory system, lies largely unexplored for other countries.[6] On the other hand, extensive attention has been given to macroeconomic adjustment, since these processes have affected a large number of countries over the last 15 years (Suleiman and Waterbury 1990; Haggard and Kaufman 1992). The value of the adjustment literature for the problem at hand is both methodological and theoretical.

On the methodological side, the strongly comparative bent of these studies, and their reliance on case studies, illustrate the value of case comparisons as a form of empirical research and testing of theoretical propositions. At the same time, this literature has greatly enriched theoretical research through a number of inductive lessons. Chief among them is the emphasis on the role of politically insulated technocratic elites – who can push consistent reform programs and resist pressures to modify or reverse the reforms – in the implementation of successful macroeconomic reform packages. Since these technocratic elites have generally had training in economics as taught mainly in English and US universities, this finding only reinforces the need to pay attention to ideology when studying microeconomic reforms. In addition, the importance of insulation from political pressures suggests that politically insulated entities, like technocratic agencies or the courts, may play a role at the micro level too. Of course, macroeconomic adjustment may differ substantially from microeconomic reform in political visibility, type and nature of opposition, technical complexity, and so forth, so the application of the macro lessons to the micro level requires careful substantiation.

Several conclusions can be drawn from this brief literature review concerning the questions about institutional change pursued here. The discussion of the neoclassical view on institutions showed that efficiency cannot be the guiding principle of institutional change. This means that theories such as mechanism design, while potentially useful as blueprints, explain little about actual changes, which are unlikely to be driven by considerations of welfare optimality. On the other hand, the emphasis of the neoclassical approach on competition suggests other possibilities; in particular, it calls for attention to the influence on institutional change of competition among rational actors for political office and for economic resources. Knight (1992) proposes a theory of institutional change based on conflict over the distributional consequences of different institutional arrangements. Knight's insight is developed below through an explicit derivation of the distributional impacts of alternative institutional choices on the various actors involved in the policymaking process.

We have also seen that sociological formulations of institutional dynamics stress the importance of symbolic or cultural elements, and thus suggest that ideology be taken into account as a powerful determinant of institutional choices. This book builds on the sociological perspective and on the more recent work of North and other new institutionalists. It does so by considering ideology, in the form of preferences that may differ from economic self-interest, perhaps because bounded rationality makes economic and political actors choose on the basis of routines reflecting stylized and incomplete views of the world rather than on a comprehensive economic calculus. The institutionalist perspective is also taken into consideration regarding the importance of path dependence. This is accomplished by examining the role of institutional constraints, inherited from the past, in the process of institutional change.

Positive political economy models offer the formal framework of game theory for purposes of modeling the interactions of the participants in the process of institutional change. The rigor of formal modeling can in turn help us establish the logic of these interactions. At the same time, the emphasis of much of the literature emanating from this perspective on formal rules is, as we have seen, inappropriate for settings where formal rules may be regularly bypassed or changed. As suggested by transaction cost politics, uncertainty about the rules of the political game, and hence inability to commit to future courses of action, can have powerful effects on institutional change. The challenge of modeling institutional change from a positive political economy viewpoint is thus to preserve the rigor while incorporating the insights of transaction cost analysis. The theoretical model underlying this book responds to these matters through the explicit analysis of bargaining over institutional change in settings characterized by commitment limitations and thus significant uncertainty about future outcomes.

Lastly, the empirical studies of macroeconomic adjustment provide a rich vein of comparative analysis on processes of fundamental economic and institutional change, as well as underscoring the importance of ideology and insulation from politics. The caveat applicable to these studies is the fact that the visibility, solutions and effects of macroeconomic adjustment may differ in significant ways from micro-level reform. The conclusions from studies of macroeconomic reform may therefore fail to apply to microeconomic reform in a general way. An important exception is Grindle and Thomas's (1991) set of case studies of different types of reforms from a public management perspective, which highlights the role of leaders' ideologies as well as leadership itself, in the implementation of reform programs in developing countries.

In sum, the literature on institutional change is hampered by the reliance on different analytic approaches and a limited empirical record. This book seeks to fill some of the gaps in the existing research, by developing and testing a model of institutional change that incorporates insights from the new institutionalism (ideology, distributional conflict, path dependence), from positive political economy (formal modeling, institutional constraints), from transaction cost politics (bounded rationality, opportunism, lack of commitment), and from studies of macroeconomic reform (role of ideology and distributional impacts). In addition, I use several complementary methodologies – formal analysis, cross-sectional tests, and case studies – to shed light on the determinants of institutional change in the electricity supply industry. The methodological approach is the subject of the next section.

## METHODOLOGICAL APPROACH

The approach followed in the book is multidisciplinary in methodology and disciplinary content, as well as comparative in scope, but focused at the same time on a specific type of economic activity, the production and distribution of electrical energy. As a work of political economy, the book spans economics and political science, drawing on theoretical perspectives and scholarly writing from both disciplines. In this sense, it transcends research written purely from either field, which tends to ignore important contributions from the other side of the academic divide, and follows Aoki's (2001: 3) call for a comparative institutional analysis that is at the same time rigorous, comparative, and historically informed. But the interdisciplinary approach taken in the book goes beyond content and involves methodology too. Because different methodologies can highlight different aspects of a given problem, the book follows several approaches to achieve a fuller treatment of the subject at hand. The use of a formal model to derive theoretical implications sharpens the logical consistency of the explanatory framework. Econometric analysis allows a systematic examination of data from a variety of countries around the world. Finally, case studies provide the detail and subtlety that statistical methods lack. In addition, the case studies are organized on a comparative basis for several Latin American cases (following a 'most similar systems design' approach[7]) in order to allow a rigorous empirical analysis even when dealing with qualitative information. In fact, the book's focus on a single economic activity responds to the same methodological concern for rigor by minimizing the need for controls in the empirical analyses due to technological differences across economic sectors. It is important to emphasize, in any case, that the theoretical approach developed in the book is applicable to many different sectors that have been organized in the past on a monopolistic, public ownership basis, such as telecommunications, water and sewerage, railroads, and oil and gas pipelines, among others.

## ORGANIZATION OF THE BOOK

After this introductory chapter, which presents the research questions in the context of recent and current research in political economy, privatization, and deregulation, the second chapter provides the theoretical grounding of the main research hypotheses. This is accomplished by means of a positive political economy model of the behavior of public enterprise, consumer electoral preferences, electoral platform choices of political parties, and side payments by production factors ('suppliers') to political parties. This model is used to analyze the political economy of choices among three alternative institutional arrangements: competition among private firms, private monopoly, or public enterprise monopoly. The analysis of the political 'game' played by these actors shows that policy outcomes can be expected to be biased in favor of public enterprise, because consumers and suppliers benefit from its behavior through subsidized prices and supply contracts, respectively. Voter and politician ideologies can temper or exacerbate this logic, however, while competition for economic spoils increases the likelihood of public enterprise by inducing suppliers to offer higher side payments to politicians, so as to capture the rents available in public enterprise supply contracts. Lastly, a weak judiciary can also make public enterprise likelier, but it creates uncertainty about parties' future actions and therefore it lowers the effectiveness of supplier side payments.

These causal factors – ideology, competition for rents, and institutional constraints – speak to existing theories of institutional change. New institutionalist perspectives emphasize the role of pre-existing factors, like a country's past history of judicial independence, or that of international forces such as pro-market ideology. Transaction cost economics suggests that economic institutions often emerge from bargaining among actors about the potential rents to be extracted under the new set of rules. Neoclassical economics also regards competition among different actors or groups as a major driver of institutional change. These fundamental factors are appropriate candidates for explanation in many developing countries, where constitutional rules and other political arrangements are too fluid to impose a significant constraint on institutional reform processes.

Chapter 3 tests the conclusions derived from the theoretical model for the ESI on a cross-section of more than 80 countries. Coding is used to compute composite scores for observed outcomes with regard to reliance on competition versus monopoly and on private versus public ownership of production assets. Multiple indicators for the hypothesized explanatory variables are aggregated using factor analysis. Ordinary least squares (OLS) regressions show that ideology plays an important role in both competition and property outcomes, and to a lesser extent, distributional conflict, while judicial independence does not in general have a clear effect.

The next three chapters examine the validity of the research hypotheses yielded by the formal model of Chapter 2 by means of a comparison of the process of restructuring of the ESI in Argentina, Bolivia, Brazil, and Chile. The focus on a single sector in four Latin American cases allows a systematic investigation of the theoretical conclusions by controlling for major technological and cultural differences that can otherwise lower the reliability of case-oriented approaches. Chapter 4 is descriptive in nature, offering a systematic comparison of the changes effected in the four countries under study. Chapter 5 presents the hypothesized explanatory factors as present in each one of the cases, while Chapter 6 looks in depth at cause and effect to draw conclusions from the comparison of the cases. The case studies show that ideology plays a major role in shaping the outcomes of the institutional change process; distributional conflict, or the conflict over the economic rents that can be extracted from the electricity industry, also has a significant influence on institutional change, although somewhat weaker than ideology; finally, the degree of judicial independence in a country can affect institutional transformation with regard to property rights, but not with regard to the degree of reliance on competitive mechanisms of resource allocation.

The seventh chapter of the book ties all of the previous material together, to recapitulate the major insights from the theoretical and empirical research, extend it to other cases and industries, point out its limitations, and suggest avenues for further work on the subject. A major section of this chapter applies the book's analytical framework to current initiatives for ESI reform in Mexico, in order to derive some predictions about the likelihood and shape of change in the Mexican electricity sector. Finally, Appendix 1 provides a summary of the data used in the statistical tests, and Appendix 2, of a methodological nature, explains how the independent and dependent variables are operationalized for purposes of empirical testing in the case studies.

## NOTES

1. Aoki (2001: 13) rightly argues that legal and regulatory changes *per se* are not institutions until they actually have an influence on the behavior of persons and organizations. It should be noted that the transformations under consideration here go far beyond changes in statutes; they involve massive changes in asset ownership and control, in financial flows among buyers and sellers of electrical energy, and in many other dimensions beyond the content of legal codes.
2. Telecommunications reforms, however, have been as much pulled by technological change as pushed by the search for greater economic efficiency; the emergence of wireless communications technologies has rendered fixed-line networks increasingly obsolete and dramatically lowered the natural monopoly and sunk-cost problems in the industry.
3. As two World Bank analysts with extensive worldwide involvement in ESI restructuring remark, 'Although many countries have expressed some dissatisfaction with the operation of their state-owned power sector, there has been a wide range of responses to the problems perceived ... The variety of responses that have already emerged globally is one of the most striking features of the power sector in the past decade' (Bacon and Besant-Jones 2001: 2).
4. The argument goes as follows: more intense conflict will result in more ambiguous legislation as a means of gaining support from the different interests, and it will make reversing existing legislation more difficult, as the cost of passing laws will be higher. Ambiguity and high reversal costs combine to push decisions into the hands of 'technocratic' agencies and the courts.
5. The formal model developed by Epstein and O'Halloran (1999) shows that greater uncertainty about the *outcomes* of an agency's work leads to greater delegation by Congress to the executive; their model, however, deals exclusively with executive–legislative relations in the US context, so it is less appropriate to analyze the issues in this book of 'delegation' by the government to independent actors through privatization and deregulation in a more general setting. The issue of uncertainty about outcomes is not considered in the theoretical model below, which assumes outcomes are deterministic and known to all actors; however, it is an important issue that is left for future research.
6. The World Bank is sponsoring research on judicial reform as part of its focus on the institutional aspects of economic growth and development. But even the bibliography cited at the Bank's judicial reform website (www1.worldbank.org/publicsector/legal/judicialindependence.htm) refers to a limited number of countries or, in the case of larger studies, provides only a limited overview of the issues concerning judicial reform.
7. Przeworski and Teune (1970).

# 2. The model

This chapter develops a formal model of the process by which policymakers make choices about ownership and competition in an infrastructure sector like the ESI. The formal model provides the theoretical basis for understanding such choices and, in subsequent chapters, for the empirical investigation of ESI restructuring. After a brief discussion of the main developments in the formal modeling of privatization and related policy choices, the chapter proceeds as follows: the first section derives the key results for the pricing and output behavior of producers under different institutional arrangements. The next section presents the political game whereby institutional arrangements are chosen. Subsequent sections extend the model to consider the effects of (i) ideology; (ii) distributional conflict; and (iii) institutional constraints on the policy process that can limit political opportunism. A final section summarizes the conclusions of the model and briefly discusses their implications.

## FORMAL MODELS OF MICROECONOMIC REFORM

The formal analysis of privatization and competition choices has been heavily focused on the issue of agency (Vickers and Yarrow 1988; Laffont and Tirole 1993). While agency is certainly very important and sure to matter when political choices are made concerning industry organization, it is not developed in the model below in order to highlight the impact of political competition without unduly complicating the analysis. Instead, by explicitly considering the electoral process, the model presented below builds on the formal political economy analyses of the processes by which governments choose to privatize and deregulate, notably Shapiro and Willig (1990), Shleifer and Vishny (1994), and Heller and McCubbins (1996). Additionally, the rich and expanding research on the political economy of macroeconomic reform, which examines the incentives of politicians, voters and other actors in dealing with inflation, balance of payments crises, and like issues, offers further insights and modeling approaches (for a comprehensive analysis, see Drazen 2000). The model presented below also draws on them (for example, Dewatripont and Roland 1992), as many of the problems, such as that of time inconsistency, are common to both macroeconomic and microeconomic reforms.   Finally, it is important to note that political institutions are not maintained by a higher authority, but are instead generated endogenously through the mutual agreement of political actors, including voters in a democratic setting.  As Aoki (2001: 2, 20) points out, the correct way to model the emergence or transformation of this type of institution is as a noncooperative game.  This is the approach followed below.

In modeling the political factors that can influence institutional choices in sectors hitherto structured mostly as public monopolies, three factors are suggested by the existing theoretical and empirical literature, as discussed in the previous chapter, as most important: first, the *preferences* of voters and politicians, which I refer to as 'ideology' following the common meaning in which this term is used;[1] second, building on the concept of competition in the political arena, on Knight's (1992) theory of distributional conflict as a driver of institutional change and emergence, and on the work of students of Latin American politics (Ames 1987; Maxfield 1997), *competition* among interest groups – termed 'distributional conflict' here after Knight (1992), but which could also be called 'rent seeking intensity'; and third, following the ideas of path dependence from the new institutionalism, and of veto points and policymaking *constraints* as specific inheritances from the past, what I term 'institutional constraints'.

As natural monopolies, infrastructure industries were traditionally organized under a single, and most often public, firm, or at most a set of local monopolies.  Such an organization offers rich rewards to those who control the firm – politicians and their agents, public managers – in the form of patronage, procurement contracts, and the like.   Interestingly, however, it is shown below that despite the strong influence of rent-seeking on institutional choice, the ideological preferences of voters and politicians still have an important role to play in the final outcome; most surprisingly, the absence of institutional constraints may temper the effects of distributional conflict, because the expected payoffs from attempts to influence political choices are diminished by the possibility of subsequent policy reversals.  This runs counter to the conventional wisdom that views rent-seeking as encouraged by insufficient institutional constraints, such as for instance an independent judiciary that can punish corruption.   While institutional constraints have been shown both theoretically (Spiller 1996) and empirically (Henisz 2000) to solve the time inconsistency problem and encourage investment in sectors plagued by this problem, such as electricity, the model shows that when it comes to reform, intended for instance to shift away from a 'bad' equilibrium, the role of such constraints may be much more ambiguous.  The silver lining is that the pessimism of the institutionalist perspective may be excessive: the absence of strong institutions may open the door to changes for the better through the agency of politicians committed to reform and voters seeking change. Of course, greater freedom from the past can also be used for the worse. In fact, in the absence of institutional constraints, the model points to the possibility of policy cycles in the organization of infrastructure sectors. The concluding section returns to this possibility as an important issue for further research.

## ECONOMIC OUTCOMES UNDER DIFFERENT INSTITUTIONAL ARRANGEMENTS

In recent decades, technological change has had a dramatic impact on infrastructure sectors that had hitherto been considered natural monopolies. In electricity, for instance, the advent of combined cycle technology heralded the end of the secular trend towards larger minimum efficient scales of production that had characterized the industry during its first hundred years of existence (Joskow 1991). In telecoms, microwave technology and, more recently, cellular telephony are quickly rendering fixed-line networks obsolete or at least ending their natural monopoly characteristics (see the discussion in Armstrong et al. 1994: 195–7); so long as network compatibility exists, rival networks can coexist and compete with each other without adverse effects on societal welfare.

Consider, then, what happens when technological change allows a given product, like electric power, to be produced efficiently at small scales, so that fixed costs become in effect negligible:

$$c(q) = \alpha q \tag{2.1}$$

where $c(q)$ is total production cost, $q$ is the firm's output, and $\alpha$ is the marginal cost of production.[2]

Assume inverse demand follows the well-known linear demand function:

$$p = a - bQ, \tag{2.2}$$

where $p$ is the product's price and $a$ and $b$ are positive parameters.

Two institutional dimensions have a key impact on the manner in which production and consumption of the good takes place: ownership of the production assets and their output, which can be either public or private, and the degree of competition among production units, which for analytical tractability is simplified to two possibilities, monopoly (one firm only) or competition (a large number of firms). The degree of competition is considered a basic determinant of firm behavior in industrial organization, while the impact of ownership has become in recent decades a central subject of microeconomic research at both theoretical and empirical levels (for a comprehensive treatment, see Laffont and Tirole 1993).

These dimensions result in three institutional alternatives for the organization of the sector: a private monopoly (M), competition among several firms (C), and public enterprise operating as a monopoly (P).[3] These alternatives are the choices open to policymakers who have to decide on a new institutional arrangement for the industry. The only requirement for any one of the choices to be available is that it be feasible, that is consistent with the structure of cost, demand, and other considerations, such as taxation, that will be made explicit later in the chapter. A feasible arrangement according to the preceding definition is assumed to be enforced by the state if chosen by the policymakers. For instance, under the assumed cost structure a monopolist might be faced with entry by competing firms; however, if a monopolistic arrangement is chosen, it is assumed to be enforced by the government through franchises or other legal devices that prohibit competitors from offering the same product to consumers.[4]

**Competition**

The usual assumptions of atomistic firms maximizing profit leads to the familiar competitive result

$$p(Q) = c'(q) = \alpha, \tag{2.3}$$

or, substituting this result in 2, the competitive equilibrium industry output level, denoted $Q^C$ is:

$$Q^C = \frac{a - \alpha}{b}, \tag{2.4}$$

where for the competitive market to exist, we require that $a - \alpha > 0$.

It is useful to think of the competitive outcome as equivalently the outcome of a regulatory process in which a regulator is vested with the authority to set the price to be charged by a regulated monopoly according to criteria of economic efficiency, and the regulator possesses the information, professional competence, and behavioral incentives to replicate the competitive outcome. Thus, when the choice of institutional alternatives is examined in the following sections, we can think of the 'competitive' alternative as also embodying an 'efficient regulation' institutional arrangement.[5]

## Private Monopoly

As before, the firm's problem is to maximize profit by choosing the appropriate output level. Again, solving the well-known monopolist's problem, the total output level, $Q^M$ is:

$$Q^M = (a - \alpha)/2b, \tag{2.5}$$

where the superscript M indicates private monopoly. Also, $p^M = (a + \alpha)/2$ and, following the standard textbook result, $Q^M < Q^C$; since the requirement for the existence of a competitive market is that $a - \alpha > 0$, it follows that $a > \alpha$, $a + \alpha > 2\alpha$ and $p^M > p^C$. The monopolist's participation constraint, that is, the requirement that it make nonnegative profits, is met since monopoly profit is:

$$\pi^M = (a - \alpha)^2/4b > 0, \text{ since } b > 0. \tag{2.6}$$

## Public Enterprise

Unlike the competitive and private monopoly cases, for which there is a canonical set of widely accepted behavioral assumptions, there is no similar consensus regarding the behavior of public monopolies. As with the behavior of politicians and civil servants more generally, we can posit a variety of motivations for the behavior of public enterprise managers and for the politicians who appoint them. A 'public spirit' perspective, which prevailed until at least the 1970s among economists (see Noll 1989, for a discussion), assumed that public enterprise, like other governmental action, is directed towards welfare maximization. However, under the production technology assumed above, this would just equal the competitive outcome. By contrast, following Stigler (1971), public monopolies may be operated like private monopolies to extract rents, either because politicians use the rents for their own purposes (such as creating 'national champions'), or because the public monopoly has been 'captured' by its managers. Again, this case would not differ from the private monopoly case in terms of outcomes.

Yet a third possibility is suggested by Laffont and Tirole (1993) and by Shleifer and Vishny (1994), although conceptually it derives from a broader range of knowledge about public monopoly and theories of the pork barrel in the US Congress (Weingast et al. 1981). The key element of this perspective is the realization that the political benefits from public monopoly need not be limited to monopoly rents or voter appreciation for maximizing social welfare. As López de Silanes et al. (1997: 451) write, 'politicians ... derive political benefits from such [public] provision, including the support of local public sector unions, the opportunity to purchase supplies from political allies, the ability to hire relatives and campaign activists, the ability to use local government employees on political projects, and so on'. In the case of infrastructure industries, we may add another, and very important, potential benefit: the possibility of providing the output to consumers at subsidized prices. This is so because as Spiller (1996) has noted, the output of sectors like electricity or water supply, or road construction, has a large impact on household welfare and is thus highly salient in political terms. For this reason, the model below also considers this third possibility for the behavior of public monopoly, following Shleifer and Vishny's (1998: 187) contention that 'the pursuit of political benefits is the principal reason for the pervasive political control over firms around the world'.

The way this third possibility is modeled is as follows. Politicians seek to obtain political support from the customers and suppliers of public enterprises. Customers can be cultivated by offering them the product of the public monopoly at subsidized prices.[6] Hence, a public monopolist is assumed to maximize both the subsidy over the competitive price and the cost of production, subject to a constraint determined by the cost of subsidies to the government. For customers, competition is the best possible alternative in the absence of public enterprise. The competitive price is thus a logical benchmark for customers when evaluating the attractiveness of public enterprise – from their standpoint, an institutional form that improves upon the competitive outcome will automatically improve upon the private monopoly outcome, since $Q^M < Q^C$ (or $p^M > p^C$) and in the simple linear demand function (2.2), consumer utility depends directly on the quantity consumed. Thus politicians can curry customer support by offering an institutional arrangement that yields prices below the competitive level. Likewise, wooing suppliers can be accomplished by buying from them the inputs of the public enterprise (labor, materials, land, and so forth), which are summarized by the cost function. Therefore, the problem of the public enterprise is:

$$\max_{q} q(p^C - p^P) + c(q) - \sigma T, \tag{2.7}$$

where $p^P$ is the price charged by the public enterprise, $\sigma$ is the cost of public funds to the treasury, and $T$ is the level of transfers provided to the firm, equal to the firm's losses or negative profits; the benefits that can be derived from suppliers are reflected in the term $c(q)$ entering with a *positive* sign. Suppliers benefit either because they are able to supply their inputs at a premium, such as higher wages and benefits, supernormal profits for construction companies, and so forth;[7] or simply because suppliers derive benefits from conducting a larger volume of business.[8]

Substituting $-\pi$ for $T$ above, and noticing that $q(p^C - p^P) + c(q) = q\alpha - qp^P + c(q) = q\alpha - \pi$ therefore results in the transformed problem:

$$\max_{q} q\alpha + (\sigma - 1)\pi. \tag{2.7a}$$

The first-order condition for a maximum is:

$$\alpha + \sigma'\pi + (\sigma - 1)\pi' = 0. \tag{2.8}$$

The second-order condition is:

$$\sigma''\pi + 2\sigma'\pi' + (\sigma - 1)\pi'' < 0, \tag{2.9}$$

which will be true if three (sufficient but not necessary) conditions are met:

$$\sigma''\pi \leq 0, \ \sigma'\pi' \leq 0 \text{ and } (\sigma - 1)\,\pi'' < 0.$$

In this model, we assume that $\sigma$ is set exogenously (see the next paragraph), so $\sigma' = 0$ and $\sigma'' = 0$. Also, since $\pi = qp - q\alpha = (a - \alpha)q - bq^2$, $\pi'' = -2b < 0$ for all $q$. The first- and second-order conditions are thus satisfied if we assume that $\sigma - 1 > 0$, or $\sigma > 1$.

In assuming that $\sigma > 1$, it is important to note that this parameter is not an interest rate or opportunity cost of government funds, as in Laffont and Tirole (1993). Rather, it is a parameter in the decision function of public enterprise managers based on the fact that negative enterprise profits may be costly to the government in political terms, since losses require higher present or future taxes, which lead voters to punish the incumbent government in the next elections.[9] We can simply assume that $\sigma$ is a parameter indirectly fixed by the treasury or by the financial markets regarding the ability of the government to incur additional indebtedness, and by the political system with regard to additional taxation, and therefore it is at least locally invariant to changes in $q$. The implications of an endogenous determination of $\sigma$ on the basis of political costs are explored in an extension to the model.

With these assumptions for $\sigma$, we can solve the first-order condition for $q$ to obtain the public enterprise output level:

$$Q^P = \frac{a - \alpha + \dfrac{\alpha}{\sigma - 1}}{2b}. \tag{2.10}$$

Note that, under the assumptions so far made ($a - \alpha > 0$, $\sigma - 1 > 0$), this level if output will always be positive and higher than the monopoly level of output; it will also exceed $Q^C$ if and only if $\sigma < a/(a - \alpha) = 1 + \alpha/(a - \alpha)$. Therefore, for the possibility that public enterprise will be of interest, the assumption about the value of $\sigma$ will be $1 < \sigma < a/(a - \alpha)$.[10]

The corresponding price under public enterprise is:

$$p^P = \frac{a}{2} + \frac{\alpha}{2}\left(1 - \frac{1}{\sigma - 1}\right), \tag{2.11}$$

which is lower than the competitive price for the range of values assumed for $\sigma$. Obviously, since output is assumed to exceed $Q^C$, which is the zero-profit level of output, the public enterprise will always be operating at a loss.[11]

As we have seen, the level of industry output is both the decision variable for firms in the model and a variable that uniquely characterizes each regime, so we can summarize the results of the regime analysis in terms of output Q:

**Proposition 1:** Under the assumptions $a - \alpha > 0$ and $1 < \sigma < a/(a - \alpha)$ (together with $\sigma' = 0$ and $\sigma'' = 0$), the institutional arrangements of perfect competition, private monopoly and public enterprise yield, respectively, the following levels of industry output:

$$Q^C = (a - \alpha)/b,$$

$$Q^M = (a - \alpha)/2b$$

and

$$Q^P = \frac{a - \alpha + \dfrac{\alpha}{\sigma - 1}}{2b}$$

where $Q^M < Q^C < Q^P$

This proposition therefore provides a complete description of each institutional arrangement. The next step is to examine how this affects institutional choices in the political system, which is the question addressed in the section that follows.[12]

## THE POLITICAL GAME

Since technological change opens up alternative institutional arrangements for the industry, it is only reasonable to suppose that the organization of the industry may be included in the political agenda. For instance, the decision by the British government to privatize and deregulate its electricity industry in 1990, although second to Chile (which carried out these reforms in 1982), made many countries around the world consider privatization and deregulation for their electricity industries, as shown by the wave of restructuring programs and proposals that took place during the 1990s.[13] Inclusion in the political agenda means that a choice has to be made about the institutional arrangement for the industry, from among the three available choices of M, C and P.[14] The process of making this choice through the political system is what I call the 'political game'.

There are three sets of actors in the political game. 'Consumers' comprise only those with the right to vote – that is, household consumers, who purchase the output produced by the sector under the supply conditions yielded by the institutional arrangements for production, vote to elect politicians who can alter these arrangements, and pay taxes. 'Politicians' seek to be elected or re-elected, and also have their own ideological preferences for institutional arrangements; and finally, 'suppliers' produce output of the good (if under private production arrangements[15]), provide capital, labor and materials to the sector, pay taxes as well and have the ability to offer 'contributions' or side payments to the politicians (which can include campaign contributions, outright purchase of favors, or other possibilities).[16]

Restricting the treatment of consumers to those with the right to vote does not do violence to the realism of the model as it might seem at first. Nonvoting consumers are numerically far fewer than voting consumers, as they involve juridical persons – mainly businesses, which are generally far fewer in number than households. Most importantly, the interest in consumers for the model lies in the influence of the ballot box on institutional outcomes, so we are primarily interested in consumers *qua* voters. In any case, consumers' non-electoral behavior (such as lobbying the government) is implicitly included in the model by positing, as one of the main objectives of public enterprise, the maximization of subsidies to consumers (subject to a public finance constraint). This reflects the fact that, when services are provided by public entities, consumers of all kinds are likely can be expected to use their political influence to consume infrastructure services at the lowest price they can bargain for.

**Consumers**

Building on the standard linear model of voting as refined by Hinich and
Munger (1994), consumers vote to maximize a linear 'political utility'
function which includes consumer surplus from their consumption of the
good produced by the sector, the disutility of taxes borne if the public
enterprise loses money,[17] and the distance between government policy and
their own institutional preferences:

$$u_i = E(bQ_j^2/2 - k_c\tau - \phi|Q_j - Q_i|), \qquad\qquad (2.12)$$

where $u_i$ is consumer i's level of expected utility, $bQ_j^2/2$ is consumer
surplus as given by the assumed demand function[18] and the institutional
choice $Q_j$ expected of party j once in power, $k_c$ is the consumers' share of
taxes (taxes are allocated between consumers and suppliers, so that
$k_c + k_s = 1$), the total level of taxes $\tau$ equals the expected level of losses
incurred by the public enterprise (therefore it equals zero under M and C), $\phi$
is the weight of consumers' political preferences, and $|Q_j - Q_i|$ is the
distance between expected ($Q_j$) and ideal ($Q_i$) institutional arrangements.

Consumers' ideal points ($Q_i$) are assumed to be of only two types: either
P or C. In keeping with common public opinion polls, particularly in
developing countries, consumers dislike M because they are aware of the
potential for abuse under this arrangement. By contrast, consumers realize
the benefits of competition in terms of choice and prices. Lastly, ideological
(as opposed to purely economic) support for P stems from the perception
that ordinary citizens have greater control over public enterprise, through
the electoral process, than over the private sector, and that competition can
be wasteful of scarce resources.

The assumption of homogeneous consumers certainly contrasts with the
diversity of users of any type of infrastructure services, where in general
there are two clearly differentiated types of consumers: large users in the
business or government sectors for which the service is often a key
production input, for example, electricity for an industrial plant; and small
users, such as 'mom and pop' shops and residential consumers, who mainly
derive 'utility' from the consumption of these services, for example,
electricity for air conditioning. However, for the reasons outlined above,
our attention is restricted to household consumers, whose diversity is far
smaller; and in any case, it is reasonable to assume that for most consumers,
the variables that affect their utility most directly are price and quantity ($p$
and $q$).[19] The assumption of a common ideal point for consumers can
represent the median position, a commonly accepted assumption in formal
models of politics.[20]

Even if we make the reasonable assumption that most voters are consumers of infrastructure services, at least in developed countries and urban areas where voter participation is highest, why should they care about infrastructure in their voting decisions? After all, such services may not figure prominently in voters' budget constraints. In reality, there is strong poll and anecdotal evidence that consumption of services such as electricity is an important issue for voters – rate increases and poor service quality are certainly noticed, as the experiences of California, Brazil, Chile and other places show.[21] This is a key assumption of the model, for the electoral visibility of infrastructure supply is what makes infrastructure fundamentally different from most other goods and services consumed by voters with regard to government policy concerning the organization of these sectors. Moreover, we can think of the electoral choice here as being 'at the margin', that is, abstracting from other policy issues, given the obvious complexity of working with a 'general equilibrium' model of voting. What matters for the research question is how expected voter reactions to institutional choices affect policymakers' decisions about infrastructure-related institutions.

Why then have two separate utility functions, one purely economic (implicit in equation (2.2), the inverse demand curve) and equation (2.12), guiding political choices? This split is a fundamental feature of the model, because it highlights the fact that voting decisions are not guided solely by expected consumption outcomes, thereby introducing the possibility that institutional choices may diverge from pure maximization of consumption utility. More specifically, equation (2.12) shows that there are two additional dimensions that voters consider when electing public officials: the tax impact of various institutional choices,[22] and ideological preferences. Ideology clearly plays a separate role from economic well-being in voting decisions, as institutional arrangements also have an impact on noneconomic issues such as national independence, supremacy of societal over private interests, and so forth, to which consumers may also attach value. Moreover, since electoral choices must be made for platforms or 'packages' of policies relating to many different issues rather than just for specific institutional choices for infrastructure services, 'ideology' provides a shorthand description of preferences over political platforms.[23]

## Politicians

Politicians (or political parties) maximize through their choice of institutional arrangements a utility function including the value of office, the contributions expected from suppliers, and the distance between their electoral platform and their institutional preferences:[24]

$$u_j(Q_j) = \mathrm{pr}(Q_j, Q_k)[h - \beta|Q_j - Q_j^*|] + [1 - \mathrm{pr}(Q_j, Q_k)] [-\beta|Q_k - Q_j^*|] + \psi\theta_j(Q_j, Q_k) \qquad (2.13)$$

for $j$, $k$ = L, R and $j \neq k$,

where $u_j(Q_j)$ is the expected utility of politician $j$ upon choosing policy platform $Q_j$, $\mathrm{pr}(Q_j, Q_k)$ is the probability of election when his or her platform is $Q_j$ and the opponents' platform is $Q_k$, $h$ is the value of office if elected, $\beta$ is the utility weight of ideological preferences, $|Q_j - Q_j^*|$ is as before the distance between implemented ($Q_j$) and ideal ($Q_j^*$) policy, $\psi$ is the utility weight of contributions from suppliers, and $\theta_j(Q_j, Q_k)$ is the contribution offered by suppliers when the choices of own and opposing platforms are, respectively, $Q_j$ and $Q_k$ (note that L and R can make the same choice of $Q$, so $Q_j$ and $Q_k$ may be equal). Since the choices for $Q$ are limited to the three institutional possibilities of M, C and P, the strategy space of each political party is precisely the set of the three possible output levels $Q^M$, $Q^C$ and $Q^P$ obtaining under each institutional arrangement.

To keep matters simple, I assume that only two politicians contend in the game, a 'left-wing' (L) politician with ideal policy P, and a 'right-wing' politician with ideal policy C or M.[25]

## Suppliers

Suppliers are assumed to be agnostic about ideology; they only care about maximizing their profits and rents; likewise, as they represent entities (firms) that are not allowed to vote, and they cannot monitor the voting behavior of consumers (balloting is secret); their only means of influencing policy is by making (nonnegative) payments to politicians.[26] Suppliers choose contribution schedules to maximize the expected sum of profits and rents accruing from a given policy platform, less their expected tax bill and expected contributions to politicians.

$$u_s(\theta_{sj}, \theta_{sk}) = E[c_s(Q_j) + \pi_s^M - k_s\tau - \theta_{sj} - \theta_{sk}] \text{ for } j, k = \text{L, R and } j \neq k \qquad (2.14)$$

where $u_s$ is the expected level of utility of supplier $s$, $\theta_{sj}$ and $\theta_{sk}$ are the contributions to parties $j$ and $k$, respectively,[27] $c_s(Q)$ is the cost of production of the good flowing to $s$ in the form of supply contracts (wages and profit margins), $\pi_s^M$ is the share of monopoly profit accruing to s (if any) if private monopoly is selected, and $k_s\tau$ is the tax bill allocated to $s$.

The initial solution of the game presented below assumes that suppliers behave as a single actor, for instance through a peak (that is, economy-wide) association of private sector firms in coalition with peak labor organizations. The consequences of assuming competition among suppliers are explored in a subsequent section.

## Timing

The timing of the game is as follows: first, suppliers announce side-payment schedules[28] to politicians, contingent upon electoral results and institutional policies (Stage 1); next, politicians choose electoral platforms (Stage 2); at the third stage, voting takes place; finally (Stage 4), the elected politician implements one among the three possible institutional arrangements (M, C or PE) and suppliers carry out their investment plans if ownership is in private hands.

The model considers future elections in a simplified way. The main reason for the simplification is that changing institutions is costly, as new organizations have to be set up, committed investment may have to be scrapped, and so forth. Therefore re-election effects are modeled as follows: if an elected party fails to implement its platform, it suffers a punishment $\Gamma$ (in present utility terms) from consumers and suppliers, who withhold, respectively, future votes and contributions.[29] In principle, this cost is assumed to be large enough so that no politician has an incentive to deviate from his or her electoral platform if elected to office, and therefore re-election considerations will not be explicitly treated in the model. A subsequent section will explicitly take the issue of electoral promises versus implemented policy into consideration.[30]

## Definition of Equilibrium

Equilibrium in the game is defined by a set of feasible and credible supplier contribution schedules $\theta$, and a set of electoral platforms $Q_L$ and $Q_R$, such that consumers and politicians maximize expected utility, suppliers maximize rents and profits, and private producers (if any) undertake production of the good, given everybody else's optimal choices and the chronology of the game. Formally, the setup of the game is:

suppliers' problem: $\max\limits_{\theta_{sj},\ \theta_{sk}} u_s(\theta_{sj},\ \theta_{sk}) = E(c_s(Q_j) + \pi_s^M - k_s\tau - \theta_{sj} - \theta_{sk})$

for $j, k = L, R$ and $j \neq k$

politicians' problem: $\max\limits_{Q_j} u_j(Q_j) = pr(Q_j, Q_k)[h - \beta|Q_j - Q_j^*|] +$

$(1 - pr(Q_j, Q_k))[-\beta|Q_k - Q_j^*|] + \psi\theta_j(Q_j, Q_k)$

for $j, k = L, R$ and $j \neq k$

consumers' problem: $\max\limits_{Q_j} u_i = E(bQ_j^2/2 - k_c\tau - \phi|Q_j - Q_i|)$ for $j = $ L, R

subject to production feasibility constraints:

$a - \alpha > 0$; $1 < \sigma < a/(a - \alpha)$ (together with $\sigma'' = 0$ and $\sigma' = 0$);

and to output constraints, reflecting the three possible institutional choices:

$$Q^C = (a - \alpha)/b$$

$$Q^M = (a - \alpha)/2b$$

$$Q^P = \frac{\alpha + (\sigma - 1)(a - \alpha)}{(\sigma - 1)2b}.$$

The chronological structure of the game, in which each set of actors makes its choice at a separate stage, makes subgame perfect Nash equilibrium appropriate for solving it. We can deal first with the decisions made by the voters in the third stage, since politicians and suppliers have already made theirs; then, we can move back to look at politicians' decisions in view of likely voter behavior; and finally examine suppliers' optimal contributions given politician and voter decisions.

In all but the discussion of institutional constraints, the fourth state (policy implementation) is not considered since, as already mentioned, implementation is only problematized when examining institutional constraints. To avoid excessive complications in results, only pure-strategy equilibria are considered in the model.

**Electoral Preferences**

Following the logic of subgame perfection, the first choice to be analyzed for the solution of the game is that of consumers. Consumer utility depends on the ideal point of each individual and on the surplus obtained under each institutional arrangement. For the reasons mentioned above, consumers whose ideal point is M are not considered in the game. That leaves those with ideal point C ('C-types') and those with ideological preference for P ('P-types').

In turn, the first step in determining voting behavior is to examine the ideology-related disutility to consumers arising from the implementation of institutional arrangements that differ from their ideal points:

- Under M (private monopoly), ideology costs are as follows:

for C-types, $|Q^M - Q^C| = \left| \dfrac{a-\alpha}{2b} - \dfrac{a-\alpha}{b} \right| = \dfrac{a-\alpha}{2b}$

for P-types, $|Q^M - Q^P| = \left| \dfrac{a-\alpha}{2b} - \dfrac{a-\alpha}{2b} - \dfrac{\alpha}{2b(\sigma-1)} \right| = \dfrac{\alpha}{2b(\sigma-1)}$

- Under C (competition):

  for P-types: $|Q^C - Q^P| = \left| \dfrac{a-\alpha}{b} - \dfrac{a-\alpha}{2b} - \dfrac{\alpha}{2b(\sigma-1)} \right| = \dfrac{\alpha - (a-\alpha)(\sigma-1)}{2b(\sigma-1)}$

- Under P (public enterprise):

  for C-types, $|Q^P - Q^C| =. \left| \dfrac{a-\alpha}{2b} + \dfrac{\alpha}{2b(\sigma-1)} - \dfrac{a-\alpha}{b} \right| = \dfrac{\alpha - (a-\alpha)(\sigma-1)}{2b(\sigma-1)}$.

Under an assumption of full information (so that we do not have to worry about expectations for the time being because all actors know each other's utility functions and the position of the median voter[31]), utility levels for the different types of consumers are:

(a) C-types

Under M,

$$u = \frac{a-\alpha}{2b}\left( \frac{a-\alpha}{4} - \phi \right). \tag{2.15}$$

Under C,

$$u = \frac{(a-\alpha)^2}{2b}. \tag{2.16}$$

Under P,

$$u = \frac{1}{8b}\left( a - \alpha\frac{\sigma-2}{\sigma-1} \right)^2 - \frac{\phi}{2b}\left[ \left( 1 + \frac{1}{\sigma-1} \right)\alpha - a \right] + k_c \tau, \tag{2.17}$$

where $\tau = [(a-\alpha)^2 - \alpha^2/(\sigma-1)^2]/4b$ is the level of losses of the public enterprise.

(b) P-types

Under M,

$$u = \frac{(a-\alpha)^2}{8b} - \phi\frac{\alpha}{2b(\sigma-1)}. \tag{2.18}$$

Under C,

$$u = \frac{(a - \alpha)^2}{2b} - \phi \frac{\alpha - (a - \alpha)(\sigma - 1)}{2b(\sigma - 1)}. \tag{2.19}$$

Under P,

$$u = \frac{1}{8b}\left(a - \alpha\frac{\sigma - 2}{\sigma - 1}\right)^2 + k_c\tau. \tag{2.20}$$

The next step is to compare the above utility levels in order to determine the ranking of regimes by each type of consumer. Since consumers value both consumer surplus and ideological preference, regime preferences need not be a trivial matter.

(a) C-types

First, we can easily see that for this type of consumer, $C \succ M$. Comparing (2.15) and (2.16), notice that consumer surplus is larger under C than under M, and the penalty under M is positive since we are assuming that $a - \alpha > 0$.

Also note that $P \succ M$ so long as taxes are not excessively high. Comparing (2.15) (for M) and (2.17) (for P) with the exclusion of the tax term in (17), we get, respectively:

$$(a - \alpha)^2 - \left(a - \alpha\frac{\sigma - 2}{\sigma - 1}\right)^2 < 4\phi\left[2(a - \alpha) + \frac{\alpha}{\sigma - 1}\right],$$

since, for the values assumed for $\sigma$, the second expression in parentheses on the left-hand side is always larger than the first expression so the LHS is negative, while the RHS is always positive.

Concerning the comparison of C and P, algebraic manipulation shows that, for the levels assumed for $\sigma$, consumer surplus is always larger under P than under C, as we would expect since consumption volume is larger and price lower under P. But the intensity of ideological preferences ($\phi$) and the tax burden under P ($k_c\tau$) can reverse this inequality if large enough. There are thus two possible rankings of institutional regimes by C-type consumers:

- $P \succ C \succ M$, and
- $C \succ P \succ M$.

(b) P-types. As before, $C \succ M$ for this type of consumer. Equations (2.18) (M) and (2.19) (C) show that consumer surplus is larger, and the ideological penalty lower, under C. The same argument applies for M versus P, equations (2.18) and (2.20) respectively, to show that P $\succ$ M, again so long as taxes are not so high that they offset the ideological and consumer surplus advantages of P.

For the comparison of C (2.19) and P (2.20), we already know from the discussion of C-types that consumer surplus is larger under P always, taxes notwithstanding. Since the ideology penalty under P is zero for P-types, we just need to check the sign of the ideological penalty under C. In this regard, we can see that

$$-\frac{\phi}{2b}\left[\alpha\left(1+\frac{1}{\sigma-1}\right)-a\right]<0,$$

since the expression outside the brackets is negative, and the expression inside the brackets is positive for the range of values assumed for $\sigma$. Thus, the ranking of institutions is unambiguously P $\succ$ C $\succ$ M for P-types.

To conclude, then, consumer preferences can take two forms: when P is preferred the most (P $\succ$ C $\succ$ M), or when C is preferred the most (C $\succ$ P $\succ$ M). M is always the least preferred option because it yields the least surplus and entails ideological costs.

## Political Platform Choices without Contributions

The first step in computing politicians' payoffs is to determine the ideological penalties they incur when policies differ from their ideal points:

- For L, ideology costs are as follows:

$$\text{under M, } |Q^M-Q^P|=\left|\frac{a-\alpha}{2b}-\frac{a-\alpha}{2b}-\frac{\alpha}{2b(\sigma-1)}\right|=\frac{\alpha}{2b(\sigma-1)}$$

$$\text{under C, } |Q^C-Q^P|=\left|\frac{a-\alpha}{b}-\frac{a-\alpha}{2b}-\frac{\alpha}{2b(\sigma-1)}\right|=\frac{\alpha-(a-\alpha)(\sigma-1)}{2b(\sigma-1)}.$$

Note that the penalty is larger under M within the range of values assumed for $\sigma$.

- For R, when R's ideal point is C:

$$\text{under M, } |Q^M-Q^C|=\left|\frac{a-\alpha}{2b}-\frac{a-\alpha}{b}\right|=\frac{a-\alpha}{2b}$$

$$\text{under P, } |Q^P-Q^C|=\left|\frac{a-\alpha}{2b}+\frac{\alpha}{2b(\sigma-1)}-\frac{a-\alpha}{b}\right|=\frac{\alpha-(a-\alpha)(\sigma-1)}{2b(\sigma-1)}.$$

In this case, the penalties can be greater under either regime, depending on the value of $\sigma$.

- For R, when R's ideal point is M:

$$\text{under P, } |Q^P - Q^M| = \left| \frac{a-\alpha}{2b} - \frac{a-\alpha}{2b} + \frac{\alpha}{2b(\sigma-1)} \right| = \frac{\alpha}{2b(\sigma-1)}$$

$$\text{under C, } |Q^C - Q^M| = \left| \frac{a-\alpha}{b} - \frac{a-\alpha}{2b} \right| = \frac{a-\alpha}{2b}.$$

Obviously, the penalty (distance from the ideal point) is larger under P than under C for the assumed range of $\sigma$ values.

The next step is to construct the payoff matrices for each party according to voter preferences. Here, we simplify the problem and assume no supplier contributions, an assumption to be relaxed in subsequent sections. As shown above, two different sets of consumer preferences must be considered: (i) $P \succ C \succ M$; and (ii) $C \succ P \succ M$. For each one of these sets, we have to consider the payoffs to each type of political actor: L, $R^M$ (when R has M as ideal point), and $R^C$, when R's ideal point is C (Table 2.1 to Table 2.4 below). The strategy space of each political actor is simply the set of the three institutional choices available: M, C or P. In other words, as explained in the description of the game, each political actor (L and R) chooses an institutional arrangement as a political platform which is then voted upon by consumers.

**Consumer preferences $P \succ C \succ M$**

*Table 2.1   Consumer preferences $P \succ C \succ M$: L's payoffs*

| L's payoffs | R's platform | | |
|---|---|---|---|
| **L's platform** | **P** | **C** | **M** |
| **P** **C** | $\dfrac{h/2}{}$ $-\beta\dfrac{\alpha-(a-\alpha)(\sigma-1)}{2b(\sigma-1)}$ | $h$ $\dfrac{h}{2}-\beta\dfrac{\alpha-(a-\alpha)(\sigma-1)}{2b(\sigma-1)}$ | $h$ $h-\beta\dfrac{\alpha-(a-\alpha)(\sigma-1)}{2b(\sigma-1)}$ |
| **M** | $-\beta\dfrac{\alpha}{2b(\sigma-1)}$ | $-\beta\dfrac{\alpha}{2b(\sigma-1)}$ | $\dfrac{h}{2}-\beta\dfrac{\alpha}{2b(\sigma-1)}$ |

*Table 2.2   Consumer preferences $P \succ C \succ M$: $R^M$'s payoffs*

| $R^M$'s payoffs | L's platform | | |
|---|---|---|---|
| **$R^M$'s platform** | **P** | **C** | **M** |
| **P** | $\dfrac{h}{2} - \beta \dfrac{\alpha}{2b(\sigma-1)}$ | $h - \beta \dfrac{\alpha}{2b(\sigma-1)}$ | $h - \beta \dfrac{\alpha}{2b(\sigma-1)}$ |
| **C** | $-\beta \dfrac{a-\alpha}{2b}$ | $\dfrac{h}{2} - \beta \dfrac{a-\alpha}{2b}$ | $h - \beta \dfrac{a-\alpha}{2b}$ |
| **M** | $0$ | $0$ | $h/2$ |

*Table 2.3   Consumer preferences $P \succ C \succ M$: $R^C$'s payoffs*

| $R^C$'s payoffs | L's platform | | |
|---|---|---|---|
| **$R^C$'s platform** | **P** | **C** | **M** |
| **P** | $\dfrac{h}{2} - \beta \dfrac{\alpha-(a-\alpha)(\sigma-1)}{2b(\sigma-1)}$ | $h - \beta \dfrac{\alpha-(a-\alpha)(\sigma-1)}{2b(\sigma-1)}$ | $h - \beta \dfrac{\alpha-(a-\alpha)(\sigma-1)}{2b(\sigma-1)}$ |
| **C** | $0$ | $h/2$ | $h$ |
| **M** | $-\beta \dfrac{a-\alpha}{2b}$ | $-\beta \dfrac{a-\alpha}{2b}$ | $\dfrac{h}{2} - \beta \dfrac{a-\alpha}{2b}$ |

*L versus $R^M$ subgame.* In this subgame, notice that choosing P always is a dominant strategy for L, and $R^M$, knowing this, will pick P so long as

$$\frac{h}{2} - \beta \frac{a}{2b(\sigma-1)} > 0, \text{ so } P \text{ is always chosen. (See Table 2.2).}$$

*L versus $R^C$ subgame.* Again, P is dominant for L here. $R^C$ thus chooses P, so long as

$$\frac{h}{2} - \beta \frac{\alpha-(a-\alpha)(\sigma-1)}{2b(\sigma-1)} > 0. \text{ Therefore, } P \text{ is always chosen. (See Table 2.3).}$$

# Consumer preferences C ≻ P ≻ M

**Table 2.4  Consumer preferences C ≻ P ≻ M: L's payoffs**

| L's payoffs | R's platform | | |
|---|---|---|---|
| L's platform | P | C | M |
| P | $h/2$ | $0$ | $h$ |
| C | $h - \beta\dfrac{\alpha-(a-\alpha)(\sigma-1)}{2b(\sigma-1)}$ | $\dfrac{h}{2} - \beta\dfrac{\alpha-(a-\alpha)(\sigma-1)}{2b(\sigma-1)}$ | $h - \beta\dfrac{\alpha-(a-\alpha)(\sigma-1)}{2b(\sigma-1)}$ |
| M | $-\beta\dfrac{\alpha}{2b(\sigma-1)}$ | $-\beta\dfrac{\alpha}{2b(\sigma-1)}$ | $\dfrac{h}{2} - \beta\dfrac{\alpha}{2b(\sigma-1)}$ |

**Table 2.5  Consumer preferences C ≻ P ≻ M: $R^M$'s payoffs**

| $R^M$'s payoffs | L's platform | | |
|---|---|---|---|
| $R^M$'s platform | P | C | M |
| P | $\dfrac{h}{2} - \beta\dfrac{\alpha}{2b(\sigma-1)}$ | $-\beta\dfrac{\alpha}{2b(\sigma-1)}$ | $h - \beta\dfrac{\alpha}{2b(\sigma-1)}$ |
| C | $h - \beta\dfrac{a-\alpha}{2b}$ | $\dfrac{h}{2} - \beta\dfrac{a-\alpha}{2b}$ | $h - \beta\dfrac{a-\alpha}{2b}$ |
| M | $0$ | $0$ | $h/2$ |

**Table 2.6  Consumer preferences C ≻ P ≻ M: $R^C$'s payoffs**

| $R^C$'s payoffs | L's platform | | |
|---|---|---|---|
| $R^C$'s platform | P | C | M |
| P | $\dfrac{h}{2} - \beta\dfrac{\alpha-(a-\alpha)(\sigma-1)}{2b(\sigma-1)}$ | $-\beta\dfrac{\alpha-(a-\alpha)(\sigma-1)}{2b(\sigma-1)}$ | $h - \beta\dfrac{\alpha-(a-\alpha)(\sigma-1)}{2b(\sigma-1)}$ |
| C | $h$ | $h/2$ | $h$ |
| M | $-\beta\dfrac{a-\alpha}{2b}$ | $-\beta\dfrac{a-\alpha}{2b}$ | $\dfrac{h}{2} - \beta\dfrac{a-\alpha}{2b}$ |

*L versus $R^M$ subgame.* In this case, M is dominated by C or P for the Left; then, C is dominant for the Right if the (C,C) payoff is $\dfrac{h}{2} - \beta\dfrac{a-\alpha}{2b}$ positive. Knowing this, L will select C if

$$\frac{h}{2} - \beta\frac{\alpha-(a-\alpha)(\sigma-1)}{2b(\sigma-1)} > 0,$$

or else it will choose P and get a zero payoff. In either case, *C is the outcome* (see Table 2.5).

*L versus $R^C$ subgame.* Here, C is dominant for $R^C$, so L will pick C always and *C will always obtain* (see Table 2.6).

The overall conclusion of the model is expressed as:

**Proposition 2:** In the absence of contributions, and even if politicians' ideological penalties are not too high, voter ideology is still more powerful than patronage: P is chosen if it is the preferred outcome of the median voter, and C is chosen if it is the preferred outcome of the median voter.

This is important because it shows that patronage is not the only determinant of institutional choices; ideology plays a significant role. For C-type consumers, a high value of $\phi$ can compensate for the higher consumer surplus available under P, to make them prefer C to P overall. In turn, this affects political strategies. On the one hand, there is a 'voter effect' that makes politicians more likely to choose C as an electoral platform; but politicians also have their own ideology. In fact, if $\beta$ is sufficiently high, it can override the voter effect and polarize politics by inducing politicians to choose their ideal points as electoral platforms. In such a case, the outcome can be strongly biased towards C (when R prefers C most) *or* towards P (when R favors M), even if consumers prefer C over P. This means that *ideological polarization in the absence of contributions increases the importance of politicians' ideologies to the detriment of voter preferences.*[32] The upshot is that accounts of public enterprise that ascribe outcomes to patronage considerations alone (Aharoni 1986: 33–40) may be incomplete – outcomes may be also due to voters' and politicians' ideological preferences. However, the foregoing ignores the role of nonvoting actors in the policymaking process. We now turn to this possibility.

## Supplier Contributions

The first step in determining the level of supplier contributions is to determine the ranking of institutional regimes from the standpoint of the suppliers. From equation (2.16), we can determine suppliers' utility levels under each regime, prior to any bribing:

- under M, = $\dfrac{(a-\alpha)^2}{4b} + \dfrac{\alpha(a-\alpha)}{2b} = \dfrac{a^2-\alpha^2}{4b}$

- under C, = $\dfrac{\alpha(a-\alpha)}{b}$

- under P, = $\dfrac{\alpha(a-\alpha)}{2b} + \dfrac{\alpha^2}{2b(\sigma-1)} + \dfrac{k_S}{4b}\left[(a-\alpha)^2 - \dfrac{\alpha^2}{(\sigma-1)^2}\right]$

Now we can compare the level of supplier utility under each regime. First, we can see that $C \succ M$ so long as $-(a - 3\alpha)(a - \alpha)/4b > 0$. By assumption, $(a - \alpha)/4b$ is positive, but $(a - 3\alpha)$ may well be negative, so we can expect C to be generally preferred to M.

We can then compare C and P. The latter yields greater utility so long as

$$\frac{2\alpha^2}{(\sigma-1)} + k_S\left[(a-\alpha)^2 - \frac{\alpha^2}{(\sigma-1)^2}\right] - 2\alpha(a-\alpha) > 0$$

Just as in the case of consumer preferences for P relative to C, this depends on the value of $\sigma$. When $\sigma$ approaches unity, the tax burden outweighs the benefit of higher production costs, so suppliers prefer C to P; at the other extreme, production volumes and costs are equal to those under C, so suppliers are indifferent between the two regimes. But for intermediate values of $\sigma$, the above inequality holds and P is the suppliers' preferred institutional regime.[33] We will therefore develop the rest of the model under the premise that supplier preferences are $P \succ C \succ M$.

The next step is to determine suppliers' optimal bribing strategy. For the time being, it is assumed that suppliers act in concert, that they act as a monopoly supplier of contributions to politicians. Since we assume that all suppliers have identical preferences, this is not an unreasonable assumption, and it is backed by numerous empirical cases of cohesive lobbies of firms engaged in a similar economic activity, or even of peak business organizations. A subsequent section will explore the consequences of relaxing this assumption.

Obviously, suppliers will offer no contributions if the median voter's preferences are of a P-type (thus with preferences $P \succ C \succ M$), since as was shown in the preceding subsection, in this case P will always be the outcome of the political process without contributions. On the other hand, if the median voter is a C-type, C would always be chosen in the absence of contributions, with L choosing a platform of C or P, and R choosing C always. In this case, contributions must therefore be such that P becomes a dominant strategy for L and for R. The least-cost strategy would be to compensate L and R for the cost of losing office (if that is the case when L or R select losing platforms), less any ideological benefits (or plus any ideological costs) of the position they are asked to take, plus an extra benefit $\varepsilon$ to sway them:

- offer L the following contributions:

$$\theta_L(P, C) = \frac{h}{2\psi} - \frac{\beta}{\psi}\frac{\alpha - (a - \alpha)(\sigma - 1)}{2b(\sigma - 1)} + \varepsilon \quad \text{and}$$

$$\theta_L(P, P) = \frac{h}{2\psi} - \frac{\beta}{\psi}\frac{\alpha - (a - \alpha)(\sigma - 1)}{2b(\sigma - 1)} + \varepsilon$$

- offer R the following contributions:

to $R^M$,

$$\theta_R(P, P) = \frac{h}{\psi} - \beta\frac{a - \alpha}{2b\psi}\frac{h}{2\psi} + \beta\frac{\alpha}{2b\psi(\sigma - 1)} + \varepsilon = \frac{h}{2\psi} + \frac{\beta}{\psi}\frac{\alpha - (a - \alpha)(\sigma - 1)}{2b(\sigma - 1)} + \varepsilon$$

to $R^C$,

$$\theta_R(P, P) = \frac{h}{2\psi} + \frac{\beta}{\psi}\frac{\alpha - (a - \alpha)(\sigma - 1)}{2b(\sigma - 1)} + \varepsilon$$

Note that the contributions simply compensate each party for the opportunity cost of choosing P, and add an infinitesimal amount $\varepsilon$ to make each party prefer P to the other alternatives.

Since the contributions are paid contingent upon the choice of a platform, and since $\theta_L(P, C) = \theta_L(P, P)$ and $\theta_R(P, P)$ is the same for RM and RC, the total cost to the suppliers is equal to $\theta_R + \theta_L = h/\psi$ plus the infinitesimal amounts that incline preferences towards P, which for simplicity are omitted from this result.

Now we have to determine whether the contribution scheme is feasible for the suppliers. Feasibility is defined in two different ways: first, whether the benefits suppliers obtain under P are enough to pay all the contributions offered – the individual rationality (IR) constraint; second, whether the increase in suppliers' utility from the no-contribution situation (C) to P exceeds the cost in contributions – the incentive compatibility (IC) constraint:

$$\text{IR:} \quad \frac{h}{\psi} < \frac{\alpha(a-\alpha)}{2b} + \frac{\alpha^2}{2b(\sigma-1)} + \frac{k_s}{4b}\left[(a-\alpha)^2 - \frac{\alpha^2}{(\sigma-1)^2}\right] \tag{2.21}$$

$$\text{IC:} \quad \frac{h}{\psi} < \frac{\alpha(a-\alpha)}{2b} + \frac{\alpha^2}{2b(\sigma-1)} + \frac{k_s}{4b}\left[(a-\alpha)^2 - \frac{\alpha^2}{(\sigma-1)^2}\right] -$$

$$\frac{\alpha(a-\alpha)}{b} = \frac{\alpha^2}{2b(\sigma-1)} - \frac{\alpha(a-\alpha)}{2b} + \frac{k_s}{4b}\left[(a-\alpha)^2 - \frac{\alpha^2}{(\sigma-1)^2}\right]. \tag{2.22}$$

The LHS of both constraints is the same (it is the sum of the optimal contributions suppliers will have to pay when they get their way). The RHS is total supplier utility under P for IR, but only the *difference* in supplier utility between C and P for the IC constraint. The RHS is thus always smaller for the IC constraint, which means that the IC is the binding feasibility constraint for the suppliers.

If the IC constraint is satisfied (which will depend on the parameter values assumed for the elements of the IC constraint), the result of the institutional choice game with contributions can be summarized in the manner of Proposition 3:

**Proposition 3:** Political decisions can be expected to be biased in favor of public enterprise monopolies as a form of infrastructure provision, because this type of institutional arrangement yields the largest surplus to consumer/voters, and also the largest rents to suppliers of inputs to the sectors. The benefits of patronage for both consumers and suppliers, resulting in support for political platforms favorable to public enterprise monopoly, will result in this arrangement being chosen over competition or private sector monopoly.

Proposition 3 shows that when suppliers' interests are included, ideological preferences may no longer hold much sway. That is why it is important, when modeling the policy-making process, to consider the role of nonvoting actors. Nonvoting actors can use a variety of means to influence policymakers, from campaign contributions to mobilization of campaign volunteers, to outright bribery. Their interests can exert a dramatic influence on policy choices, as evidenced by the large literature on state 'capture' by private interests (see, for instance, Laffont and Tirole 1993: ch. 11).

Notice that the total level of contributions needed to attain P when the median voter is a C-type, $h/\psi$, does not depend on either $\beta$ or $\phi$, the parameters that capture the intensity of ideological preferences for politicians and consumers, respectively. The intuition behind this result involves two elements of the political process as modeled here. First, consumer preferences affect political outcomes only through politicians' choices of political platforms; if all competing parties choose – by ideological conviction or bribing – not to offer consumers their preferred regime, there is nothing consumers can do about it. Hence, suppliers need only focus on affecting politicians' behavior. The second element in the explanation lies in the competitive nature of politics. Competition among political parties allows suppliers to limit contributions by offering less to the party most prone to choose P, and more to the opposing party.

## DISTRIBUTIONAL CONFLICT

Distributional conflict is modeled here as competition among suppliers for the increase in rents accruing to them under P, relative to the no-contribution outcome C (when consumer preferences favor C over P). Competition among suppliers unambiguously increases the likelihood of P. The basic reasoning behind this result is that competition produces 'Bertrand-like' results (Grossman and Helpman 1998) where suppliers spend all of their rents and profits to move away from M and C.[34] Recall that the overall utility for suppliers under different regimes is:

- under M: $u_s = (a^2 - \alpha^2)/4b$

- under C: $u_s = \dfrac{\alpha(a-\alpha)}{b}$

- under P: $u_s = \dfrac{\alpha(a-\alpha)}{2b} + \dfrac{\alpha^2}{2b(\sigma-1)} + \dfrac{k_S}{4b}\left[(a-\alpha)^2 - \dfrac{\alpha^2}{(\sigma-1)^2}\right]$

Since the level of rents is greatest for P, followed by C and then M, competition among suppliers will make P relatively more likely. Supplier rents will be dissipated up to their budget constraint, which is simply their total volume of rents under the post-contribution institutional outcome. If a supplier offers only up to the IC contribution level, another supplier can offer a higher level, but still below IR, and pocket the remainder as it obtains the supply contracts and profits, and so on until there is no money left on the table for suppliers.[35] We can restate these conclusions in a new proposition.

**Proposition 4:** Distributional conflict, in the form of competition among suppliers for the rents accruing to them under the three possible regimes, makes P more likely. In the process of competitive rent-seeking, suppliers will make contributions to politicians up to the maximum attainable level of supplier rents among the three possible regimes. Since P offers the highest rents to suppliers, the highest level of contributions will be offered to politicians that choose P and thus the likelihood that politicians pick P will be greater than when suppliers act as a single actor, other things being equal.

Competition among interest groups for the rents of various types that can be generated by infrastructure service supply will exacerbate the tendency to rely on public enterprise monopoly, further reducing the role of ideology. This contrasts with theories, going back all the way to the Federalist Papers (Fairfield 1966 [1788]), that regard interest group competition as positive, and supports instead the 'political survival' thesis originally proposed by Ames (1987). Proponents of the positive view of interest group competition believe opposing interests 'cancel each other out' with little harm to society. The 'political survival' view, by contrast, which is based on the experience of politics in less institutionalized settings than the 'Anglo-Saxon' democracies, is less sanguine about the effects of interest group competition and rent-seeking. Competing groups have an incentive to devise and support institutional arrangements that generate the maximum level of rents, so that they can access these rents to defeat their adversaries, making interest group competition far from neutral. The 'mutual cancellation' view of interest group competition may be much too naïve because it ignores the incentives generated by competition with regard to rent-seeking.

## INSTITUTIONAL CHOICE IN THE ABSENCE OF INSTITUTIONAL CONSTRAINTS

Institutional constraints are modeled here as limiting the ability of policymakers to alter policies – for instance, the existence of an independent judiciary that can strike down certain policy measures as unconstitutional, or the presence of other 'veto points' such as formal and ideological divisions in governments, or a 'Weberian' bureaucracy (Tsebelis 1990; Levy and Spiller 1996; Henisz 2000). When constraints are few, politicians are likely to have much more leeway in altering institutional arrangements at will, leading for instance to problems of time inconsistency that have traditionally plagued infrastructure provision (Spiller 1996). Institutional constraints are considered here in the following way: politicians that implement their campaign promises may be impeded, when constraints are greater, from changing the institutional arrangement later on. In other words, after the agenda 'window' for institutional choice is opened and a choice is made, the window is closed, at least partially, when institutional constraints are greater, as they limit departures from the status quo.[36]

To capture the possibility of deviations from the electoral program, I assume that after a politician is elected, with probability $\rho$ he or she will implement a purely 'electoralist' alternative, that is the one that is most preferred by the median voter, motivated perhaps by the desire of future re-election.[37] With probability $\nu$, once in power the politician will reveal him- or herself as a 'fundamentalist' and implement his or her ideal point without regard to electoral norms. Finally, with probability $1 - \rho - \nu$, the politician will maximize the mixture of electoral and ideological motives described in previous sections and will therefore implement his or her electoral platform. Following institutionalist approaches (for example, North 1990), these parameters are taken as exogenously determined by accumulated legal and political traditions.[38]

The expected behavior of politicians will now be:

- in case $P \succ C \succ M$:
$$E(Q_L) = (\nu + \rho)Q^P + (1 - \rho - \nu)Q_L$$
$$E(Q_R) = \nu Q^M + \rho Q^P + (1 - \rho - \nu)Q_R, \text{ for } R^M$$
$$E(Q_R) = \nu Q^C + \rho Q^P + (1 - \rho - \nu)Q_R, \text{ for } R^C$$

where $Q_L$ and $Q_R$ are, respectively, the announced policy platforms of candidates L and R;

- in case $C \succ P \succ M$:
$$E(Q_L) = \nu Q^P + \rho Q^C + (1 - \rho - \nu)Q_L$$
$$E(Q_R) = \nu Q^M + \rho Q^C + (1 - \rho - \nu)Q_R, \text{ for } R^M$$
$$E(Q_R) = (\nu + \rho)Q^C + (1 - \rho - \nu)Q_R, \text{ for } R^C$$

Electoral outcomes will depend on the median voter's valuation of the alternatives offered by each party under different combinations of electoral platforms, party ideologies, and consumer preferences. Since $Q$ affects consumer utility in a nonlinear manner, voting decisions are approximated by having consumers vote for the alternative closest to their preferred outcome on a weighted average basis, where weights are given by the probabilities $\rho$, $\nu$ and $1 - \rho - \nu$ previously described. For instance, if the median voter prefers P to C, he or she will vote for L if L's expected behavior is $(v + \rho)Q^P + (1 - \rho - v)Q^M$ and $R^M$'s expected behavior is $\rho Q^P + (1 - \rho)Q^M$.

We can represent these different possibilities in matrix form, where in each cell, party R's expected policy is shown at the top, L's expected policy in the middle, and the election winner at the bottom.[39]

### Consumer preferences $P \succ C \succ M$

*Table 2.7    Consumer preferences $P \succ C \succ M$: $R^M$'s platform*

| Voting outcomes | $R^M$'s platform | | |
|---|---|---|---|
| L's platform | **M** | **C** | **P** |
| **M** | **R:** $\rho Q^P + (1 - \rho)Q^M$ <br> **L:** $(v + \rho)Q^P + (1 - \rho - v)Q^M$ <br> **L wins** | **R:** $\rho Q^P + v Q^M + (1 - \rho - v)Q^C$ <br> **L:** $(v + \rho)Q^P + (1 - \rho - v)Q^M$ <br> **L wins** | **R:** $v Q^M + (1 - v)Q^P$ <br> **L:** $(v + \rho)Q^P + (1 - \rho - v)Q^M$ <br> **unclear** |
| **C** | **R:** $\rho Q^P + (1 - \rho)Q^M$ <br> **L:** $(v + \rho)Q^P + (1 - \rho - v)Q^C$ <br> **L wins** | **R:** $\rho Q^P + v Q^M + (1 - \rho - v)Q^C$ <br> **L:** $(v + \rho)Q^P + (1 - \rho - v)Q^C$ <br> **L wins** | **R:** $v Q^M + (1 - v)Q^P$ <br> **L:** $(v + \rho)Q^P + (1 - \rho - v)Q^C$ <br> **L wins generally** |
| **P** | **R:** $\rho Q^P + (1 - \rho)Q^M$ <br> **L:** $Q^P$ <br> **L wins** | **R:** $\rho Q^P + v Q^M + (1 - \rho - v)Q^C$ <br> **L:** $Q^P$ <br> **L wins** | **R:** $v Q^M + (1 - v)Q^P$ <br> **L:** $Q^P$ <br> **L wins** |

*Table 2.8*    Consumer preferences $P \succ C \succ M$: $R^C$'s platform

| Voting outcomes | $R^C$'s platform | | |
|---|---|---|---|
| L's platform | **M** | **C** | **P** |
| **M** | **R:** $\rho Q^P + v Q^C + (1-\rho - v)Q^M$ <br> **L:** $(v+\rho)Q^P + (1-\rho- v)Q^M$ <br> **L wins** | **R:** $\rho Q^P + (1-\rho)Q^C$ <br> **L:** $(v+\rho)Q^P + (1-\rho- v)Q^M$ <br> **unclear** | **R:** $v Q^C + (1-v)Q^P$ <br> **L:** $(v+\rho)Q^P + (1-\rho - v)Q^M$ <br> **R wins generally** |
| **C** | **R:** $\rho Q^P + v Q^C + (1-\rho - v)Q^M$ <br> **L:** $(v+\rho)Q^P + (1-\rho- v)Q^C$ <br> **L wins** | **R:** $\rho Q^P + (1-\rho)Q^C$ <br> **L:** $(v+\rho)Q^P + (1-\rho- v)Q^C$ <br> **L wins** | **R:** $v Q^C + (1-v)Q^P$ <br> **L:** $(v+\rho)Q^P + (1-\rho - v)Q^C$ <br> **Unclear** |
| **P** | **R:** $\rho Q^P + v Q^C + (1-\rho - v)Q^M$ <br> **L:** $Q^P$ <br> **L wins** | **R:** $\rho Q^P + (1-\rho)Q^C$ <br> **L:** $Q^P$ <br> **L wins** | **R:** $v Q^C + (1-v)Q^P$ <br> **L:** $Q^P$ <br> **L wins** |

## Consumer preferences $C \succ P \succ M$

*Table 2.9*    Consumer preferences $C \succ P \succ M$: $R^M$'s platform

| Voting outcomes | $R^M$'s platform | | |
|---|---|---|---|
| L's platform | **M** | **C** | **P** |
| **M** | **R:** $\rho Q^C + (1-\rho)Q^M$ <br> **L:** $v Q^P + \rho Q^C + (1-\rho - v)Q^M$ <br> **L wins** | **R:** $v Q^M + (1-v)Q^C$ <br> **L:** $v Q^P + \rho Q^C + (1-\rho - v)Q^M$ <br> **unclear** | **R:** $\rho Q^C + v Q^M + (1-\rho- v)Q^P$ <br> **L:** $v Q^P + \rho Q^C + (1-\rho- v)Q^M$ <br> **Unclear** |
| **C** | **R:** $\rho Q^C + (1-\rho)Q^M$ <br> **L:** $v Q^P + (1-v)Q^C$ <br> **L wins** | **R:** $v Q^M + (1-v)Q^C$ <br> **L:** $v Q^P + (1-v)Q^C$ <br> **L wins** | **R:** $\rho Q^C + v Q^M + (1-\rho- v)Q^P$ <br> **L:** $v Q^P + (1-v)Q^C$ <br> **L wins** |
| **P** | **R:** $\rho Q^C + (1-\rho)Q^M$ <br> **L:** $\rho Q^C + (1-\rho)Q^P$ <br> **L wins** | **R:** $v Q^M + (1-v)Q^C$ <br> **L:** $\rho Q^C + (1-\rho)Q^P$ <br> **L wins** | **R:** $\rho Q^C + v Q^M + (1-\rho- v)Q^P$ <br> **L:** $\rho Q^C + (1-\rho)Q^P$ <br> **L wins** |

*Table 2.10    Consumer preferences $C \succ P \succ M$: $R^C$'s platform*

| Voting outcomes | $R^C$'s platform | | |
|---|---|---|---|
| L's platform | M | C | P |
| M | R: $(\rho + v)Q^C + (1 - \rho - v)Q^M$ <br> L: $vQ^P + \rho Q^C + (1 - \rho - v)Q^M$ <br> **R wins** | R: $Q^C$ <br> L: $vQ^P + \rho Q^C + (1 - \rho - v)Q^M$ <br> **R wins** | R: $(\rho + v)Q^C + (1 - \rho - v)Q^P$ <br> L: $vQ^P + \rho Q^C + (1 - \rho - v)Q^M$ <br> **R wins** |
| C | R: $(\rho + v)Q^C + (1 - \rho - v)Q^M$ <br> L: $vQ^P + (1 - v)Q^C$ <br> **L wins** | R: $Q^C$ <br> L: $vQ^P + (1 - v)Q^C$ <br> **R wins** | R: $(\rho + v)Q^C + (1 - \rho - v)Q^P$ <br> L: $vQ^P + (1 - v)Q^C$ <br> **unclear** |
| P | R: $(\rho + v)Q^C + (1 - \rho - v)Q^M$ <br> L: $\rho Q^C + (1 - \rho)Q^P$ <br> **unclear** | R: $Q^C$ <br> L: $\rho Q^C + (1 - \rho)Q^P$ <br> **R wins** | R: $(\rho + v)Q^C + (1 - \rho - v)Q^P$ <br> L: $\rho Q^C + (1 - \rho)Q^P$ <br> **R wins** |

Now we can examine electoral strategies. First, note that P is a dominant strategy for L when confronted with $R^M$, regardless of voting preferences. No matter what $R^M$ does, L chooses P and the outcome is either P with probability one, if $P \succ C \succ M$, or C with probability $\rho$ and P with probability $1 - \rho$ if $C \succ P \succ M$. Also, P is a dominant strategy for L when confronted with $R^C$ if $P \succ C \succ M$. In this case, L always chooses P and wins, with P being the outcome with probability one. On the other hand, if $C \succ P \succ M$ then C is dominant for R; R always chooses C, wins, and C is implemented with probability one.

Thus we find that even when consumers prefer C to P, P is implemented when R's ideology is favorable to private monopoly. Relative to the case in which the judiciary is independent, *lack of institutional constraints increases the likelihood of P in the absence of contributions.*

The above results also make it clear that supplier contributions will only be necessary when consumers prefer C to P *and* R's ideal point is C. Contributions in this instance will be directed to having $R^C$ choose P as its electoral platform. $R^C$ will win the election if L chooses M or P, but may not win if L chooses C, depending on the values of the probability parameters $\rho$ and $v$. Since this is L's only chance of being elected to office, L can be expected to pick C if it knows that $R^C$ is choosing P. Hence L may need to be offered contributions too. Looking at the $L = Q^C$, $R^C = Q^P$ cell in Table 2.10, we can see that L can win if and only if $1 - \rho > v + \rho$. We can therefore distinguish two cases for contributions when the judiciary is not independent.

- *Case 1: $1 - \rho < v + \rho$.* In this case, L cannot win if $R^C$ picks P, so only $R^C$ needs to be offered contributions. The contribution is composed of two elements, the ideological penalty *if $R^C$ implements P* (therefore weighted by the probability that P is actually implemented), and the re-election penalty if instead of P, $R^C$ implements C (again, weighted by the probability of this event):

$$\theta_R(P, P) = \frac{1}{\psi}\left[(1-v-\rho)\beta\frac{\alpha-(a-\alpha)(\sigma-1)}{2b(\sigma-1)}-(v+\rho)\Gamma\right].$$

- *Case 2: $1 - \rho > v + \rho$.* Now suppliers need to offer contributions to L too, to have L choose P as the lowest-cost possibility. The contribution to L is the difference in L's utility between the choice of C and the choice of P. For the latter choice, L's utility level is zero: it loses the election, but bears no ideological cost or re-election penalty. If it chooses C, on the other hand, L wins the election, bears an ideological penalty with probability $(1 - v)$, and a re-election cost with probability $v$, so the contribution is:

$$\theta_L(P, P) = \frac{1}{\psi}\left[h-(1-v)\beta\frac{\alpha-(a-\alpha)(\sigma-1)}{2b(\sigma-1)}-v\Gamma\right].$$

The contribution to R is the same as in Case 1, so total contributions equal:

$$\theta_R(P, P) + \theta_L(P, P) = \frac{1}{\psi}\left[h-\rho\beta\frac{\alpha-(a-\alpha)(\sigma-1)}{2b(\sigma-1)}-\rho\Gamma\right].$$

Obviously, these contribution schedules must be feasible. In case 1, note that P is implemented with probability $(1 - v - \rho)$ and C with probability $v + \rho$, so we have:

IR: $\theta_R(P, P) <$

$$(1-v-\rho)\left\{\frac{\alpha(a-\alpha)}{2b}+\frac{\alpha^2}{2b(\sigma-1)}+\frac{k_s}{4b}\left[(a-\alpha)^2-\frac{\alpha^2}{(\sigma-1)^2}\right]\right\}+(v+\rho)\left[\frac{\alpha(a-\alpha)}{b}\right] \quad (2.23)$$

IC: $\theta_R(P, P) <$

$$(1-v-\rho)\left\{\frac{\alpha(a-\alpha)}{2b}+\frac{\alpha^2}{2b(\sigma-1)}+\frac{k_s}{4b}\left[(a-\alpha)^2-\frac{\alpha^2}{(\sigma-1)^2}\right]\right\}+(v+\rho)\left[\frac{\alpha(a-\alpha)}{b}\right]-$$

$$\left[\frac{\alpha(a-\alpha)}{b}\right] = (1-v-\rho)\left\{-\frac{\alpha(a-\alpha)}{2b}+\frac{\alpha^2}{2b(\sigma-1)}+\frac{k_s}{4b}\left[(a-\alpha)^2-\frac{\alpha^2}{(\sigma-1)^2}\right]\right\}$$

For case 2, the IR and IC constraints have the same RHS as the IR and IC constraints for case 1, respectively. The LHS of the constraints, however, is $\theta_R(P, P) + \theta_L(P, P)$ for both of them.

As before, the IC constraint is binding, so we can compare this constraint in cases 1 (equation 2.24) and 2 with the case where institutional constraints are strong (equation 2.22). Note that the RHS is the same for the IC constraint in all three instances (strong institutional constraints, weak institutional constraints – case 1, and weak institutional constraints – case 2). Therefore we need examine the LHS of the equations only. Also, since the $1/\psi$ factor is common to all three expressions, we can disregard it:

*Table 2.11   LHS of IC constraint*

| Judicial independence | $h$ |
|---|---|
| Weak institutional constraints — case 1 | $\left[(1-v-\rho)\beta\dfrac{\alpha-(a-\alpha)(\sigma-1)}{2b(\sigma-1)}-(v+\rho)\Gamma\right]$ |
| Weak institutional constraints — case 2 | $\left[h-\rho\beta\dfrac{\alpha-(a-\alpha)(\sigma-1)}{2b(\sigma-1)}-\rho\Gamma\right]$ |

Comparing the three expressions, we can note the following conclusions:

- $\Gamma$ forces suppliers to offer larger contributions, to compensate politicians for possible re-election penalties;
- the level of uncertainty created by the absence of judicial independence (measured by parameters $v$ and $\rho$) lowers the value of contributions (increasing the values of these parameters increases the value of the LHS[40] and thus makes the IC constraints in the absence of institutional restrictions more binding relative to the IC constraint when there are fewer such restrictions, equation (2.22)).

Therefore, incorporating contributions to the analysis nuances the preceding conclusion. These results are restated in the form of a new proposition:

**Proposition 5:** Lack of institutional constraints makes P more likely, but also makes contributions costlier and less effective. Therefore, in the (fewer) instances where C is the outcome of the institutional choice game, it is more difficult to reverse through contributions than when institutional constraints limit future policy changes.

The current conventional wisdom is that political institutions that limit policy discretion are economically efficient because they discourage rent-seeking, as interest groups find it harder to manipulate policy to create and appropriate rents (Spiller 1996). The above result shows, however, that this perspective may be excessively narrow. In the first place, as Proposition 5 makes it clear, when institutional constraints on policy are weaker, resulting in greater policy instability, the value of efforts and resources applied to rent-seeking diminishes. Rents created and appropriated today may be gone tomorrow as policy shifts in another direction in response to elections, lobbying by other interests, or other forces. Second, the conventional wisdom ignores the possibility that a 'political survival' logic may dominate interest group decisions. Such a logic would lead competing interests to redouble their rent-seeking efforts under a system with greater constraints, as the payoffs would be more likely to be sustained in the future and hence be more attractive than in an unstable system. This may explain, for instance, why in the US political system, with divided powers and significant incumbency advantages for elected politicians, the resources devoted to lobbying are so staggering rather than the opposite.[41]

Proposition 5 has important implications for our understanding of policymaking processes, at least relating to politically salient sectors such as infrastructure supply. Specifically, we need to consider more fully the conditions under which political survival imperatives may prevail. In this sense, the model above, where political competition takes place in a very simple linear context, suggests that where electoral processes are introduced with few pre-existing constraints, as is the case in many developing country democracies, the political survival logic may dominate and attempts to introduce institutional constraints on government policy may have a perverse effect as far as corruption and rent-seeking are concerned, encouraging greater public intervention in the economy through public monopolies. In turn, this means that we have to take a closer look at formal political arrangements, and also to consider informal rules that may limit or foster political survival instincts. For instance, reforms that delegate policy to meritocratic bureaucracies may be more effective at preventing opportunism than formal separation of powers provisions, because such reforms limit both the scope for policy change and the scope for rent creation and appropriation.

## CONCLUSIONS

In the process of institutional change, whereby countries choose the set of institutions that organize production in different economic sectors, the model of political choice and public enterprise behavior presented above shows that voter and politician ideology (Proposition 2), as well as distributional conflict (Proposition 4) and institutional constraints (Proposition 5), play a very important role. Despite the patronage benefits that public enterprise can confer upon voters and politicians, ideological preferences may result in other institutional choices, such as competition or even private monopoly. Yet it is nonetheless true that greater distributional conflict increases the pressure to rely on public enterprise, as competing interest groups lobby politicians for patronage through lower prices to consumers and procurement (or employment) contracts with suppliers. Lastly, the absence of institutional constraints on policy changes increases uncertainty about the outcomes of the political process, which reduces the benefits of lobbying activity. There is therefore no unambiguous relationship between institutional constraints and policy outcomes.

The implications of the model deserve some attention. They confirm the role of ideas in shaping institutions, and hence the important ideology diffusion role of institutions such as US universities, which train many foreign students. They also point to the potential long-term difficulties of introducing privatization and deregulation in highly unequal societies, insofar as higher inequality may produce higher levels of competition for office because of the higher stakes of access to office (keeping on top for some, ending subordination for others). Finally, the model questions the importance of political constraints on the choice of institutional structures. This merits some explanation. Political constraints like judicial independence restrict the choices open to policymakers and thus the ability to change the institutional framework. The model does not necessarily contradict this assertion, because the *initiation* of institutional change is not explicitly addressed by the model. Rather, it examines the factors likely to affect the *content* of reform once a window opens for it to be placed on the political agenda.

In any case, the validity of the above implications must be established empirically as well as analytically. Therefore, we now turn to testing the implications of the model, through statistical analysis first, and then through a comparison of four ESI restructuring experiences. These tests are developed in the chapters that follow.

## NOTES

1. 'Ideology' is sometimes imbued with a 'postmodern' perspective, where all choices are seen as equally valid and dictated solely by 'power', 'ideological domination', 'isomorphism' or some other such factors. My use of the term is much plainer, being closely related to economists' notion of 'preferences'. At the same time, the discussion of institutional choices in this book has no normative intent, the research question being purely positive in nature.
2. Alternatively, we can think of advances in regulatory know-how, that make it easier for regulators to determine long-run marginal costs without major problems of private information held by the regulated firm, in which case regulators would correctly set price equal to minimum long-run marginal cost $\alpha$ (see Armstrong et al. 1994). In any case, adding a fixed term only complicates the algebra without altering the basic results of the model, which hinge on the tradeoff between 'pecuniary' or 'consumption' gains for politicians, consumers and other groups, and ideological considerations in the process of choosing an institutional arrangement for the industry.
3. One or more public enterprises competing among each other or with private counterparts would either behave like private competitors and produce the P outcome or, if not bound by a profitability constraint, result in an outcome similar to P as private competitors are displaced. Hence, the analysis that follows subsumes the competitive public enterprise in either P or C.
4. There are many instances where legal rather than cost or demand considerations result in oligopoly or monopoly. A well-known case, for instance, is that of airlines, where the now-defunct Civil Aeronautics Board would 'license' a single or a few carriers to service a particular route, whether or not a larger number of airlines could service it in the absence of such licensing.
5. This assumes no principal–agent problems in regulation (also likely to be present in the other institutions), and more specifically no information asymmetries in the regulatory process. Since the purpose of viewing the competitive arrangement in this light is to explore the conditions under which independent regulatory institutions might be created, abstracting from the complexities of regulation is a reasonable simplification. For further considerations on this issue, see the concluding chapter of the book.
6. This is only a stylized rendering of public enterprise goals and as such it abstracts from other important motivations, such as preferences for domestic over foreign ownership and agency problems. The reason for focusing on patronage is that it has clear and important behavioral implications for public enterprise behavior. To the extent that domestic ownership is important, and it can only be realized through public ownership, it is reflected in the model's ideological dimension. Likewise, managerial interests – to the extent that they are of special importance for public enterprise – can be subsumed with other 'supplier' interests (see previous footnote). This is further addressed in the next section and the conclusion.
7. This would shift the cost curve out, and increase the size of $T$ *ceteris paribus*, but not otherwise impact the results of the model other than adding to its algebraic complexity. For this reason, this effect is not explicitly modeled.
8. A very extensive literature in management studies discusses why private-firm managers are likely to place a high value on revenue growth, for instance because capital markets are imperfect and larger size reduces the cost of capital (see Collis and Montgomery 1998: 77–8); for unions, larger size (greater membership) may bring greater political salience and thus greater bargaining power for their members.
9. The requirement that $\sigma$ not equal unity resembles the 'no-Ponzi scheme' requirement of certain growth models. Like private agents, the government can't create wealth out of thin air.
10. As already mentioned, it is also possible that public enterprises will produce at the private monopoly or at the competitive level.

11. At $Q^p$, the level of profits is $[(a - \alpha)^2 - a^2/(\sigma-1)^2]/4b$, which is zero at the competitive level output, that is, when $\sigma = a/(a - \alpha)$, and negative for any $\sigma$ lower than $a/(a- \alpha)$ down to the lower limit $\sigma = 1$, given the function's hyperbolic shape in $\sigma$. Because public enterprise produces at a loss, it is also possible that, over time, the burden of transfers $T$ will be such that $\sigma$ will rise and public monopolies will be privatized and perhaps deregulated too; the possibility of such cycles – as perhaps shown by the latest cycle of privatizations around the world – is considered further below. Waterbury (1993) provides evidence of 'insatiable' public enterprise expansion in Egypt, India, Mexico, and Turkey.

12. Note that I make no attempt to evaluate social welfare under the three possible arrangements, since I am trying to explain political choices rather than establish normative propositions. For the possibility that free entry produces socially inefficient outcomes, see Mankiw and Whinston (1986).

13. Since the British undertook their reforms, I have documented reforms of varying scope taking place in some 90 countries.

14. I do not explore the process by which the choice of institutional arrangements appears on the policymaking agenda. I claim that agenda considerations are analytically separable from institutional choices. In the case of infrastructure industries such as electricity supply, in addition to technological changes largely exogenous to the policymaking process, a variety of motivations have contributed to placing reform on the political agenda, such as the exhaustion of investment capacity by the public sector, or simply the desire to enhance social welfare by increasing the scope of market processes. While the financial burdens of public enterprise may place reform on the agenda, and indeed lead to policy cycles as suggested in the conclusions, it is essential to note that even in cases of severe financial crunches, for example, in most Indian states, Ecuador, or even Mexico, privatization or deregulation have not been carried out, which suggests that even when financial reasons put the issue of reform on the agenda, there is still a considerable degree of freedom regarding institutional arrangements. See the preceding chapter, especially the quote from Bacon and Besant-Jones (2001) in note 3; also, Aoki (2001: chs. 9–10) for a discussion of how the triggers of institutional change (including technological innovation) can differ from the mechanisms for selection of a new institution. 'We visualize institutional change as a process by which the agents discover a new way of doing things in response to their own crises' (ibid., p. 232).

15. Where private production occurs, that is, under M and C, producers additionally require a participation, or individual rationality (IR) constraint of nonnegative profits. This requirement is satisfied by the assumptions made in the preceding section.

16. Note that managerial interests are not separately considered. See note 5.

17. Not all consumers may bear equal tax burdens, for instance if there is widespread tax evasion. The tax term here is simply a shorthand for the costs imposed on consumers by government spending, such as inflation, indebtedness, cuts in other services, and the like.

18. To avoid aggregation problems, I use aggregate consumption Q rather than individual consumption in the calculation of consumer surplus. Since all consumers have identical demand functions, the use of Q instead of q does not alter voting outcomes.

19. For analytical purposes, quality can be subsumed as an additional dimension of quantity or as reflected in price (lower quality of service is equivalent to a higher $p$).

20. Collusion among voters is ruled out given the enormous difficulty of organizing atomistic interests and sustaining collective action. The obstacles to consumer organization are well known at least since Olson (1965).

21. For instance, the Mexican government recently scrapped plans to cut subsidies in electricity rates after street demonstrations and a call by the opposition party for a campaign of civil disobedience (Silver 2002a). According to this source, it takes a middle-class Mexican 20 hours of work to pay the monthly electricity bill, compared with only five hours in the US. The case for the importance of electoral visibility in policy decisions regarding infrastructure is clearly articulated in Spiller (1996). Of course, visibility also affects other goods and services, particularly food items in developing countries, hence the difficulty of removing food subsidies.

22. This impact would be included in a general equilibrium or public finance model of institutional choice and has a direct monetary effect on consumer income, so its inclusion here should be uncontroversial.
23. Note that in the political utility function (2.12), the ideology term enters additively to consumer surplus and tax impact to simplify the analysis, but this by no means implies that ideological and economic impacts are simply treated as additive. The coefficient $\phi$ in the ideology term is precisely intended to capture the different metrics of economic and ideological variables used by voters. See Hinich and Munger (1994).
24. Again, the assumption of vote-maximization is a modeling simplification that yields analytically tractable implications. Other dimensions of political behavior, such as public service motivations, can be conveniently included in ideology (for example, public service ideas are generally associated with competition).
25. 'Left' and 'right' are a shorthand representing typical positions on the political spectrum, not statements about the necessary positions of conservative and progressive forces. Conservative governments, for instance, may favor P out of nationalist ideas, if private ownership implies foreign ownership. The contest as modeled seems most representative of politics in many countries around the world. In fact, the consideration of right-wing parties with different ideologies partially expands the model beyond a strictly bipartisan setting.
26. I assume suppliers cannot impose actual costs on politicians, only offer positive reinforcement. In reality, labor unions do undertake stoppages, demonstrations and even violent actions that harm politicians, and businesspeople can hire thugs, militias or other agents to carry out punishment. The nonnegativity constraint simply means that any of these measures imposes a cost on the supplier.
27. A particular offer takes the form of a $\theta_j(Q_j, Q_k)$ payment to politician $j$ when politician $j$ chooses policy $Q_j$ and the contender chooses $Q_k$.
28. And investment plans, if private ownership is expected.
29. It is often argued that the existence of sunk costs in infrastructure provision renders such punishment incredible. While an assumption of this book is that technological change is reducing the importance of sunk costs, even if sunk costs are important it is difficult to understand why punishment would be incredible. Although it is costly to change course, public enterprises can be privatized, deregulated markets can be re-regulated, and private firms nationalized or expropriated, especially through the refusal to grant rate increases when production costs rise. Moreover, punishment signals displeasure with politicians who break their promises. Consumers and suppliers thus have every incentive to punish such politicians.
30. Uncertainty or informational deficiencies among voters affect policy outcomes primarily through the future electoral punishment of politicians who switch, or are perceived to switch, policies after being elected. This issue is addressed below. Uncertainty or limited information may also be the result of agency problems in public enterprise. See notes 8 and 9, as well as the concluding chapter, for a discussion of agency problems and their impact on the model presented here.
31. The assumption of full information will be relaxed in a subsequent section.
32. Another condition that increases the importance of policymakers' ideologies is, as one would expect, the absence of an electoral process for the selection of an institutional regime among the choices offered by competing parties, whether contributions are allowed or not. An analysis of this case, which is excluded here due to its lesser interest, is available from the author upon request.
33. To see this, consider the worst possible case for the above inequality, where suppliers bear the full tax burden ($k_s = 1$). In such a case, the above inequality reduces to the inequality $[(a - \alpha)^2 - 2\,\alpha\,(a - \alpha)] + 2a^2(\sigma - 1)^{-1} - \alpha^2(\sigma - 1)^{-2} > 0$. Substituting $x = (\sigma - 1)^{-1}$, this becomes a standard quadratic expression. Solving for the values of $\sigma$ at the roots, it is apparent that $1 < \sigma < \alpha/(a - \alpha)$ for one of the roots. A (partial equilibrium) proof of the feasibility of P from the perspective of public finance (that is, the financeability of P given consumer and supplier preferences) is available from the author upon request.

34. Bertrand competition occurs wherever firms compete on price rather than quantity, with the result that even with only two firms, each one has an incentive to underbid the other by offering a lower price, until they cannot reduce price further without losing money on each unit sold (that is, where price equals marginal cost). In the institutional game model, 'price' is the contribution that each supplier is willing to offer the politicians for giving him or her exclusive access to the supplier rents generated under P, so in this case suppliers outbid each other by offering more to the politicians, until the suppliers are offering the entire amount of rents available to suppliers under P.

35. Since competition among suppliers appears to be so beneficial to politicians, we would expect politicians to foster such competition. But we must bear in mind that politicians may have limited means to spur competition. For instance, setting up rival labor unions has been a common device to split workers, but it often failed because workers have seen the ruse and refused to join the alternative union.

36. Of course, politicians can renege on electoral promises even before any policy is implemented. But courts and other institutions (such as the civil service) cannot do anything about this other than enforcing the status quo. Again, since this is a model of institutional *choice*, it necessarily must be based on the assumption that a window of choice *does* appear at some point in the polity, so status quo bias of this kind is not considered in the model. Status quo bias is carefully analyzed in Fernández and Rodrik (1998).

37. Hence under the two possible preference orderings assumed for consumers, the electoralist choice will be P for all $j$ = L, R when $P \succ C \succ M$, and C for all $j$ = L, R when $C \succ P \succ M$. Again, it is important to recall that judicial and other constraints act by restricting changes in implementation once the new government has made a choice. I do not impose additional periodization here to avoid excessive complexity; what matters is that voters can expect policy to be changed in mid–course from that promised at the election and originally implemented. Alternatively, the analysis presented in this section may be regarded as extending the model to account for uncertainty or informational deficiencies among voters regarding the relationship between institutional outcomes and consumer utility. However, to avoid undue complexity, the model does not specify the motivations of politicians to switch. For a further discussion of this issue, see Stokes (2001: ch. 3).

38. To be sure, weaker institutional constraints can also affect the attractiveness and payoffs of C and M (e.g. by undermining the contract structure needed to clear the market). However, to avoid excessive complication in the model, this possibility is not considered here.

39. Where outcomes are unclear, by 'wins generally' I am making the reasonable assumption that if one party offers a weighted average of the two most favored outcomes for the median voter, whereas the opponent offers a weighted average of the most favored and least favored outcomes, the former party is more likely to win.

40. Simply consider what happens when $v + \rho \rightarrow 1$. For both cases of lack of judicial independence, the LHS expressions approach $+\infty$.

41. Landes and Posner (1975) articulated a similar argument in connection with the explanation of judicial independence.

# 3. Cross-sectional tests

Having set the theoretical argument in the preceding chapter, we now turn to the empirical testing of the propositions derived from the formal model. This chapter describes large-N empirical tests, while subsequent chapters present a comparison of several cases as a means of supplementing the rigor of econometric methods with the richness of detail afforded by case studies. Empirical studies of institutional change that go beyond the case study format have so far concentrated on comparing economic efficiency under private and public ownership, rather than on the prior question of what forces shape ownership choices in the first place. This contrasts with the analysis that follows in this chapter, as in the book as a whole, which examines the forces that influence institutional choices, such as ownership, in the first place.[1] Fortunately, in the specific case of the ESI, the large and increasing number of countries that have undertaken ESI reform since the UK did it in 1991 has made it possible to undertake statistical analyses of these changes.

The rest of this chapter provides a statistical test of the propositions derived from the formal model of the previous chapter. This is accomplished first by establishing testable hypotheses on the basis of the propositions. Next, a data set of indicators for the dependent variables is constructed; this includes a description of the scoring procedure used to aggregate dependent variable observations into overall measures of ownership and competition outcomes. The next section provides similar information about the set of independent or explanatory variable data and aggregate measures. The following section introduces and discusses the regression analyses used to test the above hypotheses. The final section concludes. In addition, Appendix 1 provides a description of the variables used, including their means, standard deviations, minimum and maximum values, number of observations available, a succinct explanation of what each variable measures, the period of measurement, and the source of data. Appendix 1 tables provide correlation coefficients, including significance levels and number of observations used to measure the coefficients, for the main right-hand-side variables used in the regression analysis.

## TESTABLE IMPLICATIONS

Some of the propositions derived in the preceding chapter cannot be easily tested by econometric techniques. Measuring most of the parameters used in the formal model is difficult because of their subjective nature and the lack of databases that might contain the required information – think, for instance, of the difficulty of determining the relative weight of politicians' ideological preferences in their utility functions, or the feasibility of optimal contributions. However, we can distill the propositions into a compact set of testable implications about how we can expect ideological preferences, distributional conflict, and judicial independence to affect institutional choices for the ESI:

1. Reliance on private ownership will be more likely to occur, other things being equal, where any one of the following conditions holds true:

   1.1 ideologies that favor private property are more prevalent in the country or jurisdiction undertaking ESI reform (Propositions 2 and 5); or

   1.2 distributional conflict is less significant (Proposition 4); but

   1.3 not necessarily under higher judicial independence (Proposition 6).

2. Deregulation will be more likely to occur, other things being equal, where any one of the following conditions is present:

   2.1 ideologies that favor private property are more prevalent in the country or jurisdiction undertaking ESI reform (Propositions 2 and 5); or

   2.2 distributional conflict is less significant (Proposition 4); but

   2.3 not necessarily under higher judicial independence (Proposition 6).

The testable implications of Proposition 6, which concerns institutional constraints in general, are expressed in terms of a specific type of constraint, judicial independence.[2] Judicial independence is taken here to be an instrument or, alternatively, a representative variable, for institutional constraints. Recent research on institutional constraints on policymaking (Tsebelis 1990; Spiller 1996; Henisz 2000) considers a much broader set of factors that effectively measure the degree to which policy can be reversed in any given polity, such as: the existence of powerful subnational levels of government; the degree of fractionalization of the legislature, the government, and even the highest court; and the internal structure of the legislature, among others. We can think of judicial independence as a concrete manifestation of these factors, and one that has particular relevance for the ESI because of the role of the courts in enforcing contracts and reviewing regulatory decisions.[3] Thus, countries where institutional constraints impede frequent and wide policy shifts are likely to have a more independent judiciary than countries with weaker constraints. When constraints are strong, governments and legislatures will have much greater difficulty in reversing judicial decisions or punishing the courts for decisions adverse to the interests of the government or legislators. In fact, as it has often been pointed out for the US, in divided polities the courts can actually come to play an important policy role by default, because a divided legislature, or a 'cohabiting' executive and legislature, cannot agree on issues such as abortion or the death penalty. Judicial independence is also a good proxy for institutional constraints because it embodies both formal and informal aspects of the institutional framework – from formal rules about appointment and promotion of judges, to informal norms about the enforcement of judicial decisions by the executive. The use of judicial independence as an explanatory variable can therefore limit excessive reliance on purely formal constraints which, although more easily measurable, can (and are) often bypassed by informal norms and habits.

## DEPENDENT VARIABLE DATA

The construction of a data set of dependent variables reflecting cross-national variation in ESI restructuring outcomes is the core of the empirical testing procedure followed in this chapter. The process of constructing the data set involved four steps: first, establishing a set of indicators of competition and ownership choices in the ESI; second, determining the values that each of these indicators can take; third, reviewing the available information, mainly of a narrative nature, to assign values to each variable for countries that have undertaken ESI restructuring; and fourth, aggregating the results into overall scores for ownership and competition.

### Establishment of Dependent Variables

On the basis of literature review, my own experience in the ESI, and the possibility of assigning values with a minimum of subjectivity and a maximum of relevance for the hypotheses to be tested, I established the following variables to measure ownership and competition outcomes in each country:

1. *Ownership measures*

- ownership structure of the generation sector;
- ownership structure of the nuclear sector (a subset of generation, in which extreme capital intensity and international security considerations tend to make public ownership or intervention more common than for other generation technologies);
- ownership structure of the transmission sector;
- ISO governance (the independent system operator, or ISO, is the basic controller of an electrical system and can operate separately from the transmission line owner; therefore, the governance structure of this operator can also be indicative of choices made concerning ownership);
- ownership structure of the distribution sector;
- reliance on concessions (where use, but not disposability, is granted over the assets, generally for a limited time period), or full ownership of productive assets for privatized utilities (the use of concessions could be construed as reflecting greater reluctance to rely on private ownership);
- distribution of utility shares to utility employees in the course of privatization, at subsidized (that is, below market) prices (which to some extent keeps utility ownership 'socialized' even after privatization, and may therefore be indicative of preference for public ownership[4]);
- possibility of direct foreign investment in the ESI (in many developing countries and small economies, privatization of a capital-intensive industry like the ESI is only possible if foreign investors can gain ownership of ESI assets);
- regulatory independence (which is an indicator of the implementing government's willingness to forego intervention in the ESI and therefore respect the property rights of private investors);
- possibility of judicial recourse of regulatory decisions (which can further limit arbitrary government intervention in the industry and with it the direct or indirect – via excessively low regulated prices – expropriation of privately-owned assets);

2. *Competition measures*

- possibility of competition in generation (whether competition is legally possible, for instance through the creation of a centralized spot market for electrical energy);
- possibility of competition in retailing of electricity (this function can be separated from distribution services and opened to competition, as in the UK);
- possibility of vertical integration (self-dealing and control over transmission lines can facilitate exclusion of actual or potential competitors in generation markets);
- existence of open access limits (limitations to the ability of consumers to participate in deregulated electricity markets and freely negotiate with generators and intermediaries; we can expect that the fewer consumers can participate, the less competitive the market is likely to be, since consumers will be less exposed to market signals);
- use of yardstick or price cap regulation (these are potential mechanisms for introducing 'market-like' factors even in segments that are natural monopolies, like transmission and distribution; 'yardstick competition' involves using benchmarks from firms engaged in similar activities to set regulated prices; price cap regulation involves mimicking competitive pressures by making regulated rates reflect the impact of productivity increases that normally results from competitive pressures);
- franchise bidding (making prospective service providers compete 'for the market' by offering the highest price for the assets being privatized, given some expected regulated prices in the future, or alternatively by offering the lowest prices for the goods produced under monopolistic conditions, wherever competition 'in the market' is impeded by natural monopoly, as a substitute for regulation of the monopoly's prices);
- competitive market structure (since in most ESI restructuring cases government ownership or influence on the sector gave it the power to alter the ownership structure of the privatized competitive segments of the industry, or have the antitrust legal instruments to limit ownership concentrations, concentrated horizontal ownership in the generation sector is indicative of greater government tolerance for monopoly).

**Range of Values for the Dependent Variables**

Most of the above variables have been structured on a binary, yes-or-no basis. The main reasons for doing so are the limitations of the available information sources for making finer distinctions, and the inherent arbitrariness of establishing 'middle categories' for variables that measure largely nonquantitative outcomes. Where it was possible to use more than two variable values, as in the cases of ownership and ISO governance, the opportunity has been taken. For ownership of generation, nuclear, transmission, and distribution assets, I have established three possible values, in ascending order from 'more private' to 'more public': entirely private, mixed, and entirely public. In some cases, the distinction between 'mixed' and the other cases is somewhat arbitrary, because there may be residual private or public ownership shares. For instance, in Argentina most generation assets are in private hands, but two nuclear stations and a large, near-complete hydroelectric facility (Yaciretá) are still in public hands because of their special characteristics (for example, Yaciretá is a joint undertaking with Uruguay, governed by an intergovernmental treaty). The exceptional nature of these still-public generation assets makes it reasonable to categorize Argentina as 'entirely private'. When in doubt, I have used the 'mixed' category to minimize arbitrariness in coding.

ISO governance is coded along a similar 'increasingly public' scale, under the presumption that public ISO ownership is more likely to facilitate competition than full private ownership, since the latter offers better opportunities for collusion. For this variable, however, I have further separated full private ownership between 'generator' (or utility) clubs and private, unaffiliated entities or mixed groups of market participants. In some countries such as Chile, generators or incumbent utilities have been allowed to control the ISO, with allegedly detrimental effects for competition.

**Assignment of Values from Narrative Accounts**

I have attempted to collect data from as many countries as possible on which I have been able to find information regarding ESI restructuring.[5] The major source of information for the assignment of values to each variable for each country in the database has been McGraw-Hill's *International Private Power Quarterly* (*IPPQ*), a periodical publication with extensive coverage of electricity markets throughout the world.[6] Where possible, I have verified or corrected the information in *IPPQ* from other sources, mainly from work by the Harvard Electricity Policy Group (HEPG) on ISO governance structures and from Yajima (1997). For the case of the Scandinavian countries, which are not covered by *IPPQ*, I have relied on information kindly supplied to me by Tor Johnsen (a former visiting scholar at HEPG), Professor Ole Jess Olsen of Copenhagen University, and Jon Sturlusson of the Stockholm School of Economics. In the few cases of countries with federal structures where there are institutional differences across subnational jurisdictions (essentially Australia, Canada, the UK, and the US), I have tried to reflect the most common type of arrangement or, for the US, the framework established by the Federal Energy Regulatory Commission in Order 888.

Ownership stakes by governments and private investors are well documented by *IPPQ* and other sources and were therefore relatively easy to code. Likewise, the use of concessions and of franchise bidding (the two are closely linked, since in most cases concessions are allocated through auctions) is extensively reported by the trade and general business press. These sources also report the allocation of shares to employees, since privatization or concession auction press releases usually include the post-auction ownership structure including employee-owned stakes. Since much of the market for business publications is oriented towards the investment community (the ESI being a very capital-intensive industry), any restrictions on foreign direct investment (FDI) are reported in the accounts of restructuring initiatives. Information about competition in generation and retailing is included in descriptions of national electricity markets. The existence of vertically-integrated utilities is available from descriptions of major utilities in the country. Open access limits are also included in descriptions of trading arrangements. ISO governance structures have been examined by HEPG, as already mentioned, or are easily identified in many cases because the ISO is the sole transmission service provider in the country, and information about ownership of the provider or concessionaire is available from the narratives.

Other dependent variables involve greater coding ambiguity. Regulatory independence can be controversial: many countries claim to have independent regulators, yet they are organizationally part of government ministries. Where possible, I have obtained information about the timing of regulator appointments (coincidence with elections for the executive and coincidence of terms for commission members if regulatory decisions are made by a commission), requirements for legislative vetting of appointments, degree of budgetary independence of regulatory agencies, appointment incompatibilities with other private or public positions, and grounds for removal of regulators.

Judicial recourse is even less clear, because in cases such as Argentina the first instance of appeal of regulatory decisions is the executive energy agency, and the courts only intervene at a higher level. My criterion has been fairly simple: I have coded judicial recourse as a 'yes' whenever I have found mention of rules that explicitly allow it or whenever I have found mention of disputes between ESI participants decided in the courts.

For the use of yardstick competition or price caps there is more limited information. Where descriptions of rate-setting principles have mentioned the use of any of these methodologies, I have coded the country as a 'yes'. In some cases, I have made the inference that the decision to split a nationwide utility into several distribution companies implies the intent to rely on yardstick competition, and thus coded these cases as affirmative as well.

I have incurred the greatest arbitrariness in coding the 'competitive market structure' variable. Not only is there very little data for most countries that would allow the construction of ownership concentration ratios, but ongoing privatization efforts would make any such indicators suspect from the outset. Instead, I have used two different criteria: first, in many cases governments have imposed ownership and control limits as a percentage if installed generation capacity in the country, or have broken up large or single utilities into many separate units and sold them to different buyers, which will guarantee competition at least for a number of years; second, when such information was not available, narrative accounts, particularly in *IPPQ*, include descriptions of 'major players' together with the number of megawatts (MW) they own. I have not used such data to attempt to compute concentration ratios, but it has given me an indication to assign more or less arbitrarily a value to the dependent variable. For example, the Spanish electricity market is dominated by two large utilities (Endesa and Iberdrola), so it is almost certainly not competitive. Even if I had sufficient information to actually estimate concentration ratios, I would still face the problem of deciding at what level does a market become 'competitive' (which is precisely why these types of measure are no longer used as benchmarks in empirical industrial organization economics).

Finally, it is worth noting that the observations are remarkably contemporaneous. Electricity restructuring for the countries in the sample has occurred, with almost no exceptions, during the 1990s. This means that to the extent that outcomes within each country change over time as new institutions 'mature' or political reactions take place, this should introduce little cross-sectional variation because of the contemporaneity of the recorded data points.

## Aggregation of Dependent Variable Data into Scores

For purposes of hypothesis testing, it makes sense to aggregate the results of the coding exercise into overall scores for competition and ownership for each country. While scoring may lead to the loss of information concerning differences across countries in the specific choices made for each variable, it has the advantage of turning the somewhat arbitrarily coded values for each variable into more consistent indicators of the outcomes observed in each country,[7] thus affording a more reliable hypothesis test. For instance, results about recourse to the courts against regulatory decisions (an ownership indicator) may be swayed by coding decisions based on ambiguous or casual references, while the aggregation of several measures will lower the effect of interpretations of such references.

In fact, aggregation is conceptually necessary as well because the factors that I am testing are not policy decisions on specific aspects of ESI restructuring, but rather broader decisions about the extent of competition and ownership, which means that hypothesis testing through the use of the individual components could be misleading. Individual component observations need not always reflect overall inclinations towards more or less competition or private ownership, and thus the results of individual analyses would be harder to interpret.

Scoring also reduces the number of dependent variables from a multiplicity to just two, which greatly facilitates the interpretation of test results, and allows the treatment of the dependent variables as effectively continuous rather than discrete. Since there are ten indicators of ownership and seven indicators of competition choices, the scoring procedure yields a substantial number of possible values for each aggregate variable.

To compute the scores, I have simply added the value of each indicator variable for competition or ownership and divided by the maximum theoretically obtainable score for that country, that is not counting the indicator variables for which there is no information. In this way, the scores vary between zero and one regardless of the number of coded indicator variables for that particular country. The two scores I have computed, for competition (CSCORE) and ownership (PSCORE), take their lowest values (zero in both cases) for competitive and private outcomes, respectively, while the highest values (one in both cases) measure full monopoly and public ownership. Competition and ownership scores are shown for each country in the database in Figure 3.1.

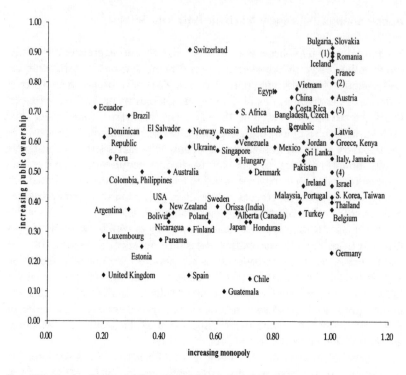

*Key:* (1) Algeria, Botswana, Cameroon, Malawi, Namibia, Niger, Nigeria, Tunisia. (2) Belarus, Ghana, Paraguay, Zambia. (3) Mauritius, Morocco, Senegal, Tanzania, Uganda, Zimbabwe. (4) Côte d'Ivoire, Indonesia, Uruguay.

*Figure 3.1    Competition and ownership scores, 1999*

Since the scores themselves are distributed only between zero and one, I have expressed them in log-odds form,[8] so that they would be distributed over the range of values that would be found with a normal distribution of error terms and thus make the dependent variable data amenable to the use of OLS regression methods.

## EXPLANATORY VARIABLE DATA

Explanatory variables were constructed from a variety of data sets providing potential instruments for any of the three causal factors established by the hypotheses (judicial independence, ideology, and distributional conflict). Other variables were used to control for other elements that could otherwise distort the results. The variables used as controls, and their importance, are discussed in the next section of the chapter. The rest of this section explains first the selection of the indicators, and then their aggregation for each hypothesized causal factor. Appendix 1 provides summary information on all indicators used.

### Sources of Explanatory Variable Data

In order to test the three hypotheses concerning, respectively, the role of judicial independence, ideology, and distributional struggles in institutional change, I selected from the available databases potential indicators for each one of the causal factors. For this purpose, I relied on the narrative descriptions of the data sets wherever such an explanation was available, from which I determined whether a given variable would be useful as an indicator for any of the hypothesized factors, or as a control variable.

The indicators of judicial independence comprise both data that measure respect for the courts more or less directly, as well as data on the actual application of the law, such as the existence of a low-quality civil service, which will generally weaken law enforcement,[9] or the level of access to legal remedies, which tells us whether the legal system is in practice a viable dispute resolution mechanism.

A major subset of judicial independence indicators are the measures of respect for the law and administrative norms compiled by Political Risk Services, Inc. (PRS), a major provider of international business risk rankings. The University of Maryland's Institute for Reform and the Informal Sector (IRIS) has made available for purchase a compilation of a subset of PRS data, for the 1982–95 period that is particularly oriented towards measuring the extent of the rule of law: contract repudiation risk (REPUD), expropriation risk (EXPRISK), level of corruption (CORRUPT), level of law and order (LORDER), and quality of the civil service (BURQUAL). For each of these indicators, the value used for each available country was simply the arithmetic average of the observations for that country over the 14-year period.

Two other measures of judicial independence were obtained from published surveys of the environment for private business in countries around the world. PROPRTS is an indicator of the degree of protection of property rights prepared for the 1998 *Index of Economic Freedom* (Johnson et al., 1998). LEGACC measures the accessibility of the judicial system to a country's citizenry, as coded for the *Economic Freedom in the World* survey of 1995 (Gwartney 1997). Although this variable does not directly measure judicial independence, it is useful to include it here because its effects are equivalent to the lack of judicial independence: a judicial system that is not available to the public is effectively nullified as a mechanism to protect rights and enforce laws, just as in the case of a judicial system subservient to the current government.

Of course, the PRS measures are oriented towards business and commercial matters, while the rule of law also concerns civil rights and political freedoms. It therefore makes sense to also examine measures of respect for these rights and liberties, as reported in Freedom House's *Freedom in the World* (Freedom House, 1990 edition), an index of political rights (POLRTS) and an index of civil liberties (CIVILFR). On a more procedure-oriented basis, the Polity II (Gurr 1989/1990) and Polity III (Jaggers and Gurr 1995/1996) data sets (averaged for the 1946–86 period for the former, and for 1946-1994 for the latter) provided a measure of the degree of formalization of transfers of executive power (EXTFR).

Finally, more direct measures of judicial independence have been compiled by other researchers: the average length of tenure of supreme court justices (CTTEN) was estimated by Witold Henisz for the post-Second World War period, and kindly supplied by him; judicial independence scores (JUDIND) are as reported by Sullivan (1991).[10]

A second group of indicators measure ideology. Ideology is difficult to capture directly, since the actions of policymakers are by no means driven by ideological concern only, and classifying party and candidate platforms into categories along the left–right axis requires condensing positions on many issues into a single dimension. For this reason, I have used not only a measure of the ideology of the party in power when ESI reform was begun in each country, but also more general measures of the 'political climate' in each country that are likely to affect the predisposition of politicians towards certain institutional arrangements. For instance, in France there is a broad consensus across the political spectrum for keeping the state, through ministries or State-owned enterprises (SOEs), firmly in control of the 'commanding heights' of the economy; not surprisingly, France has consistently opposed efforts to fully deregulate the ESI in the European Union.

The ideology of the party in power at the time of initiation of ESI reform[11] (where applicable) was obtained from Derbyshire and Derbyshire (1996) and from various editions of *The World Handbook of Political and Social Indicators* (Taylor and Jodice 1982/1983).[12] The dummy IDCL takes a value of one if the parties in government were center-left or further to the left of this point. For economic ideology, I have mainly relied on indices of 'economic freedom' such as the *World Survey of Economic Freedom 1995–1996* (Messick and Kimura 1996), *Economic Freedom in the World 1997* (Gwartney 1997, containing data for 1975, 1980, 1985, 1990, and 1995), and the *1998 Index of Economic Freedom* (Johnson et al. 1998; I have only used 1998 data). These sets are based on data culled from government and international statistics and other various sources, and are therefore less prone to bias than survey questionnaires; in some cases, moreover, they contain data predating ESI reform. From these data sets, I used rankings of the scope of government activity in the economy (SCOPE 1946–1986), the importance of the SOE sector (in all industries) in 1975 (SOE75), freedom to compete (COMPFR 1995), government interventionism (INTERV 1998), freedom for foreign investment (FDIFREE 1998), and wage and price controls (PRCONT 1998).

Ideology, however, is not only economic, but also moral and social, as concerns for instance the toleration for legalized abortion. At the same time, everyday observation shows that certain social values tend to be tied (whether logically or not) to economic values, such as 'family values' with the defense of private property. As certain of these moral and social ideas are expressed in the collective choices made by different societies about abortion, the death penalty, and other matters, I have considered measures of noneconomic values as well. Most of these measures are from compilations gathered by Sullivan (1991): contraceptive use (BIRTHC), abortion policy (ABORTP), protection of ecosystems (PROTAR), acceptance of international environmental treaties (ENVTR), and recourse to the death penalty (DEATHP). Divorce rates (DIVR) in the 1980s are from The Economist Books Ltd. (1990).[13] Lastly, female–male differences in adult illiteracy rates in 1970 (MFILLIT, from the World Bank 1998) were included as a measure of social ideology since these differences generally correspond to societal attitudes about gender roles.

The third group of indicators provide information about distributional matters. Distributional conflict is perhaps the hardest explanatory variable to measure. The first problem is that the theoretical proposition about the role of distributional conflict specifically focuses on supplier competition rather than other forms of conflict. Competition among individuals for jobs, among firms for contracts, or among investors for attractive profit opportunities may not be easily measured in a simple way. On the other hand, there are several variables that can be strongly related to these forms of competition for economic rents. Measures of inequality in the distribution of income would be prime candidates, because in highly unequal societies we can expect disadvantaged groups of workers, firms or savers to exist and exert pressure to improve their lot *vis-à-vis* the privileged groups.

Although inequality by itself need not result in conflict over the distribution of resources – political mobilization is also required to bring inequities to the political arena – high levels of inequality have given rise in many countries to mechanisms of social and political control that do put pressure on resources. Clientelism, in particular, often puts severe pressure on the resources of the public sector because social and political elites make use of these resources to buy off potential opposition from below. As a result, I use measures of inequality in the distribution of resources and of labor conflict, but I also consider the relative level of government transfers to SOEs, since the origin of losses in many SOEs lies in the claims made upon SOE output by various social groups. Lastly, measures of social or political fragmentation, like the number of political parties in the legislature or the degree of territorial decentralization, are more directly indicative of the likelihood of competition among ESI suppliers for economic rewards. For instance, the existence of a large number of parties may reflect competition among unions or pressure groups through the organization of rival party structures.

For the distribution of incomes, Gini coefficients for income as well as quintiles and deciles of income distribution were obtained from the World Bank (1998), for the late 1980s and early 1990s (YGINI). The enrollment of females in the school system, as a percentage of the total number of females in that demographic cohort (FSCH75 for 1975–91 data) is also indicative of relative inequality. The 1987–91 average number of strikes and lockouts per annum (STRKAVG) came from the 1997 edition of the ILS's *Yearbook of Labor Statistics* published by the International Labour Organization (ILO, various years). The last indicator in this group is ETHNOL, or degree of ethnic and linguistic fractionalization in a country, as measured by La Porta et al. (1998). This variable can be a useful measure of distributional conflict because it shows how divided are societies among groups that may compete for a given set of public goods and economic rents. The level of transfers and subsidies in the economy (as a percentage of national product) measures the outcome of distributional pressures. SUBSY was compiled for the *Economic Freedom in the World* database for 1985 levels (Gwartney 1997).

Information about the potential for distributional conflict among political actors came from *Political Systems of the World* (Derbyshire and Derbyshire 1996), which supplied the data on the number of major political parties (PARTIES 1996) and the number of parties with more than 10 percent of seats in the legislature (TENPCPRT 1996). The level of state centralization in a country (CENTR) came from the Polity II data set. An indicator of the degree of conflict between different regions of a country was obtained from Taylor and Jodice (1983) as the proportion of a country's population living in areas of separatist sentiment in 1975 (SEPAR).

## Aggregation of Explanatory Variables by Causal Factor

In order to make the selected instruments easier to understand, use and compare, the observations have been rescaled so that the *range* of values for each indicator varies between a minimum of zero and a maximum of one; and the *ordering* of all indicators of a certain explanatory variable is the same, that is, a larger value for the indicators means: less judicial independence; or a stronger left-oriented ideology (favoring public monopoly); or more intense conflict, respectively for each type of indicator.

The next step for the use of the indicators has then been the aggregation of the many indicators available into common factors that can be used for hypothesis testing. Because there are many potential indicators for each hypothesized explanatory variable but most of these indicators are of a discrete nature, it was not possible to use full-information methods that would take into account the information contained in the indicator values within countries. Instead, I used standard factor analysis methods to select and aggregate indicators.[14]

Prior to the obtention of indicators for each major explanatory variable, I preselected from the source databases the variables that in my judgment could be valid indicators for the explanatory variable in question. Since the database of institutional, economic and other potentially relevant variables that I assembled contained several hundred variables, it was not feasible to work without exercising a degree of prior selection and judgment.

Most of the selected indicators of judicial independence were highly correlated and yielded a single clear common factor, which I have called JUDFAC.[15] Alternative tests were also run using RCTTEN rather than JUDFAC, in order to test the explanatory power of supreme court justice tenure. Some results of these alternative tests are shown below. For economic ideology, six indicators displayed high correlation and the existence of a common factor, IDFACEC1.[16] Since the variable RSCOPE appeared to cause some ambiguity in the emergence of a common factor, a second ideological factor IDFAC2 excluded this variable. The indicators of social and moral ideology displayed a surprising degree of internal consistency, despite the fact that they had very diverse origins and referred to very different questions, from abortion and divorce to environmental protection, and were aggregated into the common factor, IDFACSO.[17] This indicator of ideology turned out, however, to be highly correlated with indicators of judicial independence (see Appendix 1), which caused the only major problems of collinearity in the tests. As a consequence, it was not used in the final set of econometric tests. As a further alternative to these ideology measures, tests were also run using IDCL, as an indicator of government ideology rather than of broader preferences.

A common factor was hardest to select for distributional conflict, mainly because the number of countries covered by many of the indicators is relatively small and this would result in a substantial restriction of the number of observations available for testing. Several common factors were selected from the group of available indicators, [18] with slight variations across the factors. Several alternative measures of distributional conflict were also used in the tests: RETHNOL and SUBSY alone; measures of redistributive behavior by SOEs (SOE average balances for 1970–75 [SOEB7075] and for 1980–85 [SOEB8085], and transfers from the government to cover SOE shortfalls during 1980–85 [SOET8085]); and government deficits in GDP percentage terms (DEFPCY).

## ECONOMETRIC TESTS

### Model Specification

As the log-odds procedure allows the treatment of the dependent variables as approximately continuous and normally distributed, we can use OLS to test the hypotheses, particularly in view of the fact that the main object of interest is not so much the magnitude of the coefficients of the right-hand-side variables as the sign of the coefficients. [19]

### Test Characteristics

With OLS, we can test the hypotheses by examining coefficient signs and applying standard t-tests to determine whether the results are significant or just random occurrences. Before running the regression equations, I examined the correlation coefficients among the explanatory variables and controls (shown in Appendix 1) to avoid multicollinearity problems (high standard errors for the coefficient estimates as well as coefficient sign reversals). In general, most of the significant correlation coefficients are below the 0.5 mid-point of possible values, so multicollinearity does not appear to be a major problem (of course, interaction variables such as JUDDEM can be expected, by construction, to be highly correlated with their components like JUDFAC). The judicial independence factor, JUDFAC, is highly correlated with IDFACSO (the moral ideology factor), as well as with some control variables like PARL (the degree of parliamentary control over the government) and per capita income. As other indicators of ideology were available that were free from this problem, I excluded IDFACSO from the regression analysis. Some of the distributional conflict factors and indicators were correlated with per capita income, but the values were just slightly above 0.5 and in any case alternative, less correlated measures of distributional conflict were available as well.

## Control Variables

I considered several control variables:

- two measures (in natural logarithm) of real per capita income in US dollars for 1985 (LYC85) and for 1994 in purchasing power parity (PPP) terms (LYC94PP), since income level may affect the choices of competition and ownership (for instance, lower-income countries may rely more extensively on certain sources of energy, which could constrain the economic feasibility of ownership and competition[20]);
- the average percentage of foreign investment in a country's total investment level for the 1970–91 period, to control for the possibility that countries that are more dependent on foreign investment may tend to favor pro-market policies to attract foreign investors and meet lender requirements (use of the lagged values of foreign investment controls for this causal direction rather than the opposite, namely that pro-market policies attract foreign capital);
- indicators of political regime (democracy versus nondemocracy, the level of policymaking constraints on the executive, and degree of parliamentary responsibility of the government, PARL), to control for distortions introduced by authoritarian rule on the role of political variables, such as the number of major political parties;
- political instability (measured by the number of political regime or government changes), which could affect choices by making politicians more oriented towards short-term goals;[21] and finally,
- a dummy variable for countries in Latin America (LATAM), since reforms have so far been greatest and deepest in Latin America, so perhaps results are entirely driven by conditions in this region.

Of these potential controls, income level had a very limited impact.[22] The degree of foreign investment and political instability had no significant effect on the choices made by different countries. Political regime was only influential through the variable PARL, but not through other characterizations. Since most Latin American countries have privatized and introduced competition in their ESIs, LATAM was highly significant, but it did not reveal any other patterns in the data.

A variation on the influence of political regime was the potential interaction of democracy with judicial independence and with distributive conflict. Judicial independence may be strongly tied to democracy, since democratic regimes are generally underpinned by the rule of law in the form of an explicit or customary constitution. Likewise, democracies may be more prone to distributive conflicts because of voting by underprivileged groups. This means that judicial independence and distributional conflict should perhaps be considered jointly with democracy rather than as variables separate from the indicators of democratic regimes. To test this possibility, I constructed two multiplicative interaction terms, JUDDEM and DISTDEM, reflecting the interaction between democracy and, respectively, judicial independence and distributional conflict. The discussion of results shows the effects of this factor on the institutional outcomes.

### Dealing with Endogeneity Problems

A major issue in the type of econometric testing carried out here is endogeneity, that is the possibility that some of the explanatory variables may be caused themselves by some of the dependent variables, producing spurious causal significance in the results. To overcome or at least minimize this problem, I have used wherever data permitted it information from years preceding reform of the ESI (1990 onwards) as much as possible. Since all countries but Chile (1978) and the UK (1989) began reform of the ESI in 1990 or after, any data from before 1990 essentially avoids endogeneity problems.

### Results from Regressions

The basic specification run to test the hypothesized determinants of institutional reform outcomes regressed competition or ownership scores on the common factors obtained for the three explanatory variables (JUDFAC, IDFACEC1, IDFACEC2, IDFACSO, DISTFAC1, DISTFAC2, DISTFAC3). Additional variations, as already mentioned, were carried out with potential control variables to test the robustness of results when other possible explanations are taken into account. The major variations run were combinations of the following possibilities:

- using economic or social measures to instrument for ideological preferences;

- for distributional conflict, using different common factors or specific indicators such as Gini coefficients or ethnolinguistic fractionalization; and
- using various control variables, mainly per capita income measures in PPP.

The main regression results are presented in Tables 3.1 and 3.2, with p-statistics shown below each coefficient value. Competition outcomes (dependent variable LCSCORE) are shown in Table 3.1, while ownership outcomes (dependent variable LPSCORE) appear in Table 3.2.

*Table 3.1   Summary of OLS results for competition outcomes (LCSCORE)*

| Regression # | 1 | 2 | 3 | 4 | 5 | 6 | 7 |
|---|---|---|---|---|---|---|---|
| N | 73 | 73 | 75 | 29 | 73 | 72 | 67 |
| R sq | 0.1730 | 0.1405 | 0.1656 | 0.2012 | 0.1733 | 0.1662 | 0.2301 |
| pr > F | 0.4% | 1.5% | 0.5% | 12.6% | 0.4% | 0.6% | 0.3% |
| constant | 3.207786 | 3.143379 | 2.24544 | 3.945476 | 3.087124 | 4.346683 | 2.285037 |
| pr = 0 | 0.0% | 0.0% | 0.0% | 0.0% | 0.0% | 0.0% | 0.3% |
| JUDFAC | -0.24801 | -0.27464 | -0.26344 | -0.91191 | | -0.56557 | 0.56248 |
| pr = 0 | 54.9% | 53.3% | 52.7% | 45.8% | | 37.2% | 34.5% |
| JUDDEM | | | | | -0.34972 | | |
| pr = 0 | | | | | 53.6% | | |
| IDFACEC1 | 1.250673 | | 1.297018 | 0.597342 | 1.213813 | 2.126028 | 1.288772 |
| pr = 0 | 0.8% | | 0.6% | 50.8% | 0.7% | 0.1% | 2.8% |
| IDFACEC2 | | 1.135269 | | | | | |
| pr = 0 | | 3.5% | | | | | |
| DISTFAC2 | | | | | | | 0.682342 |
| pr = 0 | | | | | | | 19.7% |
| DISTFAC3 | 1.471053 | 1.324536 | | | 1.429263 | | |
| pr = 0 | 3.1% | 5.8% | | | 0.3% | | |
| RETHNOL | | | 2.778518 | | | | |
| pr = 0 | | | 3.3% | | | | |
| SOET8590 | | | | 0.459114 | | | |
| pr = 0 | | | | 4.6% | | | |
| RSUBSY | | | | | | -3.47478 | |
| pr = 0 | | | | | | 11.9% | |
| PARL | | | | | | | 0.639408 |
| pr = 0 | | | | | | | 14.9% |

*Table 3.2  Summary of OLS results for ownership outcomes (LPSCORE)*

| Regression # | 1 | 2 | 3 | 4 | 5 | 6 | 7 |
|---|---|---|---|---|---|---|---|
| N | 68 | 67 | 72 | 19 | 72 | 65 | 41 |
| R sq | 0.1707 | 0.1984 | 0.2154 | 0.2858 | 0.1856 | 0.143 | 0.1667 |
| pr > F | 0.7% | 0.8% | 0.2% | 15.7% | 0.3% | 5.2% | 7.7% |
| constant<br>pr = 0 | 0.328948<br>0.9% | -2.90656<br>8.7% | 0.718007<br>0.2% | -0.17112<br>60.1% | 0.62258<br>0.1% | -0.48734<br>75.8% | 0.018306<br>96.5% |
| JUDFAC<br>pr = 0 | 0.177841<br>18.9% | 0.608405<br>2.8% | -0.15366<br>40.6% | -0.13714<br>73.8% | 0.149273<br>21.7% | -0.03442<br>90.8% | |
| RCTTEN<br>pr = 0 | | | | | | | 0.434171<br>47.8% |
| IDFACEC1<br>pr = 0 | 0.470911<br>0.8% | 0.504528<br>0.5% | 0.575146<br>0.1% | | 0.566075<br>0.2% | 0.601966<br>0.8% | 0.356011<br>14.7% |
| IDCL<br>pr = 0 | | | | 0.679839<br>11.0% | | | |
| DISTFAC1<br>pr = 0 | | | | | | | |
| DISTFAC2<br>pr = 0 | -0.01405<br>93.5% | 0.044452<br>79.3% | | | | | |
| DISTFAC3<br>pr = 0 | | | 0.160269<br>45.7% | | | | 0.332353<br>25.7% |
| SOEB8590<br>pr = 0 | | | | -0.12685<br>6.2% | | | |
| DEFPCY<br>pr = 0 | | | | | 6.08372<br>4.6% | | |
| RSUBSY<br>pr = 0 | | | | | | -1.57671<br>9.8% | |
| PARL<br>pr = 0 | | | | -0.26401<br>5.5% | | | |
| LYC75<br>pr = 0 | | | | | | 0.183453<br>43.7% | |
| LYC85<br>pr = 0 | | 0.424334<br>5.8% | | | | | |

The ambiguous role of judicial independence hypothesized by the model is supported by the data, in the sense that in most cases the judicial independence variable does not have a significant nonzero coefficient, and that the sign of the coefficient, when significant, can change across equations.

By contrast with judicial independence, economic ideology consistently and clearly plays an important explanatory role for institutional choices, for both property rights and competition. In most regression equations, the variables that measure ideology have significantly positive coefficients, indicating that the prevalence of economically orthodox ideas, for instance, tilts outcomes in favor of competition and private ownership.

The results for distributional conflict are strong in the case of competition outcomes but much less so in the case of ownership. A variety of measures of distributional conflict – except for the level of transfers and subsidies in the economy, which yields contradictory results – have significantly positive coefficients in the competition equations, showing that greater distributional conflict makes monopoly more likely. For ownership, on the other hand, coefficients are in most cases insignificant and the level of transfers and subsidies is once again contradictory (note that the negative sign on the coefficient for the level of SOE balances, SOEB8590, confirms the hypothesis, because a *lower* value for this variable indicates larger SOE losses, and hence the existence of *greater* distributional conflict over the output and rents produced by SOEs).

The cases of Argentina or Chile suggest that fierce distributional contests result in unsustainable public deficits, making privatization the only viable alternative, with or without deregulation and competition. If this is the case, then for at least some of the countries with high inequality we may observe inequality side by side with privatization, which would explain the weaker effect of distributional conflict on ownership outcomes. This explanation would suggest that the hypothesis of greater distributional conflict leading to less competition may be too simplistic and needs to take into account a richer set of possibilities.

Control variables do not seem to have much of an effect at all, or to yield sharper results. While constitutional factors such as the degree of parliamentary control over the government (PARL) do appear with significant coefficients at times, the sign of the coefficient is reversed from competition to ownership, so the role of this variable is unclear. Per capita income is insignificant in most cases. Other controls and interaction variables have even less explanatory power.

**ESMAP's Energy Sector Reform Scorecard**

As an additional test of the hypotheses about institutional change, I have regressed the hypothesized explanatory factors to a scorecard of electricity sector reforms in developing countries recently created by the World Bank/UNDP's joint Energy Sector Management Assistance Programme (ESMAP) (ESMAP 1999, Appendix A-1), and therefore free from my own coding biases. ESMAP obtained complete answers to six 'key questions' concerning the reform of the power sector for 115 developing countries, as part of a broader energy sector reform questionnaire completed during 1998 by World Bank staff with experience in the energy sector. Binary answers for each question were coded as zeroes or ones, and added to obtain a 'reform indicator' score with a maximum value of 6. The questions measure the level of reliance on competition and private ownership in a given country, and are therefore equivalent to a combination of the competition and ownership scores I compiled for the previous regression analyses.[23] Since the hypotheses of institutional change posit the same explanatory variables for competition and ownership – that is, judicial independence, ideology and distributional conflict – I applied a similar OLS approach to the reform indicator computed by ESMAP, after its transformation into a percentage of the maximum score and then into a log-odds ratio (LREFORM).[24]

The results of the analysis are shown in Table 3.3 below. When examining the results, it is important to note that a higher value of LREFORM indicates higher reliance on competition and private ownership; hence, the hypothesized coefficients for the three explanatory factors are all negative rather than positive as in the previous OLS regressions.[25]

We can see that the results for the reform scores show a positive relation between judicial independence and private ownership and competition, in some cases with significant coefficients. These results also provide strong support for ideology hypothesis, since coefficients are negative in all cases and significant in most. Regarding distributional conflict, we can see that as in the previous tests support for the hypothesis is weaker than for ideology but nonetheless clear. The coefficients are significant and negative in some cases, and where they are positive they are so insignificant as not to constitute a serious contradiction of the hypothesis. We can thus see that application of the analysis to this externally-compiled variable provides additional support for the role of ideology and distributional conflict, while pointing out that judicial independence may play a role after all.

*Table 3.3   OLS results for World Bank's Reform scores (LREFORM)*

| Regression # | 1 | 2 | 3 | 4 | 5 | 6 | 7 |
|---|---|---|---|---|---|---|---|
| N | 31 | 21 | 44 | 21 | 19 | 45 | 40 |
| R sq | 0.2716 | 0.3706 | 0.1641 | 0.3672 | 0.3683 | 0.2178 | 0.2637 |
| pr > F | 3.3% | 4.4% | 6.4% | 4.6% | 6.9% | 1.7% | 2.7% |
| constant<br>pr = 0 | 3.313608<br>1.0% | 4.373829<br>1.3% | 1.635878<br>14.3% | 4.057512<br>0.5% | 9.286415<br>1.0% | 2.603889<br>1.7% | 0.024142<br>99.2% |
| JUDFAC<br>pr = 0 | -2.87412<br>7.4% | -0.64228<br>74.3% | -2.48907<br>3.0% | | -5.84169<br>6.8% | -2.98408<br>2.1% | -2.58387<br>13.2% |
| JUDDEM<br>pr = 0 | | | | -0.59437<br>89.0% | | | |
| IDFACEC1<br>pr = 0 | -1.87749<br>6.3% | | -1.21891<br>15.1% | | | -1.22554<br>8.7% | -1.4037<br>10.5% |
| IDFACEC2<br>pr = 0 | | | | | -0.12028<br>93.3% | | |
| IDCL<br>pr = 0 | | -2.61283<br>10.3% | | -2.52328<br>11.3% | | | |
| DISTFAC1<br>pr = 0 | -0.12688<br>89.3% | -3.26801<br>3.2% | | -3.50339<br>0.9% | | | |
| DISTFAC2<br>pr = 0 | | | | | | | 0.172011<br>85.4% |
| DEFPCY<br>pr = 0 | | | -11.9999<br>42.5% | | | | |
| SOET8590<br>pr = 0 | | | | | | | |
| SOEB8590<br>pr = 0 | | | | | | | |
| SOED7075<br>pr = 0 | | | | | -6.09438<br>6.3% | | |
| DISTDEM<br>pr = 0 | | | | | | 2.52803<br>37.9% | |
| EXRESTR<br>pr = 0 | | | | | | | 0.66114<br>16.7% |

## CONCLUSION

To conclude, the data support the hypotheses regarding the importance of ideology on the institutional transformation of the ESI, and also regarding the importance of distributional conflict, although more weakly and especially so for ownership outcomes. The hypothesis about judicial independence finds partial support in the data. While some measures of ESI outcomes show no role for judicial independence, as hypothesized, a second data set shows that greater judicial independence is conducive to greater competition and private ownership.

The next task is to examine the evidence for the hypotheses listed at the beginning of this chapter 'from the bottom up', as it were, as opposed to the aggregate view provided by large-N analyses. This will permit not only a further test of the theory, but will also provide an account of how reforms have actually unfolded, in contrast to the highly stylized perspective of formal models. Therefore we turn in the next three chapters to the analysis of four case studies from Latin America.

## NOTES

1. The large–N studies of the electricity sector by Henisz and associates (Bergara et al. 1998; Zelner and Henisz 2000), address the effect of the institutional environment on investment patterns, not the determinants of the institutional framework itself.
2. Judicial independence is defined in the next chapter.
3. One way to think about judicial independence is as a 'complementary institution' (Aoki 2001: 225) that 'parametrically affects' the choices of participants in policy-making and other processes, and can thus have an effect on the direction of institutional change in the ESI.
4. Evidence collected by the author from case studies suggests that this (as a redistributive measure to protect employees' rents), and not a form of incentive compensation through profit sharing, has been the motivation for subsidized sales of shares to utility employees in Latin America, where it has been used very extensively.
5. Of course, this raises the issue of selection bias because I do not examine countries that have not restructured. But as I explained above, my theoretical presumption is that the decision to bring restructuring into the political agenda is analytically separable from the outcome of the restructuring process itself, so I should not include in my database those cases where no change has happened.
6. As a commercial publication, this periodical is not available in academic or public libraries, and subscription fees are very high. McGraw-Hill kindly provided me with a *pro bono* copy of the 3rd quarter 1998 issue of *IPPQ* for this research project.
7. Not in the statistical sense of consistent, but in the commonly used sense of likely to display a similar value above idiosyncratic differences.
8. The log-odds transformation expresses percentage scores as the natural log of the ratio of the score to one minus the score. Zero observations thus take a value of minus infinity, 50 percent scores a value of zero, and unit observations a value of plus infinity. In practice, zero and unit observations are slightly adjusted to produce, respectively, large negative and large positive log-odds values. I am grateful to Professor R. Caves for his suggestion and explanation concerning the use of log-odds ratios. See also Kalt and Zupan (1984).

9. Recall that the role of judicial institutions in the model is that of constraining the ability of politicians to change policies once they have been implemented. A less competent bureaucracy will also make it harder to put policies into practice, but we are concerned here with political feasibility rather than practical implementation issues (which, although complex in their own right, can be, as the Argentine experience shows, ameliorated through the assistance of multilateral institutions and consulting firms). See Appendix 2 for a further discussion of the measurement of judicial independence.

10. Limitations of space prevent a discussion of the quality of these indices. The PRS measures have been used by Clague et al. (1997); the indices of economic freedom are well known and widely used, as are the Polity databases and Freedom House's data. Henisz's measure of judicial independence is straightforward. I refer the reader to Sullivan's book for sources and construction of his index of judicial independence.

11. Defined as the point of passage of major restructuring legislation or of implementation of major reforms, and obtained mainly from *IPPQ* (1998).

12. I did make the following modifications to the data: (i) in the case of Argentina, I believed an error of interpretation was made by the first of these sources in classifying the Peronist party as 'right wing', so I reclassified as 'center left,' which in my opinion reflects much better the consensus opinion about the party, at least when Argentine president Menem was elected in 1990; (ii) where parties were listed as 'nationalist' or under more than one label (such as 'nationalist/right'), I dropped the nationalist label in favor of a category along the right–left axis in order to simplify the data; and (iii) where no classification was readily available, I coded the ideological position of a party using my own interpretation of the narratives of party platforms and policies in the *Handbook*.

13. These sources were supplemented with data from various other sources (all listed in the bibliography) for missing individual observations.

14. Factor loadings are computed using Stata's 'factor' routine, which calculates the loadings as the eigenvectors (scaled by the square root of the appropriate eigenvalue) of a matrix obtained from the correlation matrix of the observed variables (standardized for mean 0 and variance 1).

15. This factor (comprising the rescaled indicators RPROPRTS, RREPUD, RLORDER, RCORRUPT, RBURQUAL, RCIVILFR, RPOLRTS, RLEGACC, REXTFR, and RJUDIND) accounted for 89 percent of the correlation among the indicators of judicial independence, and had an eigenvalue of 6.68. Other factors had eigenvalues of less than 0.7 and accounted for less than 10 percent of correlation each. The full results of the factor analysis for the three explanatory variables are available from the author upon request.

16. This factor (comprising the rescaled indicators RSCOPE, RSOE75, RCOMPFR, RPRCONT, RINTERV, and RFDIFREE) explains 73 percent of correlation, with an eigenvalue of 1.72. A second factor explained 4.4 percent of the correlation among the variables but its eigenvalue did not reach 1. An analysis of factor loadings showed that while the first factor measured ideological 'orthodoxy' in favor of private property and competition, the second factor reflected a preference for competition but with public property. As a result, only the first factor was selected for hypothesis testing.

17. Only this factor's eigenvalue exceeded one; it explained 73 percent of correlation. It comprised the rescaled indicators RMFILLIT, RBIRTHC, RABORTP, RDIVR, RPROTAR, RENVTR, RDEATHP.

18. In the first two cases (comprising RFSCH759, RCENTR, RETHNOL, RPARTIES, RSTRKAVG, and RSEPAR for DISTFAC1, and all of these but RSTRKAVG for DISTFAC2), the factors retained were the only ones with eigenvalues exceeding one and explained all the correlation among the variables; in the third case (which dropped both RSTRKAVG and RSEPAR), the first factor's eigenvalue was only 0.69, but the factor explained all the correlation and is eigenvalue was more than ten times larger than the second largest eigenvalue.

19. The use of multiple-indicator, multiple-cause (MIMIC) models is impeded in this case by the binary or limited nature of much of the data, while a more disaggregated analysis of the dependent variable indicator would fail to consider the information included in the joint

data set, since the test concerns general outcomes (ownership and competition) that are likely to influence the ESI restructuring indicators simultaneously.

20. For instance, competitive markets and private ownership may be harder to sustain with hydroelectric generation because this technology has zero marginal cost and nondiversifiable hydrological risk.
21. Note that political instability is different from distributional conflict. For instance, stable regimes may be built on a foundation of clientelism that reflects fierce struggles for economic rents, as in Mobutu's long reign in Zaire.
22. A fuller discussion of test results is provided below.
23. However, I did not use the ESMAP score as the primary dependent variable because it is an aggregate containing measures of both competition and ownership together, rather than separately as I am testing in the preceding part of the chapter.
24. I used the log-odds transformation rather than ordered logit to facilitate comparison with the tests for the preceding scores, LCSCORE and LPSCORE.
25. The ESMAP scores display a significant negative correlation with my own competition and ownership scores, which constitutes a form of external validation of my own scores.

# 4.    A comparison of four Latin American cases

This and the following chapters are devoted to the analysis of several case studies as a further test of the hypotheses developed in the formal model of Chapter 2. Because of the volume and complexity of the information needed to examine four cases, their analysis is divided into several chapters. This chapter sets out the analytical methodology and the justification for the selection of the four cases. It also presents the basic facts about the restructuring of the electricity industry in each case relative to the outcomes of the restructuring process in the other three cases. Chapter 5 sets out the explanatory factors posited by the model for each one of the four countries, again in relation to each other. Chapter 6, the last chapter of the case study comparison, considers outcomes and explanatory factors together in order to assess the validity of the latter.

An empirical test of the hypotheses requires looking for evidence of causal linkages between the explanatory and the dependent variables. This involves in turn the operationalization of the dependent and the explanatory variables, that is, the identification of actual manifestations of the variables that can be observed in the sources of data.[1] Next, information about the processes of ESI restructuring in each country should be obtained in order to relate outcomes to causes, carefully taking into account the interaction between the various explanatory variables (multiple causation) as well as alternative explanations for the observed facts.

In the assessment of the empirical evidence, the relationship between explanatory and dependent variables can take a variety of forms, all of which must be carefully accounted for. In particular, the sources and content of ideology must be identified in detail, for apparent ideological homogeneity may mask important underlying differences. Within the doctrine of 'neoclassical economics' there exist important differences in the degree of preoccupation with market power issues, with scholars associated with the University of Chicago being very skeptical about the sustainability of private monopoly and the ability of the public policy process to cause welfare improvements in such situations. Nationalism is another complicating ideological factor, because it places domestic control above efficiency considerations, thus leading in practice – whether it represses or collaborates with left-wing forces – to an expansion of public sector ownership and a restriction of competition. The impacts of distributional conflict are also varied. They are not limited to the restriction of institutional choices, but can also appear in the form of compensatory payments to groups that are not direct counterparts in a privatization transaction, for instance. Many individuals may be averse to risk and thus prefer a compensatory payment today to a steady flow of benefits over a set of future periods.

## THE DEPENDENT VARIABLES

The dependent variables must refer to the specific context of the ESI to ensure the validity of the analysis, since the research question is about the institutions of the ESI. The ESI has technological characteristics that set it apart from other productive activities, namely great capital intensity (leading in some cases to natural monopoly, or at least to oligopoly), nonstorability of electrical energy, and the use of electrical networks to deliver the main output, electrical energy.

### Property

This variable refers to the control over productive assets, where control can mean operation, modification, disposition, exchange for money or other valuables, and control over the output produced with the assets (particularly the freedom to set prices). Also, the ESI has three major types of assets according to the function they perform in the electricity supply chain: Generation, Transmission and Distribution. Since the technology of control may bias ownership towards either of the two possibilities in different ways for each type of asset, it may be necessary to examine property for each type separately. Further breakdowns may in fact be required, particularly in generation (for example, nuclear plants, hydro plants, and all other generation technologies).

### Competition

This variable refers to the conditions that affect economic freedom of participants in a market, particularly the pricing (or production) and entry/exit decisions. Although in the ESI the possibilities for full competition are limited to the generation side, a number of mechanisms can be deployed in the other segments of the industry to stimulate competitive behavior.

## THE EXPLANATORY VARIABLES

In contrast to the dependent variables, the explanatory variables posited by the hypotheses are of a general nature within a given polity, affecting the process of ESI restructuring as well as other political and economic outcomes. The key empirical evidence to be sought in the case studies concerns the specific manifestations of the explanatory variables in the ESI restructuring process.

### Judicial Independence

The definition of judicial independence differs little from that of regulatory independence (see the preceding chapter). Independence requires insulation of the judicial decisionmaking process from private and political interests, by means of reasonably meritocratic appointment and career incentives, as well as a stable and adequate allocation of budgetary resources to the judiciary; and the willingness of the executive power to enforce judicial decisions (Domingo 1999; Stephenson n.d.). This suggests several types of indicators:

- At the formal level, independence can be measured by reference to: mechanisms for the appointment and removal of judges; the financial means of the court system; the common or code basis of law (greater autonomy can be expected under common law, since it gives a greater interpretive role to the courts); the career paths of judges (extensive cycling of judges between the courts and other professions can create conflicts of interest); and the existence of an enforcement apparatus under the control of the courts (such as formal control by the judiciary over a police force).
- In practice, as formal mechanisms can be subverted, and the enforcement of judicial decisions is generally in the hands of the executive power, measures of judicial independence must ideally take into account instances of judicial corruption and coercion, and the degree of actual enforcement of judicial decisions.
- A more indirect indicator of judicial independence can involve measures of the willingness of political elites to give up control over decisions and resources to autonomous agencies or organizations

within the public sector.  One example is the degree of autonomy of public enterprises.

## Ideology

As Noll has defined it, 'a person's political ideology is both a system for evaluating social outcomes and a set of beliefs about how policy decisions (including the design of public institutions) affect outcomes' (Noll 1999: 6). The logic of the hypotheses refers primarily to the second part of the definition.  While there are substantial disagreements in most societies about what is socially desirable – respect for the environment, higher incomes, 'family values', equity, and so forth – the institutional dimensions under consideration (ownership and competition) refer fundamentally to social organization rather than social goals *per se*.[2]

### Distributional Conflict

This variable is taken, according to the logic of the hypotheses, to be broadly synonymous to the level of rent-seeking activity in a society – in other words, the attempt to use the coercive power of the state to alter the distribution of income produced by the economic system, and the reaction against such attempts by negatively affected actors.  Two major phenomena are covered by this concept:

- explicit income and wealth redistribution conflicts: bargaining over wages, over ownership of productive assets (for example, over subsidies for the acquisition of privatized assets, or over land reform); taxation conflicts (including tariff policy); and conflicts over the use of explicit and implicit subsidies in the pricing of products supplied or regulated by the state;
- patronage-related pressure on distribution of income: the use of public resources to buy the loyalty of political clients, who are generally not politically mobilized and hence would not register in the explicit measures considered above.

This variable thus aims to measure the incentives that policymakers may face to maintain control over resources in order to derive political benefits. In this book, distributional conflict is taken as exogenously determined; in order to keep the analysis manageable, there is no attempt to delve into the origins of conflicts (for example, the motivations for union behavior), excepting where they may involve alternative hypotheses, or where serious issues of causal endogeneity may arise.

## CASE STUDY RESEARCH DESIGN

As mentioned in the first chapter, the complexity of the political bargaining game outlined above, and the difficulty of measuring the hypothesized causal variables, makes a case-oriented empirical test valuable, at least as a complement to a statistical exercise. The analysis of ESI restructuring cases take into account nuances and ambiguities that would be lost in a statistical analysis, and in this fashion it can hopefully highlight additional aspects of the empirics of institutional change.

Since it is impractical to devote detailed attention to a large number of cases, the case-study approach cannot rely on sampling for the selection of cases. Instead, I have attempted to approximate a 'most similar systems' design. Under this approach, cases are selected so that they display different outcomes while being equal on all explanatory variables but one. That one difference is then shown to explain the difference in outcomes.[3] This method cannot, however, be easily applied in its pure form. First, when several explanatory variables are hypothesized, more than two cases have to be compared to avoid underdetermination or insufficient 'degrees of freedom' (see King et al. 1994). Second, in practice no two countries display exactly equal values in all explanatory variables but one – there are always nuances and perceptions that must be taken into account.

For these reasons, I have sought to compare four cases rather than just two (I have three explanatory variables) as the minimum number required to determine my test, with the requirement that they display different outcomes in competition and ownership while having the degree of similarities and differences in the dependent variables that would allow me to test the research hypotheses with a maximum of rigor.

In the property area, outcome variation requires that the set of cases include countries with different degrees of reliance on private property, public ownership, or mixed forms of participation. For competition, variation means that the set should comprise countries relying on: monopoly franchises or competitive markets for electricity generation[4] or for commercial services, which are the segments in which price competition is commonly agreed to be feasible; yardstick competition or franchise auctions ('competition for the market') in transmission and distribution (T&D), where price competition is not considered feasible; and on vertically-integrated, functionally unbundled, or entirely separate firms for the products and services produced along the supply chain.

In terms of similarities and differences in the explanatory variables, I have looked for countries with a common historical and cultural background as a way of limiting variations, particularly on the cultural side, which is often invoked as an explanation for many different phenomena.

Altogether, these criteria have led me to choose four Latin American cases. Most countries in the region have restructured their electric sectors and display significant outcome variability. Furthermore, Latin American countries share many common cultural and historical elements but differ on the political dimensions that I am hypothesizing as potential explanations for institutional changes in the ESI.

Within Latin America, the comparison of Argentina, Chile, Bolivia, and Brazil is particularly appealing in relation to the criteria outlined above:

- property outcomes vary from full privatization in Chile, to a system with significant component of public ownership in Bolivia;
- competition outcomes vary from substantial reliance on competitive mechanisms in Argentina, to a largely monopolistic organization in Brazil;
- all four countries are located in Latin America and share a common Iberian colonial heritage;
- there existed significant differences in the explanatory variable levels among the four cases at the time of ESI restructuring – differences in the level of judicial independence (substantial in Chile, very limited in Argentina), ideology (from libertarian in Chile to social democratic in Brazil), and distributional conflict (low in Chile, high in Bolivia).

Having defined the overall approach to the empirical testing of the proposed hypotheses, the next step is the operationalization of the theoretical variables into observable measures of outcomes and causes. Rather than provide a detailed explanation in this chapter, a description of this methodological issue is included in Appendix 2 so as to facilitate the flow and readability of the chapter. The rest of the chapter is therefore devoted to summary descriptions of the ESI restructuring outcomes in Argentina, Bolivia, Brazil, and Chile regarding the allocation of property rights on ESI assets and the degree of competition introduced in the industry.[5]

## OWNERSHIP OUTCOMES

A summary of the distribution of property rights in the ESI of each country is shown in Table 4.1 below. The table provides information on the major components of property rights identified in the preceding section: the right to operate assets, to modify them, to dispose of them, to exchange them (buy or sell), and rights over the outputs produced with such assets (in the case of the ESI, electrical energy as well as transmission and distribution of electricity, plus related services such as billing and meter reading).

*Table 4.1    Distribution of ESI property rights at completion of restructuring process*

|  | Operation | Modification | Disposition | Exchange | Output |
|---|---|---|---|---|---|
| Chile | 100% private 1986–98 (a) | Same as for operation | Same as for operation | Same as for operation | Same as for operation |
| Argentina | Generation (G): 100% private (b) Transmission (T):100% private Distribution (D): mostly private (b) | Same as for operation | G: same T: all public (c) D: all public (c) | G: same T: all public (c) D: all public (c) | G: 100% private (b) T: 100% private D: mostly private (b) |
| Brazil | G: majority private (d) T: mostly private (d) D: mostly private (e) | Same as for operation | G: mostly public (c) T: all public (c) D: all public (c) | G: mostly public (c) T: all public (c) D: all public (c) | G: majority private (d) T: mostly private (d) D: mostly private (e) |
| Bolivia | G: 100% private (f) T: 100% private D: 100% private (f) | G: 60% private (f) T: 100% private D: 70% private (f) | Private owners cannot dispose or transfer assets for a number of years | G: 60% private (f) T: 100% private D: all public | G: 60% private (f) T: 100% private D: 70% private (f) |

*Notes:*
(a) By the end of the Pinochet regime in 1990, all major generation, transmission and distribution assets in Chile's Central Interconnected System (the main generation, transmission and load system in the country) had been privatized.   Originally (ESI privatizations were announced in 1985), only sales of minority stakes in ESI firms were envisaged (Hachette and Lüders 1993, Table 3.1).   Concessions are required in Chile to distribute electricity, but only for purposes of acquiring rights of way, and they are awarded for an indefinite period of time (Chile, National Government 1982: DFL 1, Art. 30).
(b) By the end of President Menem's second term in 1999, the Yaciretá binational dam and two nuclear stations remained in government hands.   The new Alianza administration did not pursue further privatization in the ESI.   Concessions for the largest distribution companies in terms of load and number of customers (Edenor, Edesur and Edelap in Buenos Aires), as well as many provincial distributors (which had owned the provincial distribution utilities since 1979), had been awarded by mid-2002 (in 1996, about 60% of energy was distributed to final users by private sector concessionaires, according to the Argentine government).
(c) Hydroelectric plants and transmission and distribution (T&D) assets under long-term concessions.
(d) As of mid-2002, only Gerasul (8% of total installed capacity in the south-central system), São Paulo hydro companies Paranapanema and Tietê (21% of installed capacity), and scattered projects under completion, were in private hands.   The two nuclear plants (Angra I and II) and the Itaipu binational dam (totaling some 33% of the south-central system) will remain in the public sector.   Contracts between independent power producers and distributors subject to regulatory approval.
(e) Concessions for most distribution companies awarded by mid-2002.   Major exceptions are CEMIG (Companhia Energêtica de Minas Gerais [Minas Gerais Energy Company]) and

COPEL (Companhia Paranaense de Eletricidade [Parana Electricity Company]), the former due to opposition of the Minas Gerais government.

(f) All government-owned generation and distribution companies were capitalized starting in 1994 (50% of equity sold to private investors with rights of operation); the Compañía Boliviana de Energía Eléctrica [Bolivian Electricity Company] (COBEE, owner of a generation company and two distribution companies) remained in private hands, as it had been since its founding in 1927.

*Source:* Various, elaborated by author.

The table shows a clear ranking of the cases, from greatest reliance on private property rights in Chile to least reliance (arguably) in Bolivia. In Chile, all dimensions of ownership were allocated to private actors. Although the privatization process was not complete by the end of the Pinochet regime in 1990, the main entities in the country had already been transferred to the private sector, and the process continued until its completion in 1998, when the last assets in public hands were privatized.

Argentina and Brazil have chosen to rely on concessions rather than outright property transfers of T&D companies. Under concessional agreements, the assets of these utilities remain the property of the state, so only the right to operate, modify and sell outputs is transferred to nongovernmental entities. In Brazil, the process has proceeded far more slowly and reticently than in Argentina. In part, this is due to the enormous size of many generation assets in Brazil (consisting mostly of large dams), but a greater reluctance to rely on private property can be observed in Brazil. Whereas the Menem administration in Argentina had at least announced plans to privatize the nuclear plants, the Brazilian government has no intention of doing so. Furthermore, Brazilian unwillingness to pursue means of privatizing its share of Itaipu dam (jointly owned with Paraguay) will leave a major generation asset (25 percent of total capacity in the south-central interconnected system) in public hands[6] (*GPR*, February 5, 1999). And bowing to political resistance against further privatization, by 1999 the Cardoso administration was no longer planning to sell the federally-owned generation company Furnas to strategic investors as in preceding years, but through a massive offering of small share packages (*'pulverização'*) to Brazilian investors with strict limits about concentration of share ownership.

Bolivia has been the most reluctant privatizer of the four cases. Instead of opting to fully privatize the ESI assets that were in public hands, it chose to 'capitalize' them through the sale of a 50 percent stake of each state-owned firm to a strategic investor in exchange for investment targets in each capitalized company, as well as the award of operating control to the strategic investor.[7] Although the public stake in the capitalized utilities has been transferred to pension funds for financial management purposes, the pension system remains a public assistance program rather than a true old-age savings scheme. The benefits provided by the funds are not linked to prior contributions to the funds, but are instead universally defined for any Bolivian citizen who reaches the age of 60. Such a disconnection between contributions and benefits, and governmental definition of pension benefits, is typical of public social security systems rather than private pension funds, in fact, Graham points out (1998: 161) that the political pressure to pay the initial pension disbursement before the 1997 presidential election may have resulted in an excessive payout relative to the asset base of the pension funds. It is therefore fair to characterize the Bolivian capitalization process as retaining a significant component of public ownership of ESI assets.[8] The semi-public nature of the ESI assets also affects their use in the restructured ESI. Private operators cannot dispose of or sell their stakes for a number of years, which makes their investment riskier than with fully owned assets – or transferable concessions – for which exit through sale or disposal is a fallback option.

An important caveat to the preceding discussion is the interaction with monopoly power issues. Reliance on concessions for T&D activities is not necessarily indicative of aversion to private property. It can also be a means of limiting the market power of service providers in activities that are organized as local or regional monopolies, by facilitating the periodic rebidding or even termination of concessions. But even this consideration does not change the fact that the ESI restructuring process in Chile displayed greater faith in private ownership than in the other three countries.

As pointed out in the preceding section, even when assets are in private hands, they may be subject to restrictions that limit the freedom of decision over the assets and hence the owners' property rights. Table 4.2 summarizes the major such restrictions applied to privatized ESI assets in the four cases. Restrictions relating to mitigation of monopoly power have been excluded, since they can be fairly justified by a concern for the negative welfare effects of monopoly, which is the subject of the next section dealing with competition outcomes.

*Table 4.2     Restrictions on property rights conferred on private owners
(other than related to mitigation or prevention of market
power)*

| | Foreign invest- ment | Ownership share | Output price | Public service obligations | Investment obligations |
|---|---|---|---|---|---|
| Chile | None | None | No control over hydro dispatch | G, T: none  D: obligation to serve | None |
| Argentina | None | None | Limitations on hydro dispatch | G, T:  D: obligation to serve | Indirect, for D only (quality standards) |
| Brazil | None | None | No control over hydro dispatch (a); incomplete regulatory framework | G, T, D: obligation to serve | Yes (D and concessions of unfinished hydro plants) |
| Bolivia | None | Ownership of capitalized companies restricted to 50% of equity | No control over hydro dispatch | G: none  T: obligation to meet plans  D: obligation to serve | Acquisition amount to be fully invested in physical and service assets |

*Note:* (a) Also, hydrology risk is pooled among all hydro generators.

*Source:* Various, elaborated by author.

Again, the interpretation of the table's information is that, in general, Chile imposed the least restrictions on the rights of private owners. Although owners of hydroelectric generation plants have greater freedom in Argentina than in Chile to determine the dispatch pattern (and hence the revenue stream) of these plants, in practice the significant irrigation and flood control roles of the privatized Argentine dams impose significant limitations on their operation (Bastos and Abdala 1993). Moreover, in the Argentine case investment considerations were much more explicit than in Chile for distribution companies. In Argentina, the regulatory framework includes a detailed set of quality of service parameters that, at the time the distribution concessions were awarded, implied a substantial investment requirement since existing quality of service levels were far below the standards defined in the concession agreements and sectoral regulations.

With regard to Brazil, it is essential to note the impact of centralized hydroelectric dispatch. Since 91 percent of Brazilian generation capacity is hydroelectric, compared with 64 percent in Chile, 46 percent in Bolivia, and 37 percent in Argentina, restricting control over hydro dispatch implies a very significant curtailment of property rights in the generation sector and of the positive dynamic efficiency effects of competition among generators. This restriction, combined with the lack of a well-defined ratemaking system for distribution and transmission systems,[9] means that Brazil can be characterized as more restrictive of private property rights than Argentina and Chile for the dimensions used in Table 4.2.

As for Bolivia, the limitations on ownership shares, hydro dispatch, and investment levels makes this case equally or more restrictive than the Brazilian case.

Another instance of manipulation of property rights by policymakers is the provision of subsidies and giveaways on ESI property rights to particular groups, that is, the creation of special claims on assets during the privatization process (in the sense that such claims are not acquired through fair trades in financial markets, but by government fiat). Table 4.3 shows the various groups to whom ESI property rights were allocated in the four cases in the course of their respective restructuring processes, and on what terms the rights were allocated.

*Table 4.3    Ownership composition of privatized or capitalized electric utilities*

|  | Pension funds | Foreign investors | Employees | Other domestic investors | Central government |
| --- | --- | --- | --- | --- | --- |
| Chile | Yes | Yes | Yes (at below market prices) | Yes, especially military and civil servants | Government assumption of 'stranded assets' |
| Argentina | Yes | Yes | Yes (on favorable terms) | Yes, including some transfers to provinces | Government assumption of 'stranded assets' |
| Brazil | Yes | Yes | Yes | Yes | Government assumption of 'stranded assets' see also (a) |
| Bolivia | Public pension fund system (b) | Yes | Yes | Yes | Government assumption of 'stranded assets'; see also (b) |

*Notes:*
(a) The BNDES (Banco Nacional de Desenvolvimento Econômico e Social [Brazilian Development Bank]), has taken equity positions in some privatizations to stimulate private participation and guarantee the success of the share auctions. For Rio Light, for instance, 'the government continued to be the largest shareholder of Light. Adding the shares which were not offered and remaining in the hands of the government electricity holding company, Eletrobrás, and the shares bought by BNDES (through its subsidiary

BNDESPar), the government retained a total of 39.1% of Light's shares' (Baer and McDonald 1998: fn. 42).

(b) Bolivian pension funds are not true pension funds in that they do not distribute pensions according to accumulated obligations, but according to universal benefits defined in advance by the government.

*Source:* Various, elaborated by author.

The table reveals a more complex picture than the previous tables.  In Chile, members of the military and the civil service were in some cases given subsidies for the purchase of shares in the privatized companies. Additionally, as in all other cases, the government absorbed differences between accounting and market valuations of the assets.  In the case of Endesa, for instance, the government intervened to improve the company's financial situation in 1985, two years after the first shares were sold on the Santiago stock exchange, by absorbing half a billion pesos of debt in exchange for company shares (World Bank 1993a: Box 21).  In Argentina, utility employees – and particularly union leaders – were allowed to buy shares at market prices, but with access to interest-free loans to finance the share purchases; certain generation, transmission and distribution assets owned by the federal government before privatization were transferred to the provinces.   In Brazil, the government development bank, Banco Nacional de Desenvolvimento Econômico e Social (BNDES), has invested in privatized utilities (Hinchberger 1996).

Finally, an examination of the mechanisms for the protection of the property rights of private investors (see Table 4.4) shows Chile to offer the least protection with regard to the structure of the Chilean regulatory system, which is of a purely political nature.  However, the greater risk of political intervention faced by Chilean investors has as a counterweight a more explicit reliance on judicial and para-judicial mechanisms [10] (mandatory arbitration), while in the other countries the regulatory entity or even the government is the first instance of appeal against regulatory decisions, which may reduce the protection of investors against adverse regulatory actions.[11]

*Table 4.4*    *Protection of investors from arbitrary regulatory action or regulatory capture*

| | Staggered regulator terms | Regulator appointment /removal | Funding of regulatory commission | Commission on budget approval | Judicial recourse | Public hearings |
|---|---|---|---|---|---|---|
| Chile | No; commissioners are cabinet ministers | No restrictions | General budget | Legislature | Yes, including arbitration | No |
| Argentina | Yes | Legislative approval (a); 'justified' removal only | Power market tax | Effectively executive (b) | Indirect (1st instance is executive agency) | Yes |
| Brazil | Yes | Legislative approval/ for criminal or similar reasons | Power market tax | Legislature | Indirect (1st instance is regulator) | Yes |
| Bolivia | Yes | Legislative selection (c)/ for criminal or similar reasons | Power market tax | Legislature | Indirect (1st instance is general regulator) | No |

*Notes:*
(a) Two commissioners proposed by the Federal Electric Energy Council, a joint federal-provincial entity; another three directly designated by the federal executive; all approved by the legislature.
(b) Legislative approval of budget, but in the case of a budget shortfall, the executive can approve an extraordinary charge on electricity transactions to raise the extra funds.
(c) President selects general regulator from a list of three candidates chosen by two-thirds of senators.

*Source:* Various, elaborated by author.

## COMPETITION OUTCOMES

As the primary determinant of competitive behavior, the market structures that emerged in each country after the restructuring process (or in Brazil, that are envisaged by the government) are the most important indicators of the decisions made by the respective governments concerning the choice of competition versus monopolistic systems for the production and allocation of electrical energy (Table 4.5).

*Table 4.5    ESI market structure in the four cases*

|  | Vertical integration | Generation market structure | Transmission market structure | Distribution market structure |
|---|---|---|---|---|
| Chile | Yes; Endesa owned most transmission lines in SIC until 2000, affiliated with largest distributor (Chilectra) | Concentrated; Endesa owns 59% of capacity in main system (SIC) | One major transmission company in each system (SIC, SING) | Several companies, but dominated by Santiago metro utility (Chilectra, 37% of SIC customers) |
| Argen-tina | No | Very fragmented; largest units in public sector | One major transmission company, several regional ones | Several companies, capital metro area split into two companies |
| Brazil | Partial (generation and distribution) | Concentrated, although largest units in public sector | Single entity plus concessions for specific lines | Several companies, two largest urban areas each split into several companies |
| Bolivia | No | Five generators only due to small market size | One major transmission company | Several companies, no asymmetry |

*Note:* The Chilean Central Interconnected System (SIC in Spanish) comprises about 75% of generation capacity in Chile; rest is mostly in the Great Northern System (SING in Spanish).

*Source:* Various, elaborated by author.

Chile presents the most monopolistic market structure among the four cases. A single investor group controls Endesa, which owns 59 percent of installed capacity (and all water rights), owned 82 percent of the transmission line mileage until 2000 (when, in exchange for government approval of the takeover by Endesa Spain, it agreed to sell its transmission assets to Hydro-Québec), and provides distribution service to 37 percent of customers – through control of Santiago's only distribution utility – in Chile's main interconnected system.[12] By contrast, the Argentine generation sector was sold to a large number of separate entities, and the major metropolitan areas of Argentina and Brazil are served by several distribution concessionaires, which facilitates comparisons of performance and hence stimulates efficiency in distribution services.

While the Argentine case lies at the opposite end of the market structure from Chile, with fragmentation at all three ESI levels (generation, transmission and distribution), Brazil and Bolivia represent intermediate situations, with Bolivia being more competition-oriented than Brazil. The reason for such a characterization is that while in Bolivia competition in the generation sector is limited by the small size of the country's interconnected system, in Brazil a very limited splitting of control over generation assets is planned relative to the very large size of Brazil's main interconnected network,[13] although public ownership of Itaipu, by far the largest single generation asset, may limit market power.

From a dynamic perspective, the existence of barriers to entry and exit is also an important determinant of the strength of competition, at least in the long run. As shown by Table 4.6, Chile presents a substantial number of barriers to entry and exit. The major generator in the country, Endesa, controls water rights and, until recently, transmission lines in the central system, and there is no prohibition against vertical integration in the country. This contrasts with the rest of the cases, where there exist explicit prohibitions or limitations on both vertical and horizontal market power. Further differences among the cases of Argentina, Brazil and Bolivia are unclear, for each has different limitations to entry and exit. Argentina did not impose service expansion obligations on its transmission concessionaires, which together with a deficient system for identifying expansion beneficiaries has created bottlenecks in the transmission system; in Brazil, the ongoing Petrobrás monopoly on wholesale gas and oil production and distribution is hindering entry of thermal generators; and in Bolivia, small market size limits efforts to mitigate horizontal market power.

*Table 4.6    Barriers to entry and exit*

|  | Access to capital | Access to fuel sources | Access to transmission | Bar- riers to exit | Vertical integration constraints | Horizontal concentra- tion limits |
|---|---|---|---|---|---|---|
| Chile | None | Water rights in SIC controlled by Endesa | Restricted: no obligation for service provider | None | None until recently (a) | None |
| Argenti- na | None | None | Restricted: no obligation for service provider | None | G and D allowed without physical integration | Yes, 10% of capacity control limit |
| Brazil | None | Access to gas hindered by Petrobrás monopoly | Restricted: rules unclear | None | Allowed in G and D, subject to overall limits | Yes, 20% of capacity or load nationwide limit |
| Bolivia | None | None; extensive gas reserves in country | Rate base incentive but unstable tolls | Small capital market | Vertical integration limited (b) | Yes, 35% of capacity control limit |

*Notes:*
(a)   As mentioned, Endesa finally sold (in the year 2000) its transmission operations to a separate company.
(b)   Distribution companies may own up to 15% of their generation capacity needs.

*Source:* Various, elaborated by author.

A look at the antitrust enforcement mechanisms in each country leads to similar conclusion (see Table 4.7). In Chile, the lack of legal limitations to horizontal and vertical market power prevents the regulator from taking actions to change the market structure created during the restructuring process and its aftermath. At most, the regulator could intervene through the ratesetting process to mitigate market power, but the authority of the regulator to do so is not clearly delineated in the acts that regulate the ESI, which deal mainly with regulation of the distribution component of electricity rates.[14] As a result, mitigation of market power falls mostly on the general antitrust system.[15]

*Table 4.7    Antitrust enforcement mechanisms and entities in ESI*

|  | Antitrust agency | Instruments or mechanisms |
|---|---|---|
| Chile | Regulatory commission (CNE) and competition commission | Limited, since Electricity Decree does not set limits, and existing structure is concentrated; CNE has limited freedom to alter regulated rates; antitrust commissions can order divestitures, penalize abuse of market power |
| Argentina | Regulatory commission (ENRE) | Extensive, due to rate-setting and antitrust powers of ENRE, and to concession conditions |
| Brazil | Regulatory commission (ANEEL) and competition commission | Moderate; rate-setting power limited by privatization contracts and lack of clear ratemaking framework; concessions can be revoked for public interest reasons; ANEEL empowered to penalize abuses in coordination with general antitrust commission |
| Bolivia | Regulatory commission (Super-intendencia de Elec-tricidad [Electricity Agency]) | Extensive power of regulator to terminate concessions in case of market power abuses and general antitrust powers of regulator, but conflict between market size and legal limits |

*Notes:*
CNE: Comisión Nacional de Energía (National Energy Commission).
ENRE: Ente Nacional Regulador de la Energía (National Energy Regulatory Agency).
ANEEL: Agência Nacional da Energia Elétrica (National Electricity Agency).

*Source:* Various, elaborated by author.

Brazil suffers from significant limitations too because the regulatory framework of the ESI has not been fully defined yet, thus creating substantial ambiguity about the powers of the regulator to mitigate market power. On the other hand, the limitations on ownership included in Brazil's Electricity Act do provide Brazilian authorities with greater legal grounds for antitrust interventions than in Chile. In Bolivia, the control of market power is once again limited by market size, but the regulator is equipped by the Bolivian Electricity Act with powers to check abuses of market power. Finally, Argentine regulators are in the best position to enforce antitrust policies, because the law imposes strict limits on the control over generation resources, and also because the executive power (through the Secretaría de Energía) has the capacity to alter the rules of the wholesale market and the regulator can terminate concessions in extreme cases.

The need to balance electricity supply and demand at every instant to avoid quality of service problems requires a system operator (SO) in any electrical system. Since the operator must, to carry out its duty, determine the dispatch of individual generating units, its decisions have the potential of affecting market outcomes very significantly. Control over the SO is therefore an important indicator of the viability of competition in the ESI. The governance, or control, structure of the system operating entities in each country are summarized in Table 4.8.

*Table 4.8    ISO governance*

|  | ISO name | Board composition | Decision making | Staff | Regulations |
|---|---|---|---|---|---|
| Chile | CDEC | 1 director for each generator of more than 62 MW | Unanimity, Minister of Economy arbitrates in case of conflict | No staff of its own; relies on member resources | Electricity Decree and internal regulations |
| Argentina | CAMMESA | 2 government, 2 generators, 2 transmission companies, 2 distributors, 2 large users | Majority, Secretary of Energy has veto power | Own staff | Electricity Act, implementing regulations and presidential decrees |
| Brazil | ONS (dispatch); ASMAE (market operation) | Originally formed by market participants; currently by independent professionals | Originally pre-set voting proportions; professionals now represent stakeholder groups | Own staff (formerly from Eletro-bras' ope-rations control group) | Originally agreed by market participants; superseded by regulatory order |
| Bolivia | CNDC | 1 regulator, 1 generator, 1 transmission company, 1 distributor, 1 large user | Majority, regulator can only vote to break ties | Own staff | Electricity Act, implementing regulations, and internal regulations |

*Notes:*
CDEC: Centros de Despacho Económico de Carga [Economic Load Dispatch Centres].
CAMMESA: Compañía Administradora del Mercado Mayorista, Sociedad Anónima [Wholesale Market Administrator].
ONS: Operador Nacional do Sistema [National System Operator].
ASMAE: Agente Administrador do Mercado Atacadista de Energia Elétrica [National Wholesale Market Administrador].
CNDC: Centro Nacional de Despacho de Carga [National Load Dispatch Centre].

*Source:* Gatica and Skoknic (1996), Maia (1998).

Chilean disregard for potential market power abuses is also evident here. Unlike the rest of the ISOs, the Chilean CDEC is a 'generators' club' and as such is much more subject to manipulation by existing club members to exclude new members or otherwise manipulate the rules of the game.[16] In contrast, the Argentine and Bolivian ISOs (and, to a certain extent, the Brazilian ISO) include in their boards representatives from the major stakeholders in the ESI, use majority decision rules, and have their own staff, traits which are more likely to give them the impartiality that competitive power markets require. In Brazil, the regulatory agency ANEEL exercises close control over the ISO;[17] in Argentina, the government has veto power over ISO board decisions; whereas in Bolivia, the public sector is only present through the regulator, and then only in a tie-breaking role. Public sector involvement in ISO governance need not stimulate competition, but it is unlikely to be as favorable to the exercise of market power as a generators' club. Chile can therefore be classified as having the least pro-competitive ISO governance structure.

At a greater level of detail, restrictions to bidding into the electricity spot market that are not justified by the objective of curtailing market power decrease the scope of competition and may thus be regarded as indicative of a lower commitment to competition. On the other hand, requiring cost-based bids for thermal plant bids and central dispatch of hydro units can limit market power (and hence increase economic efficiency) when structural conditions for competition are not present, as in the Chilean case, so they cannot be taken as necessarily anticompetitive. (See Table 4.9.)

*Table 4.9    Regulation of spot market bids by generators*

|  | Bidding by thermal plants | Bidding by hydroelectric plants |
|---|---|---|
| Chile | Actual auditable cost of production | Centrally dispatched using linear program |
| Argentina | Free, subject to reference price ceiling | Free, subject to reference price ceiling |
| Brazil | Free, but only uncontracted portion | Centrally dispatched using linear program; socialization of hydrological risk |
| Bolivia | Reference fuel prices | Centrally dispatched using linear program |

*Source:* Gatica and Skoknic (1996); interviews.

The format of thermal plant bidding across the four cases does not reveal any particular ordering with respect to competition, since each case appears to be tailored to its specific conditions: a less competitive market structure in Chile, a very competitive market structure in Argentina, or a potentially competitive market in Bolivia that only requires partial restrictions on bids. The same can be said about hydro for Chile and Argentina. But it is not at all justified for Brazil and Bolivia, where hydroelectric plants could perfectly well be allowed to bid freely.[18] In fact, the extreme reliance on hydrogeneration in Brazil means that central dispatch of hydro plants, together with the restriction of thermal plant bidding to uncontracted capacity, effectively eliminates competition from Brazilian generation markets (Coopers & Lybrand n.d.: 11). Competition is further dampened in Brazil by the existence of an 'energy reallocation mechanism' that spreads hydrological risk across all the hydro units built in cascade along a given river, so that operators do not have to be concerned with the decisions made by upstream units or with the effects of their own decisions on the downstream plants.

In the ESI (as in telecoms and gas), metering and other costs limit but do not impede access to direct trading in wholesale markets by small users. The absence of minimum size limitations for market access can therefore be interpreted as indicative of the desire to maximize the scope of competition. The limitations to market access by users in the four cases are as follows:

- Chile: 2 MW.
- Argentina: 100 kW, to be eliminated by 2002.
- Brazil: 10 MW to 2000, 3 MW to 2003, then at regulator's discretion.
- Bolivia: 2 MW.

Thus by this measure Argentina is the most pro-competitive of the four cases, with Brazil the least favorable to competition.

Distributor purchasing regulations limit the freedom of action of these utilities and may thus reduce market efficiency, although the lack of clear quality standards, at the other extreme of the spectrum, confers additional monopoly power to distributor over its captive customers. The pattern here is similar to most of the other competition indicators examined so far: the Chilean case displays a favorable bias towards the incumbent suppliers of distribution services, which are not subject to any clear or indirect purchasing standards; in Argentina, the recourse to quality of service standards (whereby penalties are applied to distributors for service interruptions) strikes a balance between direct intervention and potential abuse of monopoly power by the distributor; and in Brazil and Bolivia, a heavy-handed approach of mandatory minimum contract coverage levels mitigates monopoly power but at the cost of stifling distributors' initiative in meeting service obligations. In reality, however, Chile and Argentina are not as different from Brazil and Bolivia as it would appear at first because regulated consumers are insulated from spot market volatility because these customers pay for energy consumed a six-month average of spot market prices. Not surprisingly, Argentine distributors do not bother to contract for long-term supply – they just pass on the seasonal average price to their customers.

Purchasing regulations can thus be summarized as follows:

- Chile: no regulations, but seasonal price averaging for regulated customers.
- Argentina: no direct regulations, but seasonal price averaging for regulated customers and quality of service standards and penalties, as well as price regulations limiting passthrough of purchase costs; transitional contracts for the three Buenos Aires distribution utilities formerly owned by the federal government with nearby thermal plants, for about 55 percent of total needs and a term of eight years.
- Brazil: distributors required to purchase 85 percent of load under long-term contracts, and passthrough of purchase costs is subject to price caps set by regulator.
- Bolivia: distributors required to purchase 80 percent of load under long-term contracts.

The last indicator of reliance on competitive mechanisms considers the recourse by policymakers to various ways of replicating market forces for the ESI segments operating under natural monopoly conditions. Under the umbrella of 'performance-based regulation' we can include the following elements of the regulatory framework in each of the four cases:

- Argentina: use of productivity improvement factors ('X-factors') to adjust rates over time; quality standards based on industry experience.
- Chile: use of 'model company' to determine distribution rates, and of X-factors in distribution rates; return on rate base fixed, but subject to benchmarking per average rate of return of all distribution companies in Chile.
- Brazil: X-factors used for both transmission and distribution utilities, as well as benchmarking.
- Bolivia: X-factors in distribution rates; return on rate base taken from actual returns of US utilities.

The list shows that all four countries rely on 'market-like' mechanisms to induce competitive behavior in the monopoly segments of the ESI. The most comprehensive approach is the Argentine one, which uses both productivity factors and quality standards to induce increasing efficiency and productivity improvements in the concessionaires, and to pass on these improvements to ratepayers through lower rates and improved quality of service. The frameworks in the other countries are more limited, particularly in the Chilean case where the model company results must be reconciled (by law) with the parameters estimated by the distributors.

Among the substitutes for actual competition, 'competition for the market' through franchise bidding deserves special attention because it has received extensive attention since it was originally suggested by Demsetz (1968). The degree of recourse to this method in the four countries is as follows:

- Chile: no franchise bidding under Pinochet.
- Argentina: most competition-oriented system.
- T&D concessions periodically retendered for bids.
- Brazil: T&D concessions tendered for bids.
- Bolivia: all capitalized/privatized utilities tendered for bids.

We can observe yet again that in this regard Chilean policymakers relied the least on this substitute for competition, while Argentina's used the most sophisticated design, by requiring the periodic rebidding of concessions (with the possibility of bidding by the concessionaire itself) to avoid the incentive problems that can occur when the end of the concession period nears (Williamson 1985). Brazil and Bolivia are intermediate cases.


## CONCLUSIONS

This chapter has examined the outcomes of the ESI restructuring process in Argentina, Bolivia, Brazil, and Chile with respect to two key dimensions: the allocation of property rights between the private and the public sectors, and the extent of reliance on competition as an allocative mechanism for the products of the ESI.

From the examination of property rights issues, it becomes clear that Chile has relied most extensively on private property. Not only has it fully transferred asset ownership for generation, transmission and distribution activities, but it also has imposed the least restrictions on private ownership such as investment requirements, with the exception of centralized dispatch of hydro resources. Although Chile has the only clearly political regulatory entity among the four cases, arbitration provisions have been explicitly included in the regulatory framework to prevent abuses of governmental power. The greatest reliance on public property occurs in Bolivia, where even the word 'privatization' has been replaced by the term 'capitalization' to convey the idea of a different arrangement. Capitalization imposes more extensive constraints on private owners than full privatization, although the regulatory system is reasonably well protected against political encroachment. Argentina and Brazil are intermediate cases, with Argentina closer to Chile in reliance on private property and Brazil closer to Bolivia, since it plans to retain a set of large generation assets in public hands.

Concerning competition, the pattern that emerges from most of the estimators of this variable is fairly clear. For most of the indicators examined, the Chilean ESI is located at one end of the spectrum covered by the four cases. The Chilean restructuring process has in general neglected market power issues, facilitating in effect the emergence of private oligopolies. Close to this end lies Brazil, where public sector interventionism remains in the form of centralized dispatch of hydro resources and extensive restrictions on the actions of distribution companies.[19] Bolivia displays a greater reliance on competition, being limited more by a small electricity market size than by policy choices that lessen the scope of competition. Finally, in Argentina reliance on competitive or 'para-competitive' arrangements is most extensive, ranging all the way from a fragmented generation ownership structure to a sophisticated concession framework for T&D monopolies that relies on periodic rebidding and extensive quality controls.

As a visual summary of the four cases, we can place them in a simple 2 x 2 matrix for each dependent variable as shown in Figure 4.1.[20]

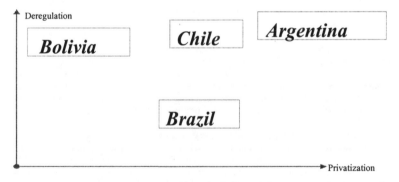

*Figure 4.1    Classification of cases by dependent variable*

Now that we know the outcomes of ESI restructuring in Argentina, Bolivia, Brazil, and Chile, we must examine in the same comparative vein the explanatory factors posited by the theoretical model. This is the task of the chapter that follows.

## NOTES

1. In order to facilitate the evaluation of the research methodology and the empirical evidence, the major variables are defined in the rest of this section, and their operationalization is discussed in Appendix 2.
2. For instance, while there are those who condemn private property as inherently immoral, the moral debate on ownership generally turns on its effects on more fundamental values, such as equity or the environment.
3. This succinct description is due to Professor Domínguez, personal communication. See also Collier and Collier (1991: 15).
4. For the purposes of this analysis, it is not necessary to differentiate further into components such as capacity, energy and ancillary services.
5. Although the data that follows is intended to reflect as accurately as possible the actual or intended state of affairs in each country as of mid-2002, the complete breakdown of Argentina's economy following the abandonment of peso convertibility in late 2001 has thrown ESI arrangements into complete disarray, with results that are impossible to predict. For instance, distribution concessions established tariffs in US dollars, effectively requiring automatic tariff adjustments for exchange rate movements away from peso–dollar parity. Such adjustments, however, were prohibited by the government when convertibility was scrapped, thus breaching concession contracts. Utilities and the government are currently renegotiating the concession contracts.
6. Argentina also faces a binational ownership issue with Yaciretá dam (with Paraguay too), but it has explored potential privatization schemes and in any case Yaciretá is only 14 percent of capacity in the national interconnected grid.
7. As indicated in note (f) of Table 4.1, there was already a privately-owned utility in Bolivia, COBEE, so after capitalization, the share of ownership in private hands exceeded 50 percent. Also, the transmission company was fully privatized rather than capitalized.
8. In the words of Bolivia's then president, G. Sánchez de Lozada: 'When you read their [the capitalization investors'] press release, they make it sound like they simply bought 50 percent of the company from the Bolivian government ... No. It's a capital contribution' (Hendrix 1995: A15).
9. Few transmission concessions have been yet awarded, and only for specific transmission lines. As for distribution, at the time of the concession auctions only temporary rate conditions were defined for an initial five- or seven-year period.
10. 'Chile has highly detailed benchmark regulation with explicit mechanisms for resolving disputes between the regulator and the utility, with the judiciary as final arbiter. These restraints are credible because the country has a long tradition of judicial independence that has restrained government discretion in areas of property rights and contracts' (Bitrán and Serra 1995: 3).
11. There are no data on the relative quality of regulatory agency staff (in fact, several of the agencies are still in the process of developing internal capacity), but the funding mechanisms appears to correlate well with quality staff: while Bitrán and Serra (1995) decry the staffing problems of the Chilean agency, ENRE in Argentina has a reputation for being one of the most competent regulatory agencies (Vispo 1999).
12. For evidence of self-dealing between Chilectra, the distribution company, and Pehuenche, a generation affiliate, see Blanlot (1993).
13. While it is true that the large size of many of the generation assets themselves (mainly large dams) is an obstacle to splitting ownership of generation assets in Brazil, the number of generation entities proposed by the government is substantially smaller than the number of separate generation stations in the main interconnected system.

14. Distribution concessions can be terminated by the President of Chile for quality of service reasons (DFL 1, Art. 40), but quality standards are not clearly defined, unlike in Argentina.
15. To be sure, there is no a priori reason why such an approach should be less able than sectoral regulation to prevent or correct market power abuses. In fact, 'light handed regulation', as this approach is known, is used in some countries, such as Germany, New Zealand and Australia. But note that the separation of transmission from Endesa was in the end achieved not through the antitrust laws (several suits brought by the post-Pinochet governments failed in the courts) but by the need for government approval of the takeover of Endesa by a Spanish utility (also called Endesa).
16. As with the issue of vertical integration and Endesa, more recent Chilean administrations have pushed changes in CDEC governance to bring in distributor and consumer participation.
17. In April 2001, ANEEL used its prerogatives to alter the governance structure of the wholesale electricity market (Mercado Atacadista de Energia Elétrica, MAE). Instead of the original board with direct stakeholder representation, ANEEL created a board of independent professionals that will represent (but have no prior, current, or subsequent financial connections to) consumers, producers and ANEEL itself.
18. In Brazil, it has been argued that the location of dams along only three major river basins (Amazon, São Francisco, and Paraná) creates too strong interdependencies (externalities) among dams to make a free market workable. But the hierarchical position of the dams in any given basin (from upriver to downriver, which means that decisions by dam operators are not simultaneously affected by hydrology), and the possibility of creating markets for water rights, makes such an objection untenable.
19. Extensive administrative intervention fails to produce acceptable results and begets more interventionism. Relatively low price caps for purchase cost passthrough and lack of market flexibility have inhibited investment in new generation, so BNDES is offering special financing packages and investment requirements are being appended to transitional Power Purchase Agreements (PPAs); low gas prices have been artificially forced on Petrobrás for power plants in order to set low price passthrough limits (Pires n.d.).
20. For purposes of a case comparison such as the present one, a graphic mapping of the dependent variables in each country is better than a numerical mapping, because the latter tends to ignore the subtleties and nuances that the case-study approach is intended to take into account in the first place.

# 5. Explanatory factors

This chapter considers, also from a comparative perspective, the explanatory variables yielded by the formal model of Chapter 2 for each one of the four cases under consideration. Each one of the three variables is discussed in turn.

## JUDICIAL INDEPENDENCE

Since there is little published information about the mechanisms for appointment and removal of judges, funding of the judiciary system, and career paths of judges in the four cases, the best indicators of relative levels of judicial independence are the indices published by a variety of sources, which are shown in Table 5.1 below. These indices measure either judicial autonomy directly, or related variables such as the quality of the judicial system (a major indicator of judicial quality is freedom from bias), and the protection of property rights (which is generally enforced by the judiciary).

*Table 5.1    Measures of judicial autonomy in Latin America (various years)*

|  | Johnson (1976a), 1945–75 total score | Supreme Court median tenure | Judicial independence perception 1997 | Judicial quality perception 1997 | Property rights security 1995–96 | Property rights protection 1998 |
|---|---|---|---|---|---|---|
| Chile | 277 | 5.72 (1951–94) | 5.18 | 4.76 | 2 | 4 |
| Argentina | 231 | 4.36 (1946–94) | 3.73 | 2.40 | 2 | 3 |
| Brazil | 230 | 7.15 (1963–96) | 4.89 | 3.85 | 1 | 2 |
| Bolivia | 150 | no data | no data | no data | 1 | 2 |

*Notes and sources:*
Measures of judicial independence developed by K.F. Johnson, based on codings of qualitative assessments by analysts of Latin American politics (Johnson 1976a), as reported by Verner (1984: Table 1). Sample comprises Argentina, Bolivia, Brazil, Chile, Colombia, Costa Rica, Cuba, Dominican Republic, Ecuador, El Salvador, Guatemala, Haiti, Honduras, Mexico, Nicaragua, Panama, Paraguay, Peru, Uruguay, Venezuela. Maximum sample score (highest independence) is 306, minimum 115.
Median tenure of Supreme Court justices from Henisz (2000). Years in parentheses indicate period used to compute median tenure figures for each country.

Perceptions of judicial independence: 7 is maximum independence, 0 minimum; World Economic Forum (1997: Table 8.08).
Perceptions of judicial quality: 10 is maximum quality, 1 minimum; IMD (1997: Table 3.37).
Security of property rights: 3 most secure, 1 least. Messick and Kimura (1996, Table 4.1).
Protection of property rights: 4 highest, 1 least. Johnson et al. (1998). Scale inverted from original for ease of comparison.

In addition to the rankings presented in the table, Verner (1984) provides a descriptive classification of Latin American Supreme Courts according to their independence. Verner labels Chile's court as 'attenuated-activist,' meaning that it was independent and vigorous prior to the 1973 coup and lost stature after that point. Lower in the independence scale, Verner places the supreme courts of Argentina and Brazil in the 'reactive-compliant' category, for courts that are active and independent during periods of civilian rule but become compliant under military dictatorships. The Bolivian court is accorded the lowest independence ranking by Verner among the four cases under consideration here, being labeled a 'minimalist' court. According to Verner (ibid.: 494), minimalist courts 'perform minimal policy functions and are completely dependent on and subordinate to external political forces'.

Judicial independence is clearly greater in Chile than in the other countries. Chile had a stable democratic political system for a substantially longer period of time than the other countries up to 1973, when the military coup occurred. Political stability in a democratic setting meant respect for the rule of law and therefore for the judiciary. Problems began under the Allende government when the Supreme Court denied the constitutionality of governmental policies and the government in turn ignored court decisions. The 1973 coup brought a further weakening of judicial independence: the Constitutional Court was dissolved right away and, while the Supreme Court was left untouched (its conservatism meant it was not regarded as a threat by the military), it slavishly accepted the numerous violations of human rights and obvious violation of the constitution by the new regime; even then, under the 1980 Constitution, Augusto Pinochet gave himself the right to appoint and dismiss justices and to determine the court's jurisdiction (Verner 1984; Domingo 1999). But the judicial system was not subject to a sweeping reorganization. The judicial machinery survived political instability and the coup relatively intact by contrast to the other cases.

Argentina is a much clearer instance of a weakened judiciary. Apart from the damage to rule of law inflicted by repeated purges of the Supreme Court since the rise of Juan Domingo Perón in the 1940s, the advent of democracy did not stop political meddling in the courts, since even during democratic periods the Argentine Supreme Court has been far weaker than the executive power. The legitimacy of the court in the restored democratic regime had also been weakened by its 'willingness to recognize and legitimize new military regimes' (Verner 1984: 487–8). The major blow in the current democratic era came after Carlos Menem's accession:

> One of Mr. Menem's first presidential decisions in 1990 was to use his party's majority in Congress to increase the Supreme Court to nine members from five. Two of the sitting justices resigned, perhaps not coincidentally ... His nominations went to congress on a Thursday afternoon and the Senate confirmed them on Friday morning, in a seven-minute secret session, without the attendance of the opposition legislators ... Mr. Menem's former legal partner is now Argentina's chief justice. (Verbitsky 1998: A17)

Ongoing cases of corruption and impropriety throughout the court system have continued to weaken judicial authority in the country, with ample evidence of corruption, the resignation of two justice ministers in 18 months, and low public confidence. The main reason is the manipulation of judicial appointments and bribery of judges by the Menem government[1] (Sims 1997; Warn 1997). For instance, Menem filled existing and newly created courts in the city of Buenos Aires with his own appointees. Of more than 100 high-ranking members of the Menem government investigated for corruption by March of 1998, none had been convicted (Verbitsky 1998).

Brazil's courts were also enfeebled by the ongoing manipulation and abrogation of the law by the military regime as the regime found it convenient (Verner 1984). This contrasted, however, with the Supreme Court's history as a relatively powerful and professionally staffed institution that was respected during the democratic regime of the New Republic (1945–64). Despite the persistent inability, lasting to the present, to enforce the rule of law in rural and remote areas of the country, including such basic tasks as the issuance and control of land titles, a difference with Argentina is that Brazil has maintained a stronger façade of continuity and even respect for the decisions of the Supreme Court by the military rulers. To be sure, several members of the Supreme Court were purged by the military regime, and the regime's Second Institutional Act of 1965 restricted the power of the court very significantly[2] and enlarged its membership to place justices sympathetic to the military; further restrictions were imposed with the Third Institutional Act in 1969, and further purges and size changes were carried out in the 1970s (Verner 1984). But even after the approval of a new constitution in 1989, the Supreme Court was not replaced or eviscerated as in Argentina. Reliance on the courts for contract enforcement, as the government envisaged for the electric utility privatization concessions, would therefore appear not as unreasonable as it would have in Argentina had it been attempted there.[3]

Bolivia has experienced more political instability – defined (simplistically) as the number of government changes through coups and other unconstitutional means – than any other Latin American country. This is linked to a poor record of effective judicial power, since it means that the rule of law is very limited.[4] Indeed, prior to the 1952 revolution, which for a while resulted in greater respect for the rule of law, the Supreme Court's independence 'was violated with impunity' (Verner 1984: 495). The return to military rule after the revolutionary episode made the court powerless once again, particularly during the 1969–79 and 1980–82 periods when the constitution was suspended. Economic reform under Paz Estenssoro of the MNR,[5] was carried out under emergency powers in order to thwart union opposition.

Further evidence of a weak Bolivian Supreme Court is provided by an examination of how justices are appointed: 'Due to historical traditions and political factors, the election of the members [of the Supreme Court] is an informal process whereby each Department [that is territorial jurisdiction] is allotted a number of justices in proportion to its size... There is a further apportionment on the basis of the governing political parties'. (Gamarra 1991: 55). 'Historically, Bolivian judges have been selected from the ranks of the private bar, to which they return after only a brief stay in the judiciary' (ibid.: p.64). The return of democracy did not end these practices: the MNR government of 1984–88 appointed the entire Supreme Court during its tenure (Gamarra 1990), which led to the further weakening of the Court as the next government perceived it as politically motivated: 'a Supreme Court ruling declaring unconstitutional a tax on beer' led to claims that 'the ruling was the product of corruption, namely the bribing of the justices by the two largest beer factories in Bolivia' on which grounds

> the executive refused to accept the Court's decision. Instead, the Acuerdo Patriótico [of the ADN[6] and MIR[7] parties] initiated a malfeasance trial in the National Congress against eight Supreme Court justices. The MNR escalated the conflict by resubmitting a lawsuit demanding that the Court declare the 1989 elections null and void. ... In mid-May 1991, ... the government allowed the eight suspended Supreme Court justices to return to their posts. (ibid.: 116)

Of greater impact for the ESI was the removal by the Supreme Court, on trumped-up malfeasance charges, of the telecoms regulator in 1997, after he required the telephone monopoly to begin interconnecting competitors; the regulator was replaced by a senator from the government party, the ADN; there have also been attacks against the banking superintendent (Friedland

1997b).  Altogether, these pieces of evidence show the low level of judicial independence in Bolivia.[8]

This section has clearly established that judicial independence at the time of ESI restructuring in each country was highest in Chile, followed by Brazil.  Although the ranking of Argentina versus Bolivia is not so clear, there are good reasons to believe Argentina's courts were more independent than Bolivia's. Despite the weakening of the courts by the Menem administration, Argentina had a slightly stronger tradition of judicial independence, which actors involved in ESI restructuring are likely to have taken into account, while the conflicts between the government and the Supreme Court in Bolivia under the democratic regime have been no less severe than the manipulation of court appointments in Argentina from the standpoint of the effect on judicial independence.  International rankings of judicial independence and related indicators also confirm such a relative ordering of Argentina and Bolivia with regard to this variable.


## IDEOLOGY

### Party Positioning at Time of Restructuring

As Table 5.2 shows, most of the parties in power at the time of ESI restructuring in the cases under study were, at least on paper, of a center-left persuasion.  However, a detailed analysis of the decisionmakers within these governments, who tended to be also the party leaders, reveals varying degrees of influence of neoclassical economic ideas concerning the importance of competition and property rights.  In the case of Chile, the absence of party competition does not preclude the positioning of the regime at the time of restructuring along a left–right axis, since the ideological preferences of major regime decisionmakers are well known and documented. For Chile the table therefore documents the overall regime orientation, and instead of competing parties I have listed competing factions within the regime, as identified by several different analysts of policymaking in the Pinochet regime.

Table 5.2    *Party/regime ideology and position relative to other major*
*parties/factions*

|  | Party in power | Ideology | Competing parties and relative position |
|---|---|---|---|
| Chile | Pinochet regime. 'Chicago boys' | Far right | Business community (at left) |
| Argentina | Partido Justicialista [Peronists] | Center-left | UCR (at right); FREPASO (at left) |
| Brazil | Partido Social Demócrata Brasileiro | Center-left | PFL (at right), PMDB (at right), PT (at left) |
| Bolivia | Movimiento Nacional Revolucionario | Center-left | ADN (at right), MIR (at left) |

*Notes:*
UCR: Unión Cívica Radical [Radical Civic Union].
FREPASO: Frente por un País Solidario [Solidarity Front].
PFL: Partido do Frente Liberal [Liberal Front Party].
PMDB: Partido do Movimento Democrâtico Brasileiro [Brazilian Democratic Movement Party].
PT: Partido dos Trabalhadores [Workers' Party].
ADN: Acción Democrática Nacionalista [Democratic Nationalist Alliance].
MIR: Movimiento de Izquierda Revolucionaria [Revolutionary Left Movement].

*Sources:* ideology positions taken from Derbyshire and Derbyshire (1996), the *Political Handbook of the World* (Council on Foreign Relations and Center for Comparative Political Research of the State University of New York at Binghamton, various dates) and E. Silva (1996b).

Another important qualification to Table 5.2 is that in some of the countries factional or party rivalry is not only, or even not primarily, oriented along a left–right axis. In particular, at the time of ESI restructuring populist and clientelist attitudes pervaded, in ascending order, the Argentine, Bolivian and Brazilian cases. Both populism and clientelism are more or less hostile to private property and competition, because both rely on the extraction and distribution of economic rents to sustain winning political coalitions, to which in the case of populism are added – at least in its traditional incarnations – a substantial amount of nationalism and emphasis on the state as an engine of national development.

**Information about Policymakers**

Orthodox economic ideas had the strongest influence in Argentina and Chile, but there were subtle differences between these two cases in the degree of influence of nationalism. In Chile, the military nature of the political regime at the time of ESI restructuring led to a greater influence of nationalism than in Argentina, given the professional inclination of military officers towards domestic interests, not perhaps in foreign trade policy but certainly in the selection of buyers for privatized firms.[9] In Argentina, by contrast, those espousing the traditions of economic nationalism were too weak and discredited by many years of crisis of nationalist policies to prevent a radical opening of the country to foreign investment. Lastly, the influence of ideas contrary to competition and private ownership was strongest in Brazil and Bolivia.

As with judicial independence, ideological influences are found at their purest in the Chilean case. Extensive documentation by scholars of the influence of the 'Chicago boys' has demonstrated a direct linkage between market-oriented policy initiatives in Chile during the military regime and the economic theories elaborated at the University of Chicago[10] (E. Silva 1996b, ch. 5; Moulián and Vergara 1980; Hira 1998).

It is important to remark that the 'Chicago' doctrine followed in Chile is strongly libertarian, in that it mistrusts all forms of government intervention, including regulation, and worries very little about market power issues in a private-property context because it believes that monopoly or oligopoly is very hard to sustain for long.

On the other hand, there are differing scholarly views on the ideology of economic policymakers during the second half of the 1980s, when the Pinochet regime was recovering from the debt crisis. According to Eduardo Silva (1996b, ch. 7), a 'pragmatic neoliberal coalition' was in power during this period, in which there was substantial influence of peak business associations because Pinochet needed upper class support in face of economic and political crisis. Patricio Silva (1991) and Paul Sigmund (1990) claim, by contrast, that technocratic influence was restored in 1985 once the worst of the economic crisis was over. The extensive biographical and relational data presented by Eduardo Silva certainly gives him greater credence, but the correlation between background and policy initiatives of some of the major economic policymakers is weak.

There is evidence that in general, the Chilean military had nationalist inclinations that set them apart from the radical internationalism of the 'Chicago boys'. For a regime that placed the return of assets expropriated by the socialist Allende administration (that it had overthrown) to its former private owners, the military junta strikingly nationalized the telephone company Compañía de Teléfonos de Chile (Chile Telephone Company, CTC) in 1974, when the 'Chicago boys' were not yet in control of the regime's economic policy. Later, the radical liberalization policies pursued by the 'Chicago boys' from 1975 on[11] were opposed by many military officers, and indeed their implementation was only possible in parallel with the consolidation of Pinochet's personal rule (Moulián and Vergara 1980; E. Silva 1996: 109; Hira 1998: 76–88 and 95).

As in all the other cases, business interests were deeply divided in Chile with regard to ideology. After the 1973 coup, business opinion was split between supporters of a 'deepening' of Chilean industrialization (Moulián and Vergara 1980) and 'internationalist conglomerates' that supported the radical policies of the 'Chicago boys' (E. Silva 1996b: 98–9). But note that on privatization there was widespread consensus: in 1974, 'business leaders demanded more than a simple return to the status quo ante [prior to the Allende nationalizations]. They also wanted the privatization of companies that had always had majority public ownership' (ibid.: 104; see also Hira 1998: 91–2). And after regaining influence on the Pinochet regime in 1985, 'more privatization' was one of the 'substantive policy demands' of business groups. Business preferences were also tinged with nationalism ('defense of national production') (E. Silva 1996b: 193 195, 205).

Argentina and Bolivia are in more complex positions when it comes to strength of ideologies. Both countries saw governments from populist or even left-of-center parties carry out economic restructuring under the influence of US advisors or US-trained experts.

As governor of La Rioja province before he became president of Argentina, Menem followed traditional Peronist policies favoring industry and social welfare programs for workers administered by unions (Palermo and Novaro 1996: 20). Menem

> ran on the traditional Peronist platform of social justice and higher industrial productivity. Most of his macroeconomic policies, however, were vague and contradictory. There was some rhetoric on a debt moratorium and traditional statist policies, but he did not mention specifics. ... Menem ... portrayed himself as a man of the people running against corruption. Menem pledged that if elected, he would faithfully adhere to the Peronist creed, which postulated economic nationalism, strong state regulation of the economy, resumption of economic growth through direct investment, and social justice in the form of income redistribution in favor of salary and wage earners. (Molano 1997: 100; see also Stokes 2001: 45–6).

Menem's campaign promises further included a sharp public sector wage increase and a foreign debt moratorium (Teichman 1997). At the same time, it is clear that Menem had little commitment to any ideology at all, only to whatever would make him win elections. He had been a founder of the Peronist party's reformist wing in 1984, which was characterized by ideological flexibility (such as the admission of Domingo Cavallo, his future economic affairs minister and a defender of free trade and economic orthodoxy) (Corrales 1996: 310). But Menem rejoined orthodox faction when he was unable to lead the reform faction (McGuire 1997: 208). Menem was above all a political chameleon who would enable Cavallo to implement orthodox policies.

Once in power, Menem and his administration demonstrated a greater commitment to economic orthodoxy. In contrast to the preceding administration, which had justified privatization on purely financial grounds, the discourse of the Menem administration appealed to microeconomic reasons, so that '[o]nly in 1989 did the Argentine government begin to promote privatization as the most efficient way to redistribute resources' (González Fraga 1991: 97). But actual economic policy was still hesitant for more than a year after the administration's assumption of power.[12] Full-blown orthodox reform did not come until the failure of half-hearted measures to tackle the country's economic problems led to the appointment of Cavallo as minister of economic affairs in 1991. Even then, Cavallo's plans caused conflict within the Peronist party, which required appeasement by allowing legislative monitoring of the economic restructuring process through a legislative oversight commission, and concessions to unions in exchange for restraint (Corrales 1996: 206–14; Acuña 1995). Like Sánchez de Lozada in Bolivia, Menem faced combative labor unions and strong nationalist and collectivist elements within the ruling party, which had traditionally espoused platforms of inward-oriented, state-led development policies, although like Menem himself, the Peronist party had already been shifting to the right, as evidenced for instance by its entering into electoral alliances with conservative parties in the late 1980s (Gibson 1997).

Cavallo's ideological commitment to privatization and competition is very well documented. He had previously established a think-tank, IEERAL,[13] which would allow him to apply to Argentine problems the perspectives learnt while a doctoral student in the US. The think-tank recruited and trained the future members of Cavallo's team during his effort to radically reshape the Argentine public sector (Domínguez 1997: 18; Yergin and Stanislaw 1998: 242–3). Moreover, Cavallo was also a committed internationalist who reversed nationalist economic policies favoring domestic producers and investors. In contrast to Chile, where the military could not be entirely ignored, the strong nationalist element in the Peronist movement appears to have been entirely overcome by Cavallo's internationalism.

International influence was also present in Argentina during the early 1990s through World Bank, United Nations Development Program and Inter-American Development Bank loans to organize the public sector restructuring process, and through the extensive use of consultants to supplement the meager resources of the Argentine public purse at the time (World Bank 1993b: 17).

In Bolivia, ideological ambiguity prevailed among the major Bolivian parties due to a very strong patronage component of party politics: the MNR, for instance, supported the dictatorial regime of General Bánzer in exchange for spoils during the years 1971–74 (Gamarra and Malloy 1995: 407). During the 1985 presidential campaign, the MNR's platform was still its traditional 'nationalist revolutionary' model of a mixed economy formed by public, private, and communal sectors, including 'rationalization' of SOEs but also agreement with labor unions. But by this time, the MNR's presidential candidate and longtime leader Paz Estenssoro was personally disenchanted with this confused, populist approach (Conaghan and Malloy 1994: 127).

As in Argentina, orthodox policies were only accepted after a period of contestation. The tension between traditional and 'neoliberal' policies within the MNR made it split on the issue of privatization during 1985–89, with technocrats in favor and old-line politicians against. The traditionalists tried to oust the reformist Sánchez de Lozada as MNR presidential candidate in 1989 (Gamarra 1990; Conaghan and Malloy 1994: 191). But the ability of the Paz Estenssoro administration to impose harsh macroeconomic stabilization measures over fierce opposition from the left, and the success of these measures, opened the door for a wider acceptance of orthodox economic ideas. 'By 1989, a remarkable consensus had emerged within the [Bolivian] political class regarding the desirability of continuing the market experiment initiated by the Paz Estenssoro government' (Conaghan 1995: 122), so that by this time, all major parties endorsed economic 'orthodoxy' (see Conaghan and Malloy 1994: 193).

Sánchez de Lozada, under whose mandate the Bolivian ESI was restructured after his election in 1989, had resided and studied (philosophy) in the US. As minister first (under the previous MNR leader, Paz Estenssoro) and president later he brought in technocrats with solid training in neoclassical economics.[14] Sánchez de Lozada does not appear to have been a pragmatic convert to market economics and private property; more of a European-style social democrat, concerned with income distribution issues but willing to accept the need to work within a market economy context (Yergin and Stanislaw 1998: 232). In fact, in Sánchez de Lozada we also find parallels with Cavallo, in that he seemed to defend a 'neoliberal' agenda but pushed from within a populist party; like Cavallo and Fernando Henrique Cardoso, Sánchez de Lozada developed many of his initiatives through the establishment of a 'think-tank' (in his case, the Fundación Milenio) before gaining power; and lastly, like Cavallo and Cardoso, he gained political fame as a successful finance minister.

Sánchez de Lozada strongly believed in the rule of law, like his political mentor Paz Estenssoro (Morales 1996: 36).

> Neither Paz Estenssoro not Sánchez de Lozada subscribed to the classic liberal argument that a market economy produces a better distribution of resources and, thus, an optimal economic outcome. Instead, they embraced the political-economy axiom that ... a reduced state would diminish influence peddling and the role of pressure groups that regard government as the best vehicle to obtain a larger share in the distribution of national income. (Conaghan and Malloy 1994: 144–5).

More strongly than in any of the other three cases, business groups played in Bolivia an important ideological role. The Bolivian peak business association (CEPB[15]) hired economists to increase its ideological coherence against the state-oriented ideologies of most political parties and the unions, and produced in 1984 a policy paper recommending elimination of price controls and consumption subsidies (Conaghan and Malloy 1994: 125). In turn, the CEPB's positions influenced the MNR's main rival, ADN, which were subsequently borrowed by the Paz Estenssoro administration.

Among ADN's economists, several had been trained at Harvard and worked with Jeffrey Sachs there to design an economic policy plan (Conaghan and Malloy 1994: 127–8). When the MNR government of Paz Estenssoro looked to ADN for policy directions, Jeffrey Sachs came to play a key advisory role in the design of a successful economic stabilization program. Other sources of foreign ideas in Bolivia came through the assistance of US AID (Gamarra 1990: 202–3). The strong international connections of Sánchez de Lozada and his collaborators, as well as his own background of several years of residence in the US, would indicate that nationalism was not a significant force under his administration, although there is no direct evidence confirming this conjecture other than the actual policies of his government, which brought foreign investors in virtually all cases of capitalization of SOEs.

Of all four countries, Brazil displays the least influence of neoclassical economics. The large size of Brazil in geographic, demographic, and economic terms has meant for Brazil a lower degree of interdependence with other countries and thus a more inward-looking orientation of its politics and policymaking, which has in turn translated into a greater strength of economic nationalism. A second element in the disinterest of Brazilian policymakers in market-oriented reform is the peculiarly non-ideological nature of contemporary Brazilian politics. Following a long historical tradition, some of the major Brazilian parties (for example, the PMDB in its current composition) are machines oriented almost exclusively to the attainment of government office and its attendant spoils, which can then be distributed to loyal constituents in exchange for votes. Brazilian voters, particularly in the poorer rural areas and in urban shantytowns populated with migrants from these areas, continue to look to the electoral system in terms of direct exchange of votes for favors, because in these poor rural areas of Brazil long-standing networks of patronage have never been broken by ideological mobilization or other influences. While business opinion surveys by the business organization Confederação Nacional da Indústria (National Industry Confederation, CNI) show significant support for economic orthodoxy (cited in Schneider 1997), business's ideological influence on parties or the government appears limited (Schneider 1997; Kingstone 1999). The Brazilian congress has therefore been very reluctant to authorize measures to reduce the role of the public sector, such as reform of the national pension system.

A further impediment to competition and privatization in Brazil has been the backlash against the perceived 'orthodoxy' of military regime since the restoration of democracy in 1985, which produced electoral support for a renewal of populism (consisting of import substitution, an acceleration of government spending on 'development' projects and some income redistribution, and tolerance of moderate inflation) (Bresser Pereira 1993: 338). Finally, nationalism did not only manifest itself in the form of resistance to foreign programs, but also in the strong opposition to the privatization of Petrobrás, the state oil monopoly.

Fernando Henrique Cardoso has little of the ideological background that could be expected to draw him to market-oriented policies. Cardoso invites certain parallels with Menem in that he appears to have placed pragmatism above the prior ideological baggage of his *dependentista* writings. His pragmatic embrace of pro-market policies came prior to the presidency, when as finance minister he was the author of the successful Real Plan, and his pragmatism continued as president (Maxfield 1999: A15). However, Domínguez writes (1997: 43) that 'Cardoso has always been suspicious of the "magic" of the market' and 'found it difficult to celebrate a market-oriented economic policy'. The difference with Menem is that Cardoso's acceptance of market-oriented reforms appears, as with Bolivia's Sánchez de Lozada, rooted not in ambition alone but also in European social democratic thought, which seeks a combination of free markets and private property with public sector programs for the reduction of inequality and poverty (Yergin and Stanislaw 1998: 258–9).

Like Cavallo in Argentina, Cardoso has appointed for senior jobs a cadre of scholars that worked with him in the prestigious research center he co-founded in 1969, CEBRAP[16] (Domínguez 1997: 18–19). In the strong Brazilian tradition of dependence theory, some of Cardoso's senior officials held in their past as academics and scholars critical attitudes to the international trading system and economic orthodoxy, but now they have been willing to participate in the administration of a largely orthodox program. The governors of the powerful and influential states of São Paulo and Rio de Janeiro belonged during the initiation of ESI restructuring (1994–98) to Cardoso's party and thus share with his ministers a mixture of technocratic training and social democratic values (Hinchberger 1996).

The ideology of Brazilian technocrats has slowly evolved from dirigisme to more liberal views (Sola 1994: 154, 157), particularly among the staff of the national development bank, BNDES (Molano 1997: 47, Schneider 1993). The military origin of many SOE managers and technocrats in Brazil has imbued them with a nationalist ideology that believes in the economic leadership of the state (Sola 1994). As in Cardoso's case, their shift towards orthodoxy is purely practical (Schneider 1993: 320, 327): 'pragmatic officials, many of whom favored a continued strategy of state-led development, have pushed privatization in order to rationalize state intervention and streamline government administration' (Schneider (1993) also points to generational and managerial change, with younger and private sector people taking charge at BNDES).

**Electoral and Public Opinion: Overall Ideological Orientation of Polity**

Public opinion surveys in the countries under study generally show support for economic orthodoxy, but contingent upon the ability of markets to improve upon the performance of the public sector (Stokes 1996; see also Armijo and Faucher 2002). In Argentina, surveys begin showing support for privatization in 1987–88. Surveys prior to the presidential election in 1989 showed 70 percent support for privatization in general. In a 1992 opinion poll, 59 percent of respondents supported competition, and 65 percent supported private provision of social services (Romer and Associates, cited in Bartell 1995, and Stokes 2001: Table 5.6). In 1990, there was strong support for privatization in Brazil, with 43 percent in favor; also, 49 percent gave priority to the private sector for the country's economic development, while 33 percent assigned such a role to SOEs, although 'nearly two-thirds of the respondents in the survey did not have a clear definition of privatization' (Molano 1997: 42). By contrast, in Bolivia opposition to the New Economic Policy (NEP) focused on privatization, 'which originally garnered considerable public support due to the perception that it would combat corruption, but … [now] political opposition and the media express fears that the sale of public companies will benefit only government functionaries rather than private entrepreneurs' (Morales 1996: 133; Sims 1998). Hence with the possible exception of Bolivia, public opinion appears to have been substantially non-ideological about ownership and competition, preferring to vote for whatever arrangement would work best in practice. This means that the key ideological preferences to consider would be those of policymakers and not of the electorate.

The overall ideological orientation of a polity, reflecting a combination of policymakers' preferences, those of political and economic elites, and public opinion, should also be reflected in the outcomes of the political process with regard to the extent of reliance on private property and competition. Table 5.3 shows some indicators of such overall orientation, as measured by various cross-national databases: the scope, or extent of involvement, of the public sector in economic activity, the relative size of state-owned enterprises in the economy, the ability of foreigners to own productive assets in the country, the degree of reliance on price controls, and the degree of regulation of labor markets. The general criterion behind the selection of these indices is that greater public sector intervention or participation in the economy is typical of left-leaning governments or polities.

*Table 5.3   Indicators of ideological orientation of the polities*

|  | Scope of govern- ment 1946– 86 | SOE activity as % GDP 1985–90 | FDI freedom 1998 | Extent of price con- trols 1995 | Labor market regulation 1997 |
|---|---|---|---|---|---|
| Chile | 5.25 | 14.4% | 1 | 1 | 3.48 |
| Argentina | 5.31 | 2.7% | 2 | 3 | 6.60 |
| Brazil | 7.00 | 7.6% | 3 | 4 | 5.37 |
| Bolivia | 6.17 | 13.9% | 2 | 6 | No data |

*Notes and sources:*
Scope of government: 10 highest, 1 lowest (Gurr 1989/1990).
SOE activity level: World Bank (1998).
FDI freedom: 1 maximum freedom, 4 minimum; Johnson et al. (1998).
Price controls: 1 least, 10 most; Gwartney (1997: Table II.C). Scale inverted from original to facilitate comparison.
Labor market regulation: 1 least, 10 most; IMD (1997: Table 3.35). Scale inverted from original to facilitate comparison.

The table's figures match the preceding discussion about the influence of orthodox economic ideology among the four cases. With the important exception of SOE activity (no doubt caused by public ownership of CODELCO, the copper mining giant, for reasons explained in the following section), Chile scores lowest in the scope of government, freedom for foreign investors, extent of price controls, and labor market regulation.

Argentina is second (excepting in this case the ranking for labor market regulation, a legacy of Peronism), while the relative positions of Brazil and Bolivia change depending on the variable (Brazil is more orthodox than Bolivia in SOE activity level and extent of price controls, while the ranking is reversed for scope of government and freedom for foreign investment).

To summarize, an analysis of ideology, both at the level of decisionmakers and of public opinion and polity orientation in general, shows that public opinion has not in general been strong enough to sway the outcome of economic policy in any specific direction. At the level of senior policymakers, Chile was the country where the most radically *laissez-faire* ideas prevailed, hostile even to the need for regulation of market power, but also under strong nationalist influence. In Argentina, an orthodox economic program was implemented (with some major exceptions, like labor market reform), although only after the failure of the historical legacies of state interventionism. In Bolivia, a similar ideological tradition combined with a more social democratic orientation of the major decisionmaker to produce a weaker commitment to orthodoxy than in Argentina. And finally, in Brazil the ideological preference for orthodox solutions was weakest due to the social democratic background of the policymakers and a greater role of clientelism and nationalism in the political system.

## DISTRIBUTIONAL CONFLICT

Table 5.4 presents comparative values for a range of indicators of distributional conflict, both in terms of actual conflict over the distribution of income, such as labor conflict, and in terms of elements of the polity that are more likely to produce such conflict, like the degree of decentralization of a country, which other things being equal can be expected to be related to the level of conflict among the different territorial units of a country over public policy, or the sheer degree of economic inequality in the country.

*Table 5.4  Indicators of distributional conflict*

|  | Gini coeff. | Annual lost work-days/ 000 pop. 1993–5 | Number of strikes or lockouts, average 1987–91 | SOE losses, % GDP, average 1985–90 | Degree of decen-traliza-tion, average 1946–94 | Average public sector deficit, % GDP | Percei-ved degree of labor conflict 1997 |
|---|---|---|---|---|---|---|---|
| Chile | 56.5 (1994) | 33.78 | 129.8 | 8.6% | 1 | 1% (1972–88) | 2.45 |
| Argentina | 43.8 (1980s) | 221.66 | 543 | No data | 2 | 6% (1980–89) | 2.55 |
| Brazil | 60.1 (1995) | 4.81 | 1889.7 | 0.6% | 3 | 8% (1980–90) | 2.76 |
| Bolivia | 42.0 (1990) | No data | 137.6 | 7.6% | 1 | 13% (1982–91) | No data |

*Notes and sources:*
Gini coefficient: higher value indicates more inequality. World Bank (1998: Table 2.8), and Taylor and Jodice (1983) for Argentina.
Lost workdays: World Competitiveness Report, various editions, IMD (various years, 1997: Table 6.25).
Number of strikes and lockouts: Yearbook of Labour Statistics, various editions (ILO, various years; Table 9A); Taylor and Jodice (1983) for Argentina.
SOE losses from World Bank (1998: Tables 5.10 and 5.8, respectively).
Decentralization: 3 = most decentralized (federal), 1 = fully centralized; Jaggers and Gurr (1995).
Public sector deficit from World Bank dataset (1993c).
Industrial relations perception: 7 = highest conflict level, 1 = lowest, World Economic Forum (1997: Table 7.14).

Table 5.4 illustrates the difficulty of measuring distributional conflict, since it can take different forms in different societies. In general, Chile appears to have a more moderate level of distributional conflict than the other countries. Although high in SOE losses and Gini coefficient, it ranks lowest in number of strikes, decentralization, budget deficits, and perception of labor conflict. The other three cases are difficult to rank. Bolivia could arguably be placed next, since it has the lowest Gini coefficient, it was until very recently a centralized country, and its major distributional problem seems concentrated in SOE and public spending. Argentina would have the second highest level of conflict, since its Gini coefficient and budget deficit are lower than Brazil's, but it displays a high level of labor conflict and is more decentralized than Bolivia or Chile. Brazil is perhaps the one with the most intense distributional conflicts, as it has the highest level of income inequality as measured by the Gini coefficient, the highest perception of labor conflict, and it is the most decentralized of all four, although it ranks lowest in number of lost workdays. In view of the ambiguity of numerical measures of distributional conflict, the rest of this section examines other evidence as well.

Chile had a strong tradition of political and labor mobilization, which played a major role in the breakdown of the democratic political system and the subsequent military coup in 1973. Under Pinochet, however, distributional conflict was suppressed through the repression of labor and the exclusion, at least under the 'Chicago boys', of most business interests from access to major economic policy decisions (E. Silva 1996a, 1996b). Policies with an obvious distributional objective, from import tariffs to subsidized prices of SOE outputs, were largely eliminated before ESI restructuring began. While the onset of the debt crisis in 1982, and the draconian adjustment policies it led the regime to adopt, caused a resurgence of political and labor contestation, the military regime remained fairly impervious to distributional pressures.

An important instance of distributional conflict in Pinochet's Chile concerned the state copper enterprise CODELCO, one of the world's top producers of copper ore. The armed forces blocked privatization of CODELCO, which was on the agenda of the 'Chicago boys', because under a law dating back to the Frei Administration of 1966–70, 10 percent of CODELCO's revenues from the sale of copper were earmarked for military procurement[17] (Allende 1988). However, there is no other clear instance of actions by a group with access to the regime's decisionmakers to keep assets in the public sector or obtain control over formerly state-owned assets under monopoly conditions. There is documented evidence of opposition to deregulation and liberalization by Chilean domestic-oriented manufacturers (Hira 1998: 98), but the diversity of business interests in the country and Chilean peak business associations prevented this position from becoming a major demand of business interests. Also, the alliance between capital and labor in import-substituting sectors that had increased their political weight under the pre-1973 democratic regime was weakened by the exclusion of labor from the Pinochet regime (E. Silva 1996b: 80–81).

Argentina's recent history has been characterized by distributional conflict along three major dimensions: class (strong labor unions), sector (agriculture versus industry) and geography (the provinces versus Buenos Aires). The advent of Peronism in the 1940s is generally considered to be the trigger for distributional conflict along these lines: the strength gained by industrial and service unions under Perón allowed them to block adverse wage and employment decisions, leading to significant wage–price inflationary spirals; nationalist interest in industrialization, together with rising industrial labor costs also made it necessary to protect domestic manufacturing, at the expense of agriculture; and lastly, the rise of industry relative to agriculture benefited Buenos Aires at the expense of the provinces. Distributional conflict thus extended not only to strikes or political infighting but to policy outcomes as well, such as relative price distortions.

To overcome the major divides of class, sector and territory, Menem's strategy for privatization 'was to build coalitions and provide side payments to ensure cooperation. ... He also redesigned the privatization program to allow the national industrial groups to participate in the ownership of the companies' (Molano 1997: 103). An important goal of such measures was to split labor and business groups through a carrot-and-stick approach (Gibson 1997). The Emergency Act of 1990 provided preferential access to the ownership of privatized companies to all groups that benefited by them: minority shareholders, employees, customers, suppliers of inputs, and marketers of outputs (Art. 16). It also provided for an emergency public works fund managed by the municipalities created to compensate workers laid off by privatized firms (Art. 59), thereby addressing both labor and provincial opposition to the reforms.

Of all the four cases, Argentina is the country in which business interests tried hardest to maintain the privileges afforded by public ownership and monopoly. In the privatization attempts under the Alfonsín administration (1986–9), '[b]usiness leaders proved to be an obstacle as well, when they endeavored to persuade the government to sweeten its offers of enterprises with future state contracts, subsidized loans from official banks, and similar concessions' (González Fraga 1991: 84). The Menem administration was forced to grant credit and tax concessions to agricultural producers due to their pressure (Acuña 1995). But in general, the internal division of business groups weakened their opposition to government policies (Palermo and Novaro 1996: 496), and the economic crisis of Argentina at the beginning of Menem's first term further weakened business influence (Acuña 1995).

The use of patronage to buy political support in a country of vast wealth and income differentials has been a common feature of Brazilian politics at least since the 'Old Republic' (1888–1930). As Hagopian (1996) has extensively documented, the military regime resorted to such a strategy when it saw its support base erode after about 1970. The return to democracy exacerbated even further these pressures as the political elites that had supported the military resorted to even greater use of patronage in order to survive electoral competition. The result has been a system of fluid, non-ideological parties vying for the spoils of state patronage in a fragmented congress. As Werneck writes (1991: 71),

> Control over public enterprises has been seen as an important source of power by ministers, top public officials, and politicians – power to appoint managers and even employees, power to affect large investment programs and the enterprises' procurement policy, and power to capitalize on successful public enterprises.

Brazilian parties are ideologically very weak: 40 percent of legislators switched party allegiance during 1994–98 session (Maxfield 1999), due at least in part to the right of incumbents to stand for re-election automatically. Electoral law reflects and reinforces the role of patronage, with an open list system in large electoral districts (the states) that makes all candidates virtual 'write-ins', pushing them to target areas within their districts in exchange for patronage promises. As a result, there is a strongly territorial dimension of clientelism in Brazil – the loyalty of legislators is generally greater to their district and state than to their party. Regionalist pressures were in fact enshrined in the 1988 Constitution in the form of provisions mandating federal revenue sharing with states and municipalities, and the legislative overrepresentation of small, backward states. As in Bolivia (examined below), campaign financing subsidies and the ability to maximize bargaining power relative to other political forces (through trading of votes for patronage) encourages extreme party fragmentation (Ames 1987; Maxfield 1999; Geddes and Ribeiro Neto 1992).

After the restoration of democracy in the mid-1980s, the nature of distributional conflict in Brazil became more complex as a result of the emergence of new unions that were independent from the corporatist unions that had been set up by previous regimes to control labor, and of a militant land redistribution movement. The 'new unionism' was an important element of intense labor conflict in the late 1980s, particularly in Brazil's industrial core around São Paulo. Moreover, this movement also had political ramifications with the foundation by some of the new unions of a political party, the PT (Partido dos Trabalhadores [Workers' Party]), whose candidate nearly won the presidential election of 1990. It is fair to say, however, that the impact of both the new unionism and the PT on the political arena and in particular on economic policy at the federal level appears to be slight. As Brazil's economic crisis deepened after 1990, and even more once the economy began to be opened to foreign trade and investment, the bargaining power of the unions was sharply curtailed since firms could no longer accommodate union demands, and Brazil's vast 'reserve army' of underemployed and unemployed labor made any extreme positions by the unions – mostly representing relatively well-paid industrial workers – increasingly untenable. Likewise, after the 1990 defeat, the PT has not been able to make major inroads at the federal level, and its candidate was easily defeated by Cardoso in 1994 and 1998.

In contrast to the 'new unionism,' patronage politics has remained dominant in much of rural Brazil, where local notables, who are generally the large landowners, control governmental matters, including police and justice. Mobilization efforts, such as the land redistribution movement (MST[18]) have had limited success, not only because of the power of the large landowners but also because land redistribution is constrained by economies of scale in agricultural production and the extremely low human and financial capital levels of the landless population.

Brazilian business has traditionally accepted a significant SOE role in the economy (Bartell 1995; McQuerry 1996), and politicians from business backgrounds appear to prefer pork-barrel deals negotiated directly with the executive over programmatic policy initiatives (Ames 1995). Yet business groups have not been a major source of opposition to reform in Brazil. The reasons lie in the diversity of their interests (as elsewhere), the weakening effects of economic crisis and, once it began, opening to foreign trade and investment (Schneider 1997; Geddes 1995), to which a further blow was added, in the Brazilian case, by the breakup of corporatism and the fragmentation of business associations that followed the restoration of democracy (Payne 1995).

In Bolivia, more than in Brazil, a combination of clientelism, militant unionism, and strong regional identities has made distributional conflict particularly severe. 'In Bolivia, the principal function of elections has been to allow competing leaders periodically to restructure patronage networks. … [A] central dynamic of politics has been to circulate the commodity of government positions (*cargos, puestos, y pegas*) among the dependent middle class' (Gamarra 1990: 122; Conaghan and Malloy 1994; Gamarra and Malloy 1995). As in Brazil, Bolivia has a large number of parties with parliamentary representation because election to the legislature can allow trading of legislative votes for state patronage (Gamarra and Malloy 1995). The clientelistic nature of the polity is also evident within the MNR itself, where patronage was the primary source of party cohesion through a clientele drawn from the middle class and a peasantry dependent on state support (Conaghan and Malloy 1994: 126). Another instance is the *Pacto por la Democracia* (Democracy Pact) between the MNR and its major competitor, the ADN, in Bolivia in 1985, which provided for political stability and continuity of policy needed to pursue NEP, 'but ratified the significance of patronage,' since patronage was the price required for MNR acquiescence (Gamarra 1990: 108). This resulted in dramatic increases in public-sector employment after cutbacks of 1986–88.[19] Problems continued under Sánchez de Lozada's administration, with the replacement of previously hired civil servants with party loyalists (Conaghan and Malloy 1994: 230).

Militant unionism led to a high level of labor conflict in Bolivia under first democratic government[20] (1981–85) (ibid.: 123). Labor conflict was only mitigated by a mixture of force (the declaration of a state of emergency, which enabled suppression of strikes by the police and military) and rewards, particularly severance payments and temporary public works programs (ibid.: 149–50). Although fierce conflicts during the 1980s weakened unions through loss and exhaustion of their members (Morales 1996), the peak labor organization COB[21] was still willing to go on strike against privatization (Sims 1998: A7).

As in the other cases, the opposition of manufacturers for the domestic market to trade liberalization was ineffectual due to the diversity of business interests, which precluded unified business lobbying against reform, and to the specific weakness of the industrial sector in a particularly poor and economically backward country, which had made industry too dependent on direct government support to enjoy any leverage over policy (Conaghan et al. 1990; Conaghan and Malloy 1994: 156–7; Conaghan 1995).

The origin of regional disputes within Bolivia lies in the great disparity of its regions, which comprise vastly different terrains (essentially the high Andes, the Amazon rain forest, and the Chaco flatlands) as well as ethnicities and languages (Spanish-speaking whites and mestizos throughout, quechua and aymara in the highlands, and guaraní in the Chaco). Regional disputes over hydrocarbon revenues from Bolivia's abundant gas and oil fields were exacerbated by the pork-barrel policies pursued by the Bánzer dictatorship during the 1970s in an effort to curry support, reappeared after restoration of democracy in 1982, and finally led to a major decentralization effort in recent years (Roca 1980, *passim*; see also Gamarra and Malloy 1995, and Conaghan and Malloy 1994).

The upshot of these various dimensions of distributional conflict was intense controversy about privatization. Distributional conflict had over time resulted in very high levels of public employment to placate the demands of the different claimants, leading one commentator to remark that '[p]rior to the NEP [the New Economic Policy of reform pursued by Paz Estenssoro], Bolivia was probably the Latin American country (with the exception of Cuba) that had the largest proportion of its urban labour force employed by the public sector'[22] (Morales 1996: 41). This made privatization 'a central issue of political and economic debate in Bolivia. ... [T]he most delicate aspect of privatization lies in its redistributive implications' (Morales 1994: 140–1). Privatization was opposed by political parties, regional civic committees, and as already noted, the COB (Gamarra

1990: 112), and indeed privatization attempts by the Paz Zamora administration of the MIR and ADN parties (1987–91) were abandoned due to such opposition.

To summarize the preceding discussion of distributive conflict, it has been least prevalent in Chile, largely as a result of the political regime, which both suppressed labor conflict and avoided the use of patronage to stay in power. At the other extreme of the ranking, Bolivia appears to have been wracked by conflicts over political patronage, over employment and employment conditions, and over the regional impact of economic policy. Nonetheless Brazil and Argentina lie very close to Bolivia on the scale of distributional conflict. Argentina has also suffered historically from significant distributional conflict, mainly of a class nature and to a lesser extent of a territorial nature, while patronage politics have been tempered by a more cohesive party structure than in the other cases. In Brazil, patronage and its territorial dimension have created very intense pressures over economic resources regardless of the political regime, but especially with the restoration of democracy that took place after 1985. On the basis of the stronger party structure of the Argentine polity, it would make sense to rank Argentina below Brazil in the degree of intensity of distributional conflict.

## CONCLUSIONS ON EXPLANATORY VARIABLES

The review of the independent variables conducted in this chapter shows the following rankings for the four cases under consideration as shown in Table 5.5.

*Table 5.5   Ranking of countries by explanatory variable*

|           | Judicial independence | Influence of *laissez-faire* ideology | Absence of distributional conflict |
|-----------|-----------------------|---------------------------------------|-------------------------------------|
| Chile     | 1                     | 1                                     | 1                                   |
| Argentina | 3                     | 2                                     | 2                                   |
| Brazil    | 2                     | 4                                     | 3                                   |
| Bolivia   | 4                     | 3                                     | 4                                   |

The clearest conclusion from the analysis is that Chile ranks highest in judicial independence (despite the authoritarian nature of the Pinochet regime), influence of *laissez-faire* ideology, and absence of distributional conflict. The ranking of the other three cases is somewhat more complex, since there is no other case with a uniform position across the three explanatory variables. Nonetheless, some conclusions can be reached regarding the relative position of the cases. At the other extreme from the Chilean case lies Bolivia, which ranks lower in judicial independence and has the highest level of distributional conflict, being only above Brazil in the degree of influence of economic orthodoxy. Argentina's overall rank is second to Chile, since it is only below Brazil with regard to judicial independence. This leaves Brazil in third place with regard to the overall likelihood of espousing competition and privatization in the restructuring of its ESI. How well these rankings explain the outcomes described in the previous chapter is the subject of Chapter 6.

## NOTES

1. In 1994, a major constitutional modification was agreed with the main opposition party (Unión Cívica Radical [Radical Civic Union], UCR) as part of the 'Pact of Los Olivos' to create a new council to nominate all judges prior to their appointment, as well as a new General Accounting Office to audit governmental accounts and prevent corruption (Domínguez and Giraldo 1996). But the council was not actually created until 1998.
2. Jurisdiction over political matters was transferred to special military tribunals (Domingo 1999).
3. Other evidence provides a similarly mixed picture. Schneider (1993) shows that relative to Mexico and developed countries, the Brazilian federal civil service is insulated from outside pressures by widespread circulation of personnel within the bureaucracy at large, and few ex-bureaucrats jump to the private sector. At the same time, extensive presidential appointment powers put great pressure on weak presidents to yield to patronage criteria for filling senior civil service positions.
4. Bolivia had 17 Supreme Courts between 1950 and 1990, which is relevant here because judicial independence is observed by looking at the recent history of relations between the courts and other branches of the government. Wholesale dismissals of the Supreme Court occurred during this period in 1952, 1957, 1961, 1964, 1967, 1972, 1974, 1979, 1980 (twice), and 1982 (Gamarra 1991: 64 and 86, fn).
5. Movimiento Nacional Revolucionario (Nacional Revolutionary Movement).
6. Acción Democrática Nacionalista.
7. Movimiento de Izquierda Revolucionaria (Revolutionary Left Movement).
8. As in Argentina, recent changes may herald an unprecedented increase in judicial independence: an ombudsman's office, a constitutional court, and an independent judicial commission were recently created, and seven new Supreme Court justices appointed by then-President Bánzer under the new arrangements 'owe their seats to professional competence and hard work, not to political connections' (*The Economist*, April 10, 1999: 34).
9. Note that the controls on short-term capital flows imposed in Chile in 1982 are not appropriate indicators of nationalist ideology, however, because they were meant as an emergency solution to a severe financial and foreign exchange crisis, not as a deliberate attempt to curtail the influence of foreign capital (I am grateful to Professor J. Domínguez for pointing out this fact to me).
10. Under an agreement concluded in 1955, the Catholic University of Santiago began sending students to Chicago for their PhD training in economics. These students came back to Chile with strong convictions about the proper role of the state in the Chilean economy and set up a think-tank, CESEC (Centro de Estudios Económicos) in 1968.
11. '[I]n 1973 ... the Armed Forces advocated a strategy of 'inward looking' national economic development as a requirement of territorial defense' (Moulián and Vergara 1980: 105).

12. There is some question about the timing of Menem's shift away from traditional Peronist policies. For an excellent discussion of this issue, see Stokes (2001: 71–7).
13. Instituto de Estudios Económicos de la Realidad Argentina y Latinoamericana.
14. 'Sánchez de Lozada's involvement in politics [the government of Paz Estenssoro 1982–86] had a profound impact on the course of economic policy and the entire ideological climate in Bolivia. He became one of the most effective advocates of the free market' (Conaghan 1995: 122).
15. Confederación de Empresarios Privados Bolivianos.
16. Centro Brasileiro de Análise e Planejamento (Brazilian Center for Analysis and Planning).
17. Other productive assets benefiting the military were also left untouched, such as several factories producing a variety of products; in addition, military salaries and pensions were increased under the Chicago Boys' tenure to allay military opposition to their programs (Hira 1998: 96).
18. Movimento dos Sem-Terra.
19. The Paz Zamora administration (1989–1993) created three new ministries, 16 new vice-ministerial posts, and 20,000 public-sector jobs (Conaghan and Malloy 1994: 230).
20. Nine general strikes were launched between December 1983 and March 1985 (Conaghan and Malloy 1994: 149).
21. Central Obrera Boliviana (Bolivian Labor Federation).
22. 245,000 public sector employees, or some 11 percent of the labor force, in 1985 (Morales 1996, Table 2.3).

# 6. Putting the pieces together: ESI restructuring in Argentina, Bolivia, Brazil and Chile

This chapter ties the observations on the dependent and explanatory variables together. The approach followed below, however, is not limited to pointing out correspondences between dependent and explanatory variables (an exercise that would in any case have little value in a small-N context). Instead, the analysis traces out the effect of each one of the explanatory variables, as discussed in the preceding chapter, on the observed outcomes as described in Chapter 4. For expositional purposes, the chapter is organized by explanatory variable. Nevertheless, as reality seldom presents itself so neatly, the interaction between explanatory variables is pointed out where necessary.

## EFFECTS OF JUDICIAL INDEPENDENCE

Recall the mechanism through which judicial independence affects outcomes. Judicial independence decreases uncertainty about the future actions of regulators and politicians because it limits their freedom of action in accordance with previously promulgated statutes. In particular, arrangements based on private property and competition will face lower chances of reversal when judicial independence is greater, thereby eliciting the commitment of private investors and hence the success of the arrangements. In testing the effect of this variable, we should look then for specific elements of ESI restructuring outcomes that rely on judicial enforcement in countries with higher judicial independence, or conversely that keep enforcement in the hands of the executive or the legislature in cases of low judicial independence.

### Chile

There are several elements of the Chilean ESI restructuring that imply a substantial degree of reliance on judicial enforcement. First comes the degree of specificity of the legal texts regulating the restructured ESI. In general, greater vagueness of legal statutes requires greater judicial interpretation to clarify specific instances of the law. While the basic Chilean ESI restructuring act, DFL No. 1, is fairly detailed about the various aspects of rate-setting and other matters, implementing regulations were never written, which increases the possibility of disagreements between regulators and utilities over the aspects that the decree defined most vaguely. For instance, disputes over distribution rates between the regulatory commission and the utilities are to be solved by means of a 'Salomonic' weighted average of the rate-setting parameters obtained by each side. This has invited, of course, high cost of service claims by the utilities, sometimes even 50 percent higher than the CNE numbers, which has in turn increased mistrust between the CNE and the utilities and led to numerous requests by the utilities for court injunctions against the CNE (Blanlot 1993). This would seem to indicate that the drafters of the decree were confident of the ability of Chilean courts to inspire trust in ESI investors, a confidence which was proven correct in the investors' willingness to go to the courts rather than to attempt to circumvent them (of which there is no evidence whatsoever).[1]

Even more strikingly, the Chilean ESI reform eschewed entirely the attempt to create a quasi-judicial independent regulatory entity and simply relied on the courts and quasi-judicial mechanisms like arbitration to protect the rights of investors and other stakeholders. Faced with a regulatory commission (the CNE) entirely formed by government ministers (three of whom head 'political' ministries) and thus devoid of any semblance of independence, the subsequent privatization of utilities could have failed if private investors did not have the confidence that arbitration and the courts would protect their interests adequately. Without independent courts, investors would have demanded instead more rigid mechanisms, such as very detailed implementing regulations, or would have sought the favor of the government to obtain preferential treatment in case of disputes. Nothing like this has happened since ESI privatization, despite acrimonious fights between utilities and the CNE over issues such as the passthrough of productivity improvements to ratepayers. Such disputes have been solved through the courts rather than through the previously mentioned political expedients (which has not prevented the government, after the resolution of some of these disputes, from acknowledging imperfections in the law and making amendments to correct the flaws).

Legal ambiguity and lack of regulatory independence cannot be attributed in Chile to a rush to restructure the ESI. The CNE was created in 1978, the DFL No. 1 was issued in 1982, and privatization began in 1985 and was in fact not completed until 1998, with the sale of the last remaining ESI assets in public hands.

The promotion of competition also displays extensive reliance on the independence of judicial and quasi-judicial bodies. The antitrust system, created in 1973, consists of a series of antitrust commissions organized along the same pyramidal structure of the courts, where lower-level commissions are restricted to a smaller geographic area and their decisions can be appealed to higher-level commissions. As explained in the next subsection, the ideology of the Pinochet regime's decisionmakers, the 'Chicago boys', led them to create a highly concentrated ESI market structure. When subsequent governments and competitors hurt by Endesa's market power sought to reverse the situation, they made use of the antitrust system rather than seeking to sidestep it through new legal acts or even extralegal measures.

The fact that decisionmakers under Pinochet chose to rely on a fairly independent judiciary might seem puzzling, since authoritarian regimes are by definition interested in controlling all levers of power. However, it is less puzzling when we consider the avowed objectives of the regime and its allies, such as the 'Chicago boys'. Pinochet and the 'boys' saw their tenure in power as a transformational period, in which they would radically alter the economic and social structures of Chile to prevent the future recurrence of the pre-coup political and social conflict. They were thus keenly interested in creating or strengthening institutions that would preserve their policies after the end of the Pinochet regime. As Horn (1995) has pointed out, the usual channel for ensuring the permanence of institutional transformations is to delegate decisions and policies to independent bodies, so that future executives and legislatures will find it harder to reverse such transformations. The existence of a relatively independent court system in Chile offered the Pinochet regime a useful commitment mechanism for its project of economic and social transformation.

## Argentina

As shown in the preceding chapter, Argentina has a history of political manipulation of the courts. Even the creation of the independent ESI regulatory commission, ENRE, was plagued by problems over the appointment of commissioners. The entity representing provincial interests, the Federal Electricity Council (Consejo Federal de la Energía Eléctrica, CFEE), wished to follow its own selection procedure for its allotted commissioner appointments, which conflicted with the government's attempt to control the appointment process; Menem further strained the spirit of the Electricity Act by imposing a candidate without congressional consensus (Bastos and Abdala 1993: 264). In the Act itself and its regulations, the executive asserted its will to intervene in the regulatory process by making the sectoral executive agency (the Secretariat of Energy) the first instance for appeals of regulatory decisions, with judicial review only at higher instances.[2] The executive also retained veto powers over decisions by the ISO (CAMMESA), which has been a cause of concern among ESI stakeholders (ibid.: 274). The fact that such a context offers fewer assurances to ESI stakeholders than Chile's is not, however, reflected in either the overall ownership or competition choices made in the restructuring process.[3]

Despite the fact that a high level of political intervention in the regulatory system diminished the degree of protection of investors' interests, the government chose to privatize its ESI holdings to the greatest extent possible. Likewise, a highly competitive market structure was created, together with extensive reliance on mechanisms to emulate competition wherever possible, even when the regulatory commission (ENRE), which is also the primary antitrust agency for the ESI, had been the object of political manipulation. But if there was little assurance that their property rights would be respected and competition would be fair, why did private investors agree to participate in the Argentine market? As Cavallo himself has pointed out (1997), Argentine's judicial problems were reflected in the restructuring process through the deliberate reliance on simple, clear rules that would provide minimal room for disputes and judicial interpretation. But the next section shows that this is only part of the story: ideological commitment made up for the lack of judicial independence in the Argentine case.

## Brazil

Stakeholders in Brazil's ESI have ample precedent not only about political influence on the courts but more directly on the deleterious effects of political control over ESI regulation. DNAEE,[4] the predecessor of the current regulatory agency, was perceived as highly politicized;[5] of special importance was the meddling of the Ministry of the Economy to try to control inflation during the 1980s, because it decreased electricity rates in real terms so much that by the mid-1990s most electricity distribution utilities were practically bankrupt (Kirkman 1997), which in turn motivated subsequent ESI restructuring efforts. But the new agency appears so far to suffer from some of the same problems as its predecessor. In response to 'a storm of public and media criticism' against blackouts experienced by Rio's residents in early 1998, it stepped out of the bounds of local utilities' concession contracts to fine them, require them to fulfill a set of minimum investment requirements, and threaten them with exclusion from future privatizations (Dyer 1998). Moreover, the new agency's regulatory practice has generally consisted of 'erratic' inflation adjustments rather than a consistent rate-setting policy (*IPPQ* 1998: 12).

To deal with such precedent and the absence to this day of a regulatory framework that sets minimal ratemaking and other criteria (such as, for instance, the statutes enacted in Argentina,[6] Bolivia[7] and Chile[8]), the Brazilian government has relied instead on concession contracts that offer very generous margins and limit regulatory intervention during a transitional period, so as to allow concessionaires to recover their investment quickly. Although contract enforcement falls under the responsibility of the courts, reliance on contracts is actually a *stronger* form of governmental commitment than regulation by commission. The reason is that the concession contracts executed by the Brazilian government are in principle far less discretionary than regulatory supervision (as allowed in Chile, Argentina, Bolivia or even Brazil after the transitional period), and therefore limit the potential need for court interpretation substantially. Rather than stating general principles of ratemaking, for instance, that are then interpreted by a regulatory commission and overseen if need be by the courts, the Brazilian concession contracts specify rigid pricing formulas based on official price indices,[9] and offer few ratemaking guidelines after the end of contract terms.

Brazilian distribution contracts are also notoriously generous, an indication that large returns have been offered to concessionaires by the government in order to attract interest to the concession auctions. For 1998, the average distribution rate in Brazil was R$67.90 per MWh, against an average cost of supply of R$27.59/MWh, only 40 percent of the average rate, while the international average cost was 60 percent of the average rate in 1996. Also, X-factors have been set at zero for the initial seven- or five-year contracts (Pires n.d.).

The restriction of competition in Brazil's restructured ESI matches the fact that Brazil's courts are not as autonomous as Chile's. As explained in the following section, the major reason for such a choice is ideological. But weak judicial institutions may also have played a role. Brazil's generation asset structure would require greater market power monitoring than that of the other cases, thereby making the need for judicial independence potentially greater too. Brazil's generation structure is almost unique in the world: it is dominated by a relatively small number of huge dams, including the largest dam in the world, Itaipu, which at 13,000 MW of capacity constitutes one-quarter of installed capacity in Brazil's main interconnected system; and the dams are located on three river basins and have relatively little storage capacity. This creates greater potential for market power than in Argentina or Chile (Bolivia faces other difficulties due to small market size), where the role of thermal generation is greater[10] and (in Chile) hydro plants are less concentrated in a few basins. Dams like Itaipu could affect market prices due to their sheer size, while upstream dams can affect the behavior of downstream units. While a competitive market appears to be feasible in such a system, an aggressive antitrust stance may be part of the formula needed to make such a market work. A more aggressive antitrust stance is therefore needed in Brazil to make a competitive generation market work. But with relatively low historical levels of judicial independence, an impartial antitrust system may not be attainable.

## Bolivia

In Bolivia even more than in Brazil or Argentina, the regulatory system began its life already politicized, as Sánchez de Lozada filled regulatory commissioner positions with his own appointees (Bowen 1997). The consequences were soon evident: transmission rates were increased without a proper regulatory process prior to the privatization of the transmission company, to make it more attractive. Moreover, as shown in the preceding section the politicization of the regulatory system was not limited to electricity but was even worse for telecoms and banking regulators.

Given the magnitude of political meddling in the judiciary and in regulatory commissions, capitalization may result not only from ideological and distributive opposition to privatization, but also from the need to provide additional safeguards to private investors about the future governmental behavior towards the utilities. Recall that capitalization involved not simply keeping 50 percent of utility shares in public hands, but using them to fund a pension plan for all Bolivians. By putting at stake the ability of the government to deliver on its pension promises – promises, because the pension plan is based on defined benefits, not on past contributions – the Bolivian government created a powerful commitment to respect the property rights of investors in the capitalized utilities, which included effectively all Bolivians. Therefore the creation of a formally independent regulatory commission, which by itself would have been rightly regarded with skepticism by private investors, was powerfully supplemented by a mechanism that put the future pensions of all Bolivians at stake.

As shown in Chapter 4, Bolivia chose to promote competition in generation through a diversified ownership structure, and in distribution through yardstick competition. Keeping competition vigorous in a small power market like Bolivia's[11] requires, in addition, aggressive monitoring and sanctioning by the regulator of any signs of market power abuse or collusion, as it would in Brazil although for different reasons. The choice of competition is thus hardly compatible with the very low judicial independence record of Bolivia.[12] Ideology, moreover, is a less powerful predictor for Bolivia than for Argentina, so interaction with other explanatory variables cannot be argued in the Bolivian case.

Other predictions of the analytical framework are, however, borne out by the evidence, indicating that the failure of the Bolivian case to conform to the competition hypothesis does not lie in the theory behind the hypothesis but in a miscalculation on the part of Bolivian policymakers (note that 'miscalculation' does not imply lack of rationality, but simply inadequate information about the perceptions of private investors concerning judicial independence in Bolivia). As the analytical framework predicts, generators have protested adverse regulatory decisions directly to the government rather than to the judicial channels specified in the regulatory commission statute (*GPR*, June 13, 1998: 16–7), since undertaking litigation under a politicized judiciary is less efficient than trying to influence the government directly. In contrast to the Argentine case, the lower ideological commitment to private property and competition of Bolivian policymakers encourages lobbying by private actors to obtain favorable outcomes in disputes with other participants or with regulators.

## Conclusions

To conclude, three of the four cases confirm the hypothesis about the relationship between judicial independence and ownership choices, while competition and judicial independence are more weakly related. Although a crude evaluation casts doubt on the effect of judicial independence on property choices (three of the four countries rely essentially on private property despite their different levels of judicial independence), an analysis of the cases that considers the specific circumstances guiding policymakers' choices is more favorable to the hypothesis. In Chile, reliance on private property is greatest, and so is judicial independence. Substantial confidence in the ability of the courts to protect stakeholder interests led policymakers to pass a somewhat general legal text and rely on an openly political regulatory commission. In Brazil, the extent of privatization is more limited than in Chile, and the courts less independent. Lower judicial autonomy has forced the government to minimize the scope for intervention by regulators, politicians or the judiciary through the use of concession contracts. In Bolivia, very low levels of judicial independence have required supplementing a formally independent regulatory system with an ownership arrangement that can impose substantial political costs on the government if it tries to meddle in the regulatory process. Argentina, on the other hand, contradicts the hypothesis because it has privatized extensively despite a weak court system.

The relationship between judicial independence and competition is weaker than between judicial independence and ownership, perhaps reflecting the smaller role of the judiciary in protecting competition. In Chile, the antitrust system reflects a high degree of confidence in the independence of judicial and para-judicial entities, but the market structure is highly concentrated. In Argentina, the highly competitive structure created through restructuring is not supported by judicial independence. Brazil is the clearest case in favor of the hypothesis, since lack of full judicial autonomy appears in conjunction with severe limitations to competition as a result of an unusually complex generation asset structure. Lastly, while judicial limitations have not hindered the creation of a competitive framework in Bolivia, attempts by market participants to bypass regulatory and judicial channels are consistent with the predictions of the analytical framework.

## EFFECTS OF IDEOLOGY

Countries with a stronger influence of orthodox economic ideas should show a greater reliance on private property and competition, while greater influence of nationalism or economically unorthodox ideas, such as structuralism or socialism, should be more inclined toward public ownership and monopoly.

### Chile

The key ESI restructuring act (DFL No. 1 of 1982) was issued at the peak of radical orthodox influence, as shown by E. Silva's analysis of policymakers' backgrounds and decision structures in the Pinochet regime (1996b, ch. 6). Since a major hallmark in the law is the introduction of the competition in the activity of generation, and the use of a theoretical benchmark or 'ideal company' for distribution ratemaking, issuance of DFL No. 1 clearly confirms the hypothesis linking ideology and choices. The result is further confirmed by the fact that in 1982, deregulation of generation activities was still a purely theoretical possibility, since no country in the world had tried it yet. The willingness of Chilean policymakers to test uncharted waters adds further evidence about the strength of their pro-competition ideology.

Likewise, ESI privatization took place in 1985 and beyond, confirming also the hypothesis relating property choices to policymaker ideologies. In Chile, however, belief in the superiority of private property was not the only motivating ideology behind ESI privatization: nationalism also played an important role. Among the forces that opposed ESI restructuring are the military, who saw a strategic role for utilities (the left, as expected, opposed restructuring due to their belief in public enterprise) (Bernstein 1995; see also Allende 1988, for 'national security' opposition to privatization). Ideological opposition to privatization also came from the staff of the state monopoly (Endesa prior to privatization), who justified their position by claiming that electricity was too much of a public good for private provision to be efficient (Hachette and Lüders 1993: ch. 8). Of these two 'insider' groups (the military and utility staff), the military were the key actor. The major ESI privatization decisions made under Pinochet were carried out in 1985–88 by a commission formed by ministers of finance, economy, planning (Organismo de Planificación [Planning Agency], ODEPLAN), the development bank (Corporación de Fomento [Development Bank], CORFO) and a representative of Pinochet, in which 'the only civilians were the ministers of finance and economy' (E. Silva 1996b: 195). There is thus a very explicit linkage between the major privatization push under Pinochet and the influence of nationalist ideology during this period. The heavy presence of the military, imbued with nationalism, in the privatization commission may explain the low participation of foreign investors in this process as implemented under Pinochet,[13] and shows that although privatization was carried out after the onset of Chile's debt crisis (which began in 1983 with the government's assumption of much of the foreign debt of domestic firms), the macroeconomic objective of debt reduction was not a primary motivator for privatization.

As the data in Chapter 4 made clear, privatization created an oligopolistic market structure. This raises the puzzle of why would an orthodox, pro-competition regime produce such a skewed market structure. To solve this paradox, we need to recall from the previous chapter that the antitrust thought emanating from the University of Chicago has always been consistent with the rest of 'Chicago' economic doctrine, which is notoriously libertarian. Chicago school economics is suspicious of natural monopoly arguments, and even more suspicious of the effectiveness of monopoly regulation and antitrust interventionism. As a result, in this school there is far less concern for market concentration and vertical integration than in other strands of neoclassical economics. This would explain why the 'Chicago boys' were impervious to the privileged position given to the post-privatization Endesa. Further confirmation comes from other industries: in telecoms market power issues were weakly regulated (Galal 1996), and in urban transport, high cartelized fares were allowed until 1991, after the advent of democracy (Gómez-Ibáñez and Meyer 1992). An alternative explanation, of course, would be that Endesa was sold to regime insiders or clients as part of a political exchange. Such a possibility will be explored in the next section.[14]

## Argentina

That ESI restructuring in Argentina bears the stamp of Cavallo is clearly shown by the sequence of events that led to the restructuring program. As the discussion of ideology in Argentina showed, policies favoring privatization and deregulation (that is, to increase competition) were not implemented immediately upon accession of the Peronists to the presidency in 1989. State interventionism and public monopoly, or tolerance of private oligopoly if a consequence of import substitution, were still popular ideas in the Peronist party. Menem's own preferences appeared to lie with such ideas so long as they proved effective. The Menem administration was therefore reluctant to accept ESI privatization and deregulation for more than a year, until there were few alternatives left. In 1990, a first reform attempt was undertaken along the lines of the French state monopoly model: there would be a single wholesale price for the entire country, with differences only in distribution charges, since distribution services were provincially controlled; and there would be no privatization, but instead creation of a holding SOE, run through management contracts. This reform attempt failed because public finances were too weak to provide the required capital and to retain managerial expertise, while there were few incentives for the efficient use of electricity (Bastos and Abdala 1993: 81).

The new restructuring program, as described in Chapter 4, was implemented upon Cavallo's accession and under his close supervision as Minister of Economy, Public Works and Services (Rausch 1994), with the assistance of his appointee, Secretary of Energy Carlos Bastos, an academic and longtime associate of Cavallo from the think-tank IEERAL (Friedland and Holden 1996). Other domestic influences in the program were minimal. Although the program was carried out under the special powers delegated to the executive under the Emergency Act, and as such it was subject to congressional approval (Emergency Act, Arts 8 and 9), federally-owned electric utilities had already been pre-approved for restructuring (including privatization if necessary) in the Emergency Act (Annex I). A subsequent requirement for legislative approval of the privatization process that had been included in the Electricity Act (Art. 93) was eliminated in the Electricity Act's implementing regulations (Decree 1398/92).

The role of the World Bank as lender to the Argentine government has already been mentioned in the general context of Chapter 5, and is worth repeating here. The World Bank's loans were used to hire consultants to help plan the restructuring effort, since the managerial and general human resources of the Argentine government were very limited after years of erosion of public salaries. The best-known consulting firms in the energy sector were, in the early 1990s, overwhelmingly from the US, which means that they were generally familiar, and tended to advocate, an organization of the ESI in the fashion of the US, with preponderance of private property and (after the Chilean and UK restructuring experiences in 1982 and 1991, respectively) competition in generation markets. The World Bank's loans thus had in all likelihood a direct ideological impact on the Argentine restructuring process. A further channel for World Bank influence in favor of private property was the participation of the International Finance Corporation (IFC) in the privatization process. The IFC's expertise in tapping international financial markets for developing countries offered the Argentine government important insights into the actual mechanics of privatization, practical knowledge that could supplement any theoretical preferences for private property.

The strength of ideological commitment accounts, in fact, for much of the success of the Argentine restructuring program despite the poor quality of the country's judicial institutions, as noted in the discussion of the role of judicial independence. The preceding chapter showed how the architect of Argentina's economic reform, Cavallo, was fully committed to economic orthodoxy; some of his writings convey very explicitly his support for privatization and competition (Cavallo 1997). His determination to privatize and introduce competition in spite of the lack of judicial independence would have sent a strong signal about the strength of his ideological commitment, which to some extent could substitute for the lack of judicial independence. Investors would not mind a certain potential for government influence on regulation (and hence on property rights) and on competition if they were reasonably assured that the government would take a position in favor of private property and competition, and if future changes in government would not affect risk very much (either because the opposition party shared a similar ideology, or because investment was expected to be recouped quickly).[15] This possibility is also supported by the lack of direct lobbying of the executive by ESI participants since restructuring was undertaken. Judicial and regulatory weakness induces participants to lobby the government directly in the case of disputes. But a government with a strong ideological position in favor of property rights and competition is unlikely to overturn judicial and regulatory decisions, since judicial and regulatory independence is needed to support private property and competition. Thus market participants are unlikely to lobby the government if they perceive it to be ideologically committed to private property and competitive forces.

## Brazil

The pragmatism and ambivalence of the Brazilian government towards restructuring is reflected in the hesitant evolution of the process. After the privatization of most of the distribution utilities in 1997 and 1998, the privatization of the transmission lines is still unclear, and there are no well-defined objectives either for the structure of the generation entities to be privatized. The federally-owned legal entities that currently own most generation assets cannot be privatized as they are, because they would have substantial market power, they are simply too large for the level of liquidity in international financial markets for developing countries, and in some cases like Furnas, because they own assets that the government will not or can not privatize, like Itaipu and the nuclear plants. Such a lack of well-defined objectives, after several years into the privatization process, is the direct result of the ideological influences on the restructuring process; ideology has also had a major impact on restricting competition in Brazil's restructured ESI.[16]

The Brazilian ESI restructuring process appears to be under substantial influence from technocrats in the former public monopoly Eletrobrás and in the state development bank, BNDES, which is in charge of the privatization side. The old regulatory agency, DNAEE, and the new one, ANEEL, have had a limited impact, because they have not – so far, at least – been equipped with the level of technical expertise needed to provide a credible input into restructuring initiatives. The highly technical nature of some of the issues raised by restructuring in Brazil, such as the possibility of competition among large hydroelectric generators sited on a common hydrological basin, have kept the number of ideologically influential actors small.

The only other major participant in the restructuring debate has been a foreign consulting firm, Coopers & Lybrand (now Pricewaterhousecoopers or PWC), which was commissioned by the Ministry of Energy and Mines to draw a restructuring blueprint for the ESI in 1995. But the role of Coopers & Lybrand is itself debatable, for it amended its original report recommending an English-style structure[17] in order to please the anti-competition stance of Eletrobrás's staff and management (Thomas and Tiomno Tolmasquim 1997). Whatever the reasons of Coopers & Lybrand for doing so, its willingness to accept Eletrobrás's views diminished very substantially its ability to make an independent ideological contribution to restructuring in Brazil.

Foreign and domestic investors, and particularly the different utilities that are acquiring Brazilian ESI assets, are certain to influence restructuring as well, particularly through *ex post* negotiations with the government and regulators to improve their prospects. So far, however, such influence has been limited to negotiations with BNDES over the terms of the concession contracts for the distribution utilities, and even then primarily in the case of the first major distribution privatization, that of Light Rio, where the success of the privatization was crucial for the government and therefore potential buyers had a great deal of leverage to seek better terms. More recently, foreign investors such as AES Corporation have made loud announcements of their intentions not to invest further in the Brazilian ESI until the regulatory framework is defined more clearly (Karp 2001), but in view of strong investor pressure to retrench due to domestic scandals (the Enron bankruptcy) and poor returns from overseas investments, such threats appear empty – fresh foreign investment into Latin America's ESI is unlikely to be forthcoming for some time even if the Brazilian regulatory climate improves significantly.

The generally statist ideology of the *técnicos* (technocrats) of Eletrobrás and BNDES was explored in the previous chapter, and certainly extended to restructuring. 'Many top-level managers of the state enterprises in question, along with part of their respective technocracies, engaged in systematic obstruction [of privatization]' (Sola 1994: 157; also Werneck 1991: 70). Eletrobrás is no exception, and opposes competition and privatization. BNDES, by contrast, has a more ambiguous attitude. It favors private property but is cooler to competition, since greater competition will make it more difficult for BNDES to get high prices for the assets put on the block.[18] As an example of the tension between the two agencies, Eletrobrás is trying to keep transmission under its control, against the wishes of BNDES (Dyer 1997b; Friedland 1997a). Also, in a privatization advertisement published in 1998, Eletrobrás's Chief Operating Officer Mário Santos was quoted as stating: 'The strategy for expanding production must be kept under government control from the outset' (Brazil, National Government 1998a). The result of having left the major restructuring initiatives to Eletrobrás and BNDES is thus determined by the juxtaposition of the ideological interests of the two entities: in the area of privatization, where ideologies conflict, overall objectives have been muddied, while competition has been significantly restricted because the ideologies of the two entities in this regard are quite similar.

## Bolivia

Bolivia's restructuring blueprint – and particularly the capitalization program – emerged as a compromise between a strongly nationalistic and collectivist ideology, still present in sections of the MNR and the main labor unions, and the market-oriented ideas of foreign-trained officials with international backing as well as Bolivian business associations. As in Argentina, ideas favoring public monopoly or concentrations of private ownership in import-substituting sectors were still common in the government party and especially in the union movement, while Bolivian business associations and 'Washington-based privatization groups' had helped set up the think-tanks COMTRAIN[19] and the Center for Privatization around 1987 (Gamarra 1990: 202–3). However, ESI restructuring was more heterodox in Bolivia than in Argentina. The difference between Argentina and Bolivia can be explained by the greater strength of ideologies hostile to orthodoxy in Bolivia relative to Argentina, and by the ideological biases of the top policymakers in each country.

Conflicting views between nationalism and collectivism on one side, and economic orthodoxy on the other, predicted if anything a compromise or a stalemate rather than the success of either ideology. In fact, stalemate did prevail for a number of years, and it was only broken by the country's economic tailspin, which gave a justification to the supporters of orthodoxy for the implementation of their ideas at the macroeconomic level. Although by 1989 a consensus had emerged among the major parties favoring orthodox ideas, preferences for public monopoly or concentrations of private ownership in import-substituting sectors were still common in the government party and especially in the union movement.[20] As the urgency of new reforms diminished, the value of compromise increased, given the high political costs of direct confrontation in a fragile democracy. ESI restructuring is thus the product of compromise: introduce competition, but leave a substantial public component in ownership through the capitalization program. And even in the case of competition, some restrictions were introduced to appease ideological opponents: the utilities were given a three-year initial monopoly in order to boost privatization revenues and preempt accusations of 'selling cheap' (Hendrix 1995).

The existing evidence points to Sánchez de Lozada as the undisputed originator of the idea of capitalization, rooted (according to his own statements in published interviews) in the traditions of kinship-based exchange of Bolivian society and dissatisfaction with the various methods of privatization in use around the world, especially in former socialist economies (Yergin and Stanislaw 1998; Bolivia, National Government n.d.; *The Economist* 1997; Revollo 1998). The discussion of ideologies in

Bolivia in the preceding chapter showed that Sánchez de Lozada is neither an ambitious pragmatist with only a weak attachment to traditional nationalist and interventionist ideas, like Menem, nor an ideologue of orthodoxy like Cavallo. Rather, the closest resemblance in terms of ideology is between Sánchez de Lozada and Cardoso, since both appear to profess social democratic ideas even if they have reached this point from different origins. The social democratic credo of Sánchez de Lozada would make him far more comfortable with the compromise of capitalization than Cavallo in Argentina would have been with such a heterodox solution; at the same time, Sánchez de Lozada's international background, and extensive international connections with foreign and multilateral institutions gained as finance minister, make it possible for him to accept foreign investment as part of the capitalization program, and to promote competition in the ESI following the models of Argentina and Chile, which had already been implemented at the time of restructuring in 1995.[21] Research on economic reform in Bolivia has in fact identified the ambivalence of the Paz Estenssoro administration, in which Sánchez de Lozada was finance minister, towards private ownership but not towards competition: 'Privatization ... was not included in the nucleus of essential NEP reforms advocated by Paz Estenssoro ... During his administration, some national public enterprises were transferred, as opposed to privatized, to regional development corporations (RDCs) and municipal governments' (Morales 1994: 134–5). The Paz administration pursued deregulation but not privatization (Conaghan and Malloy 1994: 144–5).

**Conclusions**

The effects of ideology on ESI restructuring are strong: in all cases, there exists a documented connection between the ideology of the main actors involved in the restructuring process, and the outcomes of the process. In Chile, the 'Chicago boys' imposed a model that relied radically enough on deregulated markets and private property so as to neglect issues of market power, just as they had done before 1982 with the privatizations of assets in other sectors and the rise of unregulated financial intermediaries. Additionally, the participation of military officers in the privatization decision was reflected in the preference given to domestic investors, since the nationalist orientation of Chilean military officers, particularly with regard to basic infrastructure industries like the ESI, has been documented. In Argentina, Menem and significant sectors of the Peronist party favored traditional policies, and this resulted in a period of experimentation with solutions within a framework of public monopoly, until their failure led to the appointment of a man of impeccably orthodox ideology, Domingo

Cavallo. Cavallo went on to introduce full deregulation and privatization of the federally-owned ESI assets. In Brazil, domination of the debate by technocrats from Eletrobrás and BNDES, together with a president who accepts private property out of pragmatism about fiscal needs rather than out of ideological conviction, has biased the restructuring process towards their ideas, which in the former case favor public monopoly and in the latter, private ownership and monopoly or oligopoly. The result has been a slow and hesitant privatization process, and the practical elimination of the scope for competition. Lastly, the existence of a powerful left in Bolivia, despite the defeats it suffered in the late 1980s, and the social democratic ideology of the president have led to a compromise solution where competition is introduced but ownership remains to a significant extent in public hands.

## EFFECTS OF DISTRIBUTIONAL CONFLICT

In countries with higher levels of distributional conflict, a higher level of public ownership and monopoly organization should be present at the end of the ESI restructuring process. Distributional conflict induces policymakers to preserve higher levels of public ownership and higher levels of monopoly, since they facilitate the extraction of rents to appease the parties involved in the conflicts.

### Chile

Since political repression under the Pinochet regime kept levels of distributional conflict low relative to its previous history and to the other cases in the study, the allocation of subsidized utility shares to employees and other domestic interests during the ESI privatization process of 1985–89 would seem to contradict the hypothesis regarding distributional conflict and ownership. To some extent, this is the case: the onset of debt crisis in 1982 forced a sharp contraction in public spending and led to a rise in political and labor contestation, thereby inducing the government to increase redistribution in order to ensure that its reforms would not be reversed after the end of the regime (P. Silva 1991; E. Silva 1996b: 183). Chilean utility privatizations did have the distributional objective of making the new ownership structure politically irreversible, by widely distributing the property and by buying off employees[22] (Maloney 1994). Even the official announcements of privatization objectives were structured to avoid strong adverse reactions, through a strategy of gradually increasing the targets for private ownership (Hachette and Lüders 1993, ch. 3).

But distributional objectives were not the only objective, or even the main one, of the Pinochet regime in the mid-1980s (many other unpopular measures, particularly of macroeconomic stabilization, were also implemented). The relatively broad allocation of shares was also carried out to avoid the concentrations that led to widespread business failures in 1982 (when dollar interest rates shot up and Chile devalued its currency) and the subsequent assumption by the government of one of the heaviest foreign debt burdens in Latin America (Hachette and Lüders 1993; Maloney 1994; Graham 1998: 75). Allowing workers and other Chilean citizens to acquire shares was in tune with the nationalist ideology discussed in the preceding subsection. Since at the time of the privatizations Chilean stock markets were small (pension fund reform was only undertaken in November of 1980) and had been adversely affected by the debt crisis (which wiped out important financial intermediaries and dried up foreign portfolio investment), the most practical way of keeping ownership in domestic hands while avoiding undue concentrations of ownership was through the special allocation programs used by the government, rather than through direct offerings in the stock market.

The design of the share allocation policy casts further doubt about the importance of distributional objectives for the government. The policy's effects on the distribution of income were actually rather limited. Preferential sales to employees favored mainly white-collar and management employees because the fragmentation of ownership into many shareholders with small holdings allowed the existing management teams to consolidate their control over the privatized firms in at least one major case[23] (Bitrán and Serra 1996). The 'popular capitalism' program of subsidized sale of shares to the population had even more modest effects: from 1985 to 1988, the number of owners of stock only increased 'as a share of the adult population ... from roughly 0.3 percent to about 2.1 percent, far from the rise from 5 percent to 10–14 percent in the United Kingdom' (Maloney 1994: 146–7). These results were the direct consequence of the program's design: its 'peculiar limitation that investors could only contract loans up to the value of their previous year's tax payments posed a very rigid barrier to participation by the bottom 50 percent of the wage earners, since under Chile's progressive income and property tax system, they pay nothing' (ibid.). Only the most indirect means of ESI share distribution, the sale of shares to the privatized pension funds, probably had a significant income redistribution effect. But even in this case, it is worth noting that in the Chilean case, pension recipients comprise only persons with legal employment contracts and thus many individuals who are not particularly poor – in a typical Latin American economy the poorer segment of the working population is composed of persons working in the informal sector without legally mandated benefits;[24] according to Graham (1998: 40), Pinochet's economic reforms failed to reach the poorest segments of the population.

Other authors suggest other channels through which distributional conflict might have affected ownership decisions. Hachette and Lüders (1993: 34, 38, 42) argue that a major regime motivation for the initial wave of privatizations prior to 1982 (which did not involve ESI assets) was income redistribution, being intended to 'maximize public sector revenues' in order to fund social expenditure; but they go on to add that 'sectors connected to the government itself' resisted the second-wave privatization of the larger SOEs because among other factors 'they had been used as income redistribution tools'. Bernstein (1995) mentions opposition to privatization from groups favored under public ownership, such as politicians, employees and industrial customers. Whatever the case, neither reason matches other published research.[25] Relative to the left-wing government of Salvador Allende, social expenditure was cut rather than increased by the fiscally conservative Pinochet regime, particularly when the latter was attempting to lower inflation and cut trade and budget deficits. In fact, fiscal restraint meant that public enterprises were forced to adjust their prices and costs to become self-sustaining, so when they were privatized after 1982 the impact on consumers was very limited. More specifically, employment losses had already occurred with the reform of public enterprise management in the pre-1982 period. Galal writes (Galal et al. 1994: 289) that excess labor in public enterprises was already made redundant in the 1970s, so no major layoffs would be observed by examining only the periods of divestiture and after.[26] The same author (ibid.: 219) evaluated the welfare effect of the privatization of Chilgener and found only modest gains for the domestic population (although within a large range of possible outcomes due to uncertainty about the causes of productivity improvements over the period of study). In the author's 'most likely' case, the government suffered a large loss of revenue (dividends), employees only made slight gains, consumers stayed the same, and shareholders were the clear winners. Only for Chilectra Metropolitan (the distribution company for the city of Santiago), did the same author find that privatization was distributionally regressive, since in this case the substantial reduction in theft of electricity that occurred after privatization hurt the poor (ibid.: 240, 242, 248).

Finally, it is possible that ESI restructuring in Chile might have had elements of 'cronyism' in the form that Chilectra Metropolitana was privatized, and in the dominant market position that it was allowed to gain in 1989 when, through its parent company Enersis, it became the main shareholder of Endesa, turning these entities into a vertically-integrated conglomerate that dominates Chile's central electric system. José Yuraszek, a 'right-wing firebrand' before 1973 and a regime 'insider' afterwards, was appointed by the government to prepare Chilectra for privatization. At Chilectra, he and his management team used the shares received under the employee share-ownership plan (ESOP) as collateral to borrow from outside sources the capital needed to acquire the final 10 percent share package sold by the government, thus gaining control over the company.[27] The management buyout was further facilitated by important biases in the privatization process. Company statutes restricted the voting rights of shareholding workers, and share-backed loans used for the buyout were provided by a state-owned bank. Later on, the wide diffusion of Endesa share ownership that resulted from the share ownership program allowed Chilectra's managers to gain control over Endesa while owning only 11 percent of the latter's shares[28] (Bitrán and Sáez 1994; Friedland 1996b). Insider privileges were also granted to military officers close to the privatization process (Moguillansky 1997).

Yet such a corruption story does not fit with the agile performance of Enersis-Endesa after privatization, when energy losses in the distribution networks were cut from 23 percent to 9 percent and the conglomerate became a major regional force (Bitrán and Serra 1995), all of which would indicate that the Yuraszek team was successful in gaining control over Enersis-Endesa more because of its competence than because of its connections.[29] The corruption story does not match the chronology either, since Endesa began to be privatized as a vertically integrated (generation and transmission) utility with a dominant position in the generation market two years before the Enersis takeover. Furthermore, insider deals are not documented for either the initial Endesa privatization or ESI privatization processes other than Chilectra Metropolitana/Enersis. It is thus reasonable to claim that distributional conflicts did not play a major role in privatization in Chile, and that the choice of an oligopolistic structure was influenced more by ideology than by the desire to extract rents in favor of privileged regime insiders.

**Argentina**

ESI restructuring in Argentina faced actual or potential opposition by strong unions, by provincial authorities, and by utility customers and suppliers. The potential for these forces to derail the restructuring effort was serious enough to influence the manner in which privatization took place.

To overcome the major divides of class, sector and territory, Menem's strategy for privatization 'was to build coalitions and provide side payments to ensure cooperation ... He also redesigned the privatization program to allow the national industrial groups to participate in the ownership of the companies' (Molano 1997: 103). An important goal of such measures was to split labor and business groups through a carrot-and-stick approach (Gibson 1997). The Emergency Act of 1990 provided preferential access to the ownership of privatized companies to all groups benefited by them: minority shareholders, employees, customers, suppliers of inputs, and marketers of outputs (Art. 16). It also provided for an emergency public works fund managed by the municipalities created to compensate workers laid off by privatized firms (Art. 59), thereby addressing both labor and provincial opposition to the reforms.

Utility employees faced substantial losses under restructuring. Under public ownership, the utilities had offered very favorable employment conditions (Murillo 1997), and not surprisingly utility employees had opposed privatization when the subject was brought up under the Alfonsín administration (González Fraga 1991). In fact, privatization was marred by union opposition in several provinces well after the election of Menem and the passage of ESI restructuring legislation. In Río Negro, the privatization of the provincial distribution utility, Energía de Río Negro SA (ERSA), was contested by the local union for fear of job losses, despite the reservation of 10 percent of shares for the employees (*GPR*, 23 August 1996). Union opposition is also documented in Misiones, Córdoba, Mendoza and Santa Fe (*GPR*, 18 April 1997), and in Eseba's case in Buenos Aires province (*GPR*, 2 May 1997). Workers' concern was justified: just in SEGBA[30] (the metropolitan Buenos Aires utility), almost 5,000 jobs (out of the starting workforce of 17,000) were shed in the first year after privatization.

To defuse the threat of industrial conflict, which could have adversely affected the success of the privatization auctions, the government used a 'carrot-and-stick' strategy. For the privatization of SEGBA (the first one to take place), it reached an agreement with the company union on September 29, 1989, including a provision to set 10 percent of the shares for the employees[31] (González Fraga 1991). The unions, and particularly the major union of the Argentine ESI, FATLyF,[32] were subsequently able to negotiate other favorable deals as other utilities were privatized (Murillo 1997). For instance, FATLyF was able to acquire between 20 percent and 40 percent of the shares of fourteen generating plants throughout Argentina and participation in partnerships that own another three generators and a provincial distribution utility (Murillo 1997). In the province of Córdoba, the local branch of FATLyF obtained a concession of the provincial utility's generation assets (331 MW), acting in a joint venture with provincial user cooperatives. For the recalcitrant unions, the 'stick' was the enforcement of decrees passed by the Menem administration that restricted strikes and wage increases (Murillo 1997; McGuire 1997: 224–40; Acuña 1995).

A major problem of the Argentine ESI prior to restructuring was the arrears or even nonpayment of wholesale power purchases by the provincial distribution utilities, which contributed significantly to the cash-flow problems of the federally-owned generators and through them, to poor maintenance, equipment degradation, and ultimately a burden on the national treasury. In effect, the distribution utilities enjoyed a 'soft budget constraint' because the federal government was unwilling to cut off supply to recalcitrant provincial utilities. At the same time, to make restructuring fully successful, the federal government needed the cooperation of the provinces to impose hard budget constraints on the purchases of electricity of the provincial utilities (thereby avoiding the disruptive potential of higher credit risk and bankruptcies on the wholesale electricity market) and ultimately to privatize the distribution segment in full, as well as privatizing most of the hydroelectric units, which perform important flood control, irrigation and potable water supply functions in the provinces where they are located. In order to compensate the provinces for the need to pay for power purchases, the government created a number of tax and subsidy schemes meant to counteract the most adverse effects of competition for the provinces while preserving the viability of a nationwide wholesale power market. A National Electric Energy Fund was created in 1992 under the administration of the Federal Electric Energy Council,[33] with the objective of making disbursements for rate subsidies to isolated or dispersed consumers (60 percent of the total disbursed) and the rest for rural electrification, and financed by means of a surcharge on electricity transactions (Electricity Act, Art. 70; Bastos and Abdala 1993: 161). In the Buenos Aires metropolitan area and province, an additional fund was set up in 1994 to subsidize electricity bills of formerly illegal customers of Buenos Aires' distribution utilities, although in this case the fund's revenue was to come from the dedication of federal and provincial electricity tax revenues.

Another set of interests adversely affected by ESI restructuring were the private subcontractors and suppliers of the public sector utilities (known in Argentina as the 'patria contratista' or 'contractor homeland'), who due to lax audits of the utilities' books, poor managerial practices, and sheer corruption, were able to overcharge the SOEs. Logically enough, they opposed restructuring and lobbied the legislature to derail restructuring (Armijo and Faucher, 2002). Also benefiting from the 'soft budget constraints' were firms and even government agencies that engaged in theft of electricity, as an investigation into this problem revealed (Palermo and Novaro 1996: 315). Although many industrial customers stood to benefit from better quality of service and possibly lower prices through direct access to the wholesale electricity market, and thus supported restructuring (Bastos and Abdala 1993: 161ff.), two aspects of the restructuring package were added to preempt the opposition of large suppliers and customers. First, the Emergency Act that vested the executive with the power to privatize public assets, made major suppliers and customers eligible for purchases of shares of the privatized firms under favorable conditions, just as in the case of ESI employees. In the end, no special set-aside was made for customers and suppliers, but the legal provision was clearly a sop intended to appease opposition from these groups. Second, in contrast with Chile (which was at the time of ESI privatization the only case of deregulation in Latin America and one of the few cases in the world), large users were allowed to participate in the wholesale electricity market, and competition was vigorously pursued through fragmentation of control over the privatized generation assets and other means. Also, the government's macroeconomic goal of price stability worked in favor of the interests of utility ratepayers, since the government preferred not to increase rates to get higher bids.

It is worth noting that in Argentina, unlike Brazil (see below) pressures on the public purse were not strong enough to influence the restructuring process. Apart from the restriction on rate increases mentioned in the previous paragraph, the use of debt–equity swaps yielded little cash inflow to government, and the competitive structure of the wholesale market lowered the bids (ibid.: 97–8).

## Brazil

The effects of distributional conflict in Brazil have been most clearly reflected in the severe restrictions to competition in the wholesale power market, rather than on ownership outcomes. The highly territorial orientation of Brazilian politics, together with a pre-existing ownership structure of the distribution utilities organized on a state-by-state basis, came together to force the government to maximize the rents obtained from privatization by restricting competition and granting generous concession contracts. The economic and lobbying weight of business conglomerates has also pushed the government in a similar direction, inducing it to sell the conglomerates the attractive shares of utilities operating in conditions of minimal competition.

In the ESI, union opposition has been minimal, despite the substantial layoffs that have followed the process. Union mobilization did not increase after the massive layoffs of utility employees that followed the first privatizations, such as Light's.[34] Major job reductions have even occurred under federal ownership in utilities to be privatized.  In the northeastern utility CHESF,[35] for instance, employment was cut from 12,000 in 1990 to 6,500 in 1998 (although accompanied by expenditure of some $5 million in training programs for the remaining workers; see Brazil, National Government 1998b).  Furnas, the third-largest generation company in Brazil, cut its workforce from 10,000 in 1990 to about 6,200 in 1998, excluding employees transferred to Eletrobrás (ibid.).  While Furnas's workers have struck against privatization, the conflict has been focused on the specific issue of protecting the employee pension fund, rather than on privatization *per se* (*GPR*, 6 August 1999: 20).  Low labor opposition to restructuring has led to a reduction in the scale of the ESOPs in at least one major privatization.  The employees of Rio Light, one of the first and major privatizations of distribution companies in the country, were only able to obtain 4 percent of shares at a subsidy, instead of the 10 percent that had originally been promised by the government (Kirkman 1997).

By contrast, at the federal and state parliamentary levels the resistance has been more substantial.  In Brazil's patronage-ridden politics, utilities have traditionally provided an excellent vehicle to deliver favors in exchange for votes (Dyer 1997a).  In the larger cities, utilities provide employment; in town and country alike, access to the distribution grid can significantly enhance the quality of life of previously unserved residents.  Legal electricity purchases open up credit and strengthen property rights for shantytown dwellers (Moffett 1998).  Finally, vast projects such as hydroelectric facilities are not only a source of publicity but also a major source of business for 'the large public works contractors, who have played a crucial role in campaign financing' (Geddes and Ribeiro Neto 1992: 648).  Not surprisingly, distributional conflict with regard to privatization and competition has revolved around opposition to privatization from 'employees of state enterprises, earning salaries that were substantially higher than market averages; private firms that sold goods to government enterprises at great profits; firms that received goods and services from public enterprises at subsidized prices; and politicians who made use of public enterprises for their own purposes' (Baer and Villela 1994: 8; also Sola 1994).

The many political benefits of control over electric utilities at the state level have forced the Cardoso administration to negotiate with reluctant legislators in order to pass ESI restructuring laws in a highly territorialized legislature, and with the state governors to privatize the distribution utilities, which are mainly organized on a statewide basis. The federal nature of Brazil's political system and the patronage-oriented nature of electoral politics create strong allegiance to the home turf on the part of federal legislators, as pointed out in Chapter 5, so that the effects of utility ownership are felt at both the federal legislature and state government levels. Newly-elected governors in Minas Gerais and Rio de Janeiro have opposed the sale of Furnas, and attempted, in Minas, the reversal of the partial privatization of CEMIG, the state utility.[36] Municipalities have objected to the privatization of Companhia Energêtica de São Paulo (São Paulo Energy Company, CESP), a large utility in São Paulo, out of concern for water rights and loss of jobs (*GPR*, 30 April 1999: 2). The need to provide favors in exchange for supporting votes has increased pressure on federal and state governments to provide generous concession contracts to the potential buyers, since favorable terms translate into higher sale prices which can then be used to alleviate the fiscal impact of buying off opponents of privatization. Resistance to privatization has only been overcome at the expense of the future political sustainability of the new structure of the industry. The creation of private monopolies is unlikely to be well received by voters in future elections, while the regulatory authorities will find themselves in conflict with the utilities if their attempts to restrain market power are interpreted by the utilities as a breach of the terms of sale.[37]

The distributional impact of restructuring on Brazil's utility suppliers and customers appears to have disproportionately affected decisions about competition more than the decisions about ownership. Traditionally, Latin American business conglomerates have preferred the for them desirable mixture of private property and concentrated ownership, which has given them access to market power rents in the domestic scene. Brazil is no exception (see the preceding chapter on the attitudes of Brazilian business groups), and as already mentioned, the country's utilities were a major source of business for construction companies through the construction and equipment supply contracts for the large hydroelectric plants built by the utilities. The government, however, was able to attract these business interests towards restructuring by pointing out the possibility of acquiring ownership stakes in the privatized utilities. Although the conditions of purchase were the same as for foreign investors, as suppliers to the public sector and thus government creditors, the domestic business conglomerates would have had large amounts of government paper that they could redeem at face value to acquire ESI assets. Since government paper sold in financial markets at a substantial discount, the cost of acquisition was discounted as well. Diversified groups like Votorantim (with a basis in the production of concrete) or Camargo Correa (construction) are as a result becoming significant ESI shareholders.

Among the other three cases, Argentina also had a federal structure and provincially-owned distribution utilities at the time of restructuring. It is thus necessary to examine why the effects of territorial conflict were less harmful in Argentina than in Brazil. Apart from the interaction of different causal factors, such as ideology, the key reason for the difference lies in the more institutionalized nature of Argentine political parties. Greater central control over party finances and candidate slates give Argentine parties greater organizational resources to buffer conflicts between provincial and federal politics. Relative to Brazil, territorial issues are also diluted in Argentina by the enormous concentration of population and economic activity in the federal district of Buenos Aires, which gives the federal government significant power over a major area of the country in demographic and economic terms. In the context of the ESI, for instance, the federal government was able to begin privatization of major generation and distribution assets through its control over the Buenos Aires utility SEGBA. By contrast, Brazil is not only a more dispersed country, but also the main concentrations, in São Paulo and Rio de Janeiro, are under the jurisdiction of powerful states that can challenge the federal government. These differences between Brazil and Argentina do not mean, however, that the focus of the analysis of institutional change in the ESI should be directed to the specific issue of party organization, since party organization is itself likely to reflect distributional conflicts; rather, what matters is understanding how distributional conflict is expressed and handled within the political system.

## Bolivia

As explained in Chapter 5, Bolivian politics are also driven to a large extent by patronage. Prior to restructuring, electricity supply was not an exception to the effects of such pressures, and as a result pre-capitalization electricity rates contained 'a strong element of cross-subsidization between "general" customers and other categories (domestic, industrial)' (ESMAP 1992: 25), that is, domestic and industrial customers were subsidized by commercial and possibly public sector customers. Such a rate structure made it likely that, in addition to the unions, restructuring would be opposed by residential and industrial customers, who would face a loss of the subsidies (since deregulation and vertical separation increase price transparency, making cross-subsidies politically costlier to maintain).[38]

The design of the capitalization pension payoff, the *bonosol*, seems undoubtedly linked to the intention of dispelling public opposition to the restructuring of the ESI and other capitalized sectors, which remains significant (Graham 1998: 165). The government put extreme pressure on the newly-created pension funds in order to ensure that the first distribution of dividends would be made before the 1997 presidential election, as indeed was the case (*The Economist* 1997; Graham 1998: 160–61), although it failed to win Sánchez de Lozada's party a second electoral victory. Large customers or suppliers, on the other hand, do not appear to have influenced restructuring outcomes as they did in Brazil or Argentina, because as already noted above, Bolivia's industrial interests are far more limited due to the country's lower level of industrial development. With a much smaller level of per capita generation capacity than Brazil, and no large generation projects, Bolivia lacked a powerful construction industry that could lobby against restructuring. Bolivia's largest electricity users are the mining operations, which use electricity for smelting. Either because some mines already had their own generation facilities (or their energy usage economics could easily justify installing their own generation plant if rates were increased), because some of them were under the government's control as part of the public mining company Corporación Minera Boliviana (COMIBOL), or because most of the mines were allowed direct access to the wholesale power market and thus to lower prices through competition, there is no evidence that mining interests played a role in restricting competition in the design of a restructured Bolivian ESI.

Capitalization faced strong union opposition. The main union, Central Obrera Boliviana, attempted a 24-hour general strike in November 1996 to stop the program (Graham 1998: 160). Given the recent history of militant labor opposition closely experienced by Sánchez de Lozada as finance minister of Paz Estenssoro, he was well aware of the potential for union opposition to disrupt the ESI restructuring process, and unlike Paz Estenssoro, Sánchez de Lozada had political ambitions for the future.[39] In dealing with labor, Sánchez de Lozada wished to avoid 'the way of doing politics in the dictatorship years, based on confrontations and unnegotiable positions' (Morales 1996: 32); hence, '[a]n important objective of the reform team was to obtain the support of the [electricity] enterprise workers early in the process' (Graham 1998: 156). To mollify union opposition, the government reserved a package of shares in each capitalization for its sale at book value to company employees for a year prior to the capitalization auction and in a second stage after the auction, still at the original price. Shares could be purchased with only a 5 percent downpayment and 24 monthly installments. More than 15,000 workers purchased shares of capitalized companies in the first year of the program (ibid.).

ESI restructuring was thus accompanied in Bolivia by substantial side payments to mollify public and union opposition to the end of patronage benefits and rate cross-subsidies, as the country's high level of distributional conflict would have led us to expect. As another important dimension of distributional conflict in Bolivia has been the territorial aspect of income distribution, we would expect side payments to be directed as well towards the various subnational jurisdictions. However, there is little evidence that any specific compensation programs were set up as in Argentina, or that territorial interests within the legislature obtained benefits in order to approve the reform of the ESI, as happened in Brazil. On the other hand, as a universal benefit the *bonosol* is a form of territorial compensation, particularly if we take into account that several parts of Bolivia are not connected to the central grid yet. Since the capitalization of utilities mainly concerned entities operating in the central system, the bonosol program effectively transferred part of the future profits of these entities to the isolated areas. The territorial dimension of distributional conflict may also have been limited by the fact that one of the most assertive regions in the country, the province of Santa Cruz, is likely to experience a substantial net gain as a result of restructuring. As the country's gas-producing region, if ESI restructuring leads as expected to an expansion of electricity consumption in Bolivia (due to increased investment levels and potential exports of power from Bolivia to Brazil), Santa Cruz will reap some of the gains from increased production of natural gas.

**Conclusions**

To conclude this section, distributional conflict has also played a large role in shaping the choices made by policymakers during the restructuring of the ESI in the four cases, either by limiting such choices or by imposing the need for compensatory payments that have in turn affected the shape of the restructuring programs. In Chile, an authoritarian regime repressed distributional conflict and thus enjoyed substantial freedom to deregulate and privatize the ESI. While restructuring did nonetheless involve some side payments to utility employees and other groups to ensure its long-term viability, the primary motivations for such programs were not redistributional. Privatization may have involved some cronyism, but the privatized entities have not subsequently behaved just as rent-seeking monopolists, at least outside Chile. In Argentina, specific compensatory programs were put in place for utility employees and unions, for the provincial governments, and for low-income users in parts of greater Buenos Aires, while large users were allowed direct access to the wholesale power market and suppliers were able to acquire privatized ESI assets. In Brazil, minimal labor opposition was more than matched by state and legislative resistance to privatization. This induced the government to offer generous terms to the buyers of privatized distribution utilities in order to obtain higher privatization revenues that could compensate states and legislators. Suppliers to the ESI were compensated, as in Argentina, through their ability to acquire ESI assets in competition with foreign investors. Finally, restructuring in Bolivia involved using part of the capitalization proceeds to make a pension payment to the country's older citizens, to buy off popular and territorial opposition to capitalization. Additionally, utility employees were rewarded with subsidized share purchase programs in response to a history of militant unionism among public sector employees.

## CONCLUSIONS FROM THE CASE STUDIES

This chapter has brought together the information discussed in the previous two chapters in order to examine the linkage between the hypothesized explanatory variables and the ESI competition and ownership outcomes found in each one of the four case studies. A summary of the position of each country with regard to the hypothesized explanatory variables and the restructuring outcomes is shown in Figure 6.1, by way of addition to the two-dimensional matrix in Figure 4.1:

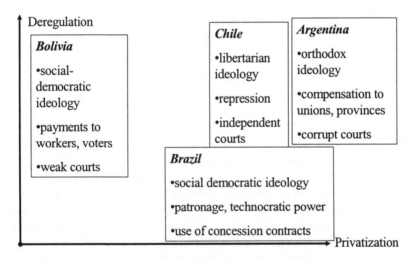

*Figure 6.1 Summary of results from comparative analysis of cases*

Several conclusions can be drawn from the figure. First, the hypotheses regarding property choices fit the case information more closely than the competition hypotheses. For all of the three explanatory variables, the property outcomes generally line up with the explanatory variable rankings: ideology coincides with the heavier emphasis on privatization in Argentina and Chile, and the weaker outcome in Brazil and Bolivia; judicial independence coincides in three cases but not in Argentina's. For distributional conflict, interpretation is complicated by the fact that the distributional payments made to certain groups, such as utility employees, during the restructuring process, must be taken into account. Even on this basis, the Argentine case remains exceptional. As for competition outcomes, judicial independence and distributional conflict hardly explain outcomes. Explanatory power is only increased when compensatory payments and ideological distinctions between 'mainstream' and 'libertarian' (or 'Chicago') economic doctrines are made.

Turning to the explanatory power of each causal variable, we can observe that ideology is confirmed by the cases more than the other causal variables; in fact, ideology alone seems to explain the choices made about competition, perhaps as a reflection of the lower prominence of competition in the policymaking process, which gives policymakers greater freedom to follow their own ideological preferences. Next in terms of empirical confirmation comes distributional conflict, and finally judicial independence, which has a poor record regarding the outcomes for competition. The specific results of the case-study analysis for each explanatory variable are discussed in the rest of this section.

Judicial independence was shown to have played a very important role in the privatization of the Chilean ESI, since the government relied extensively on the existence of a fairly independent judiciary to protect the rights of stakeholders before an openly political regulatory commission and a vague legal text. On the other hand, judicial independence did not lead to the creation of a competitive market structure. Chilean decisionmakers relied instead on the country's independent antitrust system to remedy the worst cases of market power abuse, guided by a libertarian ideology that did not regard market power as a serious public policy problem. The Argentine experience also contradicted the judicial independence hypothesis at first blush. Vigorous privatization and emphasis on competition were pursued despite a history of political meddling with the courts and widespread evidence of judicial corruption. Lacking a solid institutional basis, Argentine decisionmakers relied instead on their ability to project an image of ideological commitment to convince other stakeholders about the sincerity of the government's intentions. In Brazil and Bolivia, however, judicial independence played an important role. To reassure investors in Brazil's ESI, the government used concession contracts that minimized regulatory discretion, and limited competition to avoid the need for extensive antitrust intervention given its complex generation asset structure. The Bolivian government chose instead to make a public commitment to pension payments tied to the preservation of property rights, since the judiciary lacked credibility, although on the matter of competition no equivalent remedy was pursued and the government has had to face protests from market participants.

Ideology is clearly the most important explanatory variable for the choices made in each country. A libertarian credo emanating from the University of Chicago resulted in widespread privatization with very few limitations on market power in Chile. Economic orthodoxy came to Argentina only after the failure of the attempts to salvage Peronism's traditional preference for public monopoly; subsequently, the impeccable commitment of Domingo Cavallo to neoclassical economic doctrine resulted in a textbook case of privatization and promotion of competition. The technical complexity of Brazil's generation asset structure, combined with the executive's lack of enthusiasm for private property and markets, left ESI restructuring in the hands of governmental technocracies that were uniformly hostile to competition and divided about privatization. The similar ideology of Bolivia's president led to the reliance on mixed private–public enterprises rather than to straight privatization, although it did not prevent the introduction of a competitive market design.

Distributional conflict has also been shown to be a powerful explanatory variable. In Chile, an authoritarian regime repressed distributional conflict and thus enjoyed substantial freedom to deregulate and privatize the ESI. Side payments to utility employees and other groups responded to nondistributional motivations as well as the desire to ensure the long-term viability of restructuring, and were in any case limited. Specific compensatory programs were put in place for the major groups affected by restructuring in Argentina: utility employees and unions, provincial governments, low-income users, and suppliers. In Brazil, opposition came mainly from state governments and territorially-oriented legislators. This induced the government to offer generous terms to the buyers of privatized distribution utilities in order to obtain higher privatization revenues that could compensate states and legislators. Suppliers to the ESI were compensated, as in Argentina, through their ability to acquire ESI assets in competition with foreign investors. Finally, restructuring in Bolivia involved using part of the capitalization proceeds to make a pension payment to the country's older citizens, to buy off popular and territorial opposition to capitalization. Additionally, utility employees were rewarded with subsidized share purchase programs in response to a history of militant unionism among public sector employees.

In short, the conclusions arising from the case studies are consistent with the statistical evidence and by and large with the predictions of the theoretical model. The implications of the preceding theoretical and empirical exercises, for reform in the ESI as in other sectors or areas and countries, as well as the limitations of the analysis, are examined in the next, and last, chapter.

## NOTES

1. The regulatory framework for telecommunications is similarly ambiguous, and disputes about regulatory ambiguities have also been taken to the courts (Galal 1996: 136).
2. Likewise, the new antitrust law creates an antitrust commission under the control of the government, since its president is an undersecretary at the Ministry of Commerce (Rowat 1997).
3. This is not to mean that it has had no effect at all. As we have seen, regulated consumers are largely insulated from price volatility; also, the concession contracts grant a 10-year period before the first rate review, rather than the five-year periods that will follow afterwards, and limit the size of the productivity improvement (or X) factors in the rate adjustment formulas.
4. Departamento Nacional de Águas e Energia Elétrica.
5. 'Many [of DNAEE's] decisions were based not on improving operations or on making efficiency gains, but on alleviating political situations or repaying political favors' (Kirkman 1997: B2).
6. Argentina, National Congress, Law No. 24,065 of 19 December 1991, on Electrical Energy ('Electricity Act').
7. Bolivia, National Congress, Law No. 1604 of 21 December 1994, on Electricity ('Electricity Act').
8. DFL 1 1982.
9. Hence a macroeconomic anti-inflationary goal cannot explain the choice of the concession terms, since indexing would defeat such a purpose.
10. Hydro plants account respectively for 60 percent, 44 percent and 93 percent of capacity in Chile, Argentina and Brazil.
11. 'Small' in relation to the typical scale of efficient generation plants. Total installed capacity in Bolivia's interconnected system is about 600 MW, the size of a high-efficiency coal plant or of a single gas-fired cogeneration plant, although the minimum efficient scale for the latter can be as low as 50 MW.
12. For the same reasons as in Argentina, it is also incompatible with macroeconomic goals of deficit and debt reduction, or of inflation reduction.
13. Stakes by foreign pension funds only appear in Enersis in 1989, and in ENDESA in 1990 (Moguillansky 1997: Tables 2 and 3).
14. At the very least, such a market structure choice is inconsistent with a macroeconomic goal of inflation reduction, since greater market power would in principle make it easier for generators to pass on general price increases to their customers.
15. By contrast, it would not have made sense to privatize with a competitive market structure if all the government wanted was to maximize privatization revenue due to budget deficit pressures. And an anti-inflationary goal could have been met more simply through a monopoly concession with a price cap.
16. Although it must be pointed out that Brazil's antitrust statute and the creation of an independent anti-monopoly commission (CADE) date back to 1994, when Cardoso was finance minister (Rowat 1997).
17. In 1991, the British government privatized the ESI in England and Wales and created a competitive electricity pool with mandatory participation for all generators and distribution utilities, as well as voluntary participation by large consumers.
18. The fact that BNDES is in charge of the privatization program does not explain its preference for privatization, since the causality runs the other way: successive Brazilian governments have assigned this mission to the BNDES as in most other countries with similar institutions (CORFO in Chile, Banco Nacional de Desarrollo, in Argentina, Banco de Fomento in Puerto Rico, Nacional Financiera in Mexico).

19. Comisión para la transición industrial.
20. In fact, a new populist movement, Conciencia de Patria (Fatherland's Conscience, CONDEPA), made important inroads against the major parties on the basis of a populist platform, until the death of its founder sapped its appeal.
21. Unfortunately, there is no direct evidence about the decisionmaking process that led to the competitive choice for the Bolivian ESI. Note, however, that creating several competitive generation and distribution entities weakens the position of their respective foreign investors relative to the government and is therefore consistent with the wish to placate nationalists.
22. By contrast, there were no egalitarian intentions *per se*: 'In Chile, however, there is simply no mention in any discussions of the [share distribution] program as a means of distributing wealth within society.' (Maloney 1994: 140). Also, survey data show little fear of employers about labor militancy (Payne 1995).
23. In fact, there is a possibility that the allocation of shares was distributionally motivated, but as a case of 'cronyism' rather than as an attempt to buy off potential opposition. This possibility is discussed below.
24. By contrast, the Bolivian 'bonosol' program (discussed below) provides defined benefits to all persons 65 years old and older, which makes it more obviously redistributive.
25. It must be pointed out that Hachette and Lüders are not impartial observers. Both have ties to the 'Chicago boys' through the Catholic University, and the latter was in fact finance minister in 1982–83 (E. Silva 1996b: Table 6.1). Contrast their assessment with Graham's (1998: 79), who notes that at the height of the unemployment crisis in 1982, only 1.5 percent of GDP was allocated for unemployment benefits for 600,000 workers, while another 600,000 unemployed got no benefits at all.
26. Note that the modest welfare gains of restructuring reported above from Galal's work thus understate the true benefits because Galal's analysis does not include the 1970s.
27. Another 40 percent of the shares was apparently bought at auction by two US banks in January 1988 when the government put the shares on the block (World Bank 1993a: Box 21). But the banks appear to have bought the shares for portfolio considerations alone, as the Yuraszek team remained in control of Chilectra.
28. The simmering resentment of other shareholders exploded in 1997 when the Yuraszek team agreed to sell their controlling stake in the conglomerate to Spain's utility Endesa (hitherto unaffiliated with its Chilean namesake) at a disproportionate gain for the management team. A non-controlling shareholder revolt forced the Chilectra management team to leave the conglomerate altogether.
29. Further evidence of the standing of Yuraszek and his associates was revealed by the fact that part of the strategic value attached by Endesa Spain to the partial takeover of Enersis-Endesa (see previous note) lay in keeping him and his team in charge of the conglomerate. Such value could not be derived from political connections, since Chile was under the democratic rule of a center-left government, and since Endesa Spain's strategy concerned not just Chile but Latin America as a whole (*GPR*, various issues).
30. Servicios Eléctricos del Gran Buenos Aires.
31. Other measures, of a more general nature that did not affect ownership or competition, included severance payments and voluntary retirement programs funded by the government and the World Bank (Harteneck and McMahon 1996).
32. Federación Argentina de Trabajadores de Luz y Fuerza.
33. The council was set up in 1961, with representatives from each province and from the federal executive.
34. The sequential nature of the privatization offered unions in the yet-to-be-privatized utilities a unique opportunity to 'see the writing on the wall' and try to fight privatization. For instance, in the first 18 months after privatization, Light's workforce was reduced by 40 percent, a loss of 4,500 jobs (Dyer 1998). But I have nowhere seen evidence of increasing contestation of privatizations by the unions; in fact, Light management's fears of personal harm from disgruntled ex-workers turned out to be unfounded (Moffett 1998).
35. Companhia Hidrelétrica do São Francisco.

36. Abuse of patronage by state governments has been limited, however, by the parlous situation of most state treasuries. In past years, bankruptcy allowed Eletrobrás to take over the state utilities of ten states, including Rio de Janeiro and Mato Grosso.
37. Conflicts are already appearing. The concession contracts with the Rio utilities Light and Companhia de Eletricidade do Rio de Janeiro (Rio Electricity Company, CERJ) apparently had no mention of service quality and penalties, so the utilities are contesting the fines imposed by ANEEL for blackouts in January 1998.
38. Revollo (1998), who was Minister of Capitalization under Sánchez de Lozada, notes the opposition to the program, for ideological and distributional considerations, by the Ministry of Mines and Energy, SOE managers, unions, political opponents, and the military.
39. The Bolivian constitution prohibits the immediate re-election of presidential incumbents, but re-election is possible after at least one term outside of office has elapsed.

# 7. Understanding institutional change

This book has examined the determinants of institutional change in a specific industrial activity, the production and delivery to final users of electric power, using as the empirical basis four case studies from Latin America. The analysis of institutional change has focused on two dimensions: the ownership structure of the various elements of the industry, and the degree of reliance on competitive mechanisms emerging from the change process. Three explanatory variables were posited to explain the outcomes for these two dimensions: the degree of judicial independence in the country, the preferences of policymakers as shaped mainly by their own ideology and where relevant by electoral or interest-group preferences, and the level of distributional conflict in the country.

The four cases provide substantial evidence about the impact of the hypothesized explanatory variables on the institutional transformation of the ESI. Empirical confirmation is more extensive for ownership outcomes than for competition outcomes. Of the three hypothesized explanatory variables, ideology has the greatest explanatory power, accounting especially for the outcomes in Argentina and Chile. In particular, ideological considerations appear to play a leading role in determining competition outcomes.[1] The poorer explanatory power of the other two causal variables for competition outcomes may be the result of a lower public policy salience of competition decisions, which would give policymakers greater freedom to follow their own policy preferences. Certainly, the greater paucity of information about competition decisions would confirm that this dimension of restructuring has lower salience; even in widely publicized restructuring efforts like that of England and Wales, much greater attention was devoted to privatization than to market structure, at least outside of the industrial organization literature. While ownership involves politically charged issues like foreign control and capital flows, competition is a technically more complex problem, particularly in the ESI where technological constraints are very significant. This is exacerbated in developing countries by many decades of import substitution, which accustomed consumers to highly concentrated domestic markets.

Distributional conflict also plays an important role in shaping institutional change, although often in the form of side payments to influential groups that are affected negatively by the changes rather than through a direct effect on the choice of ownership and competitive structures. This may contrast with political economy models of interest-group competition, in which greater competition leads to the mutual cancellation of the influence of opposing interest groups (just as greater competition among firms erodes oligopoly profits). The reality of politics is that greater competition can lead to paralysis and even chaos, as opposing groups resort to strikes, lock-outs, and other forms of protest and mutual punishment. Under these conditions, politicians may prefer to buy off any interest groups that have the potential to disrupt policymaking and implementation.

In keeping with evidence collected elsewhere, judicial independence has the weakest effect on either ownership or competition.[2] This may be due to the transformational nature of the institutional changes that have been examined above. By this I mean that the reform of the ESI and similar infrastructural sectors entails the creation of entities and forms of public sector behavior *ex novo*, that is without precedent in the country's political and legal history. Policymakers may therefore disregard institutional precedents, such as the country's prior record of judicial subservience, because they provide a poor guide for shaping the new institutions, or even an example of what *not* to do.

## UNDERSTANDING ESI REFORM ELSEWHERE IN LATIN AMERICA

In the Latin American context, macro-level analyses of market reforms lead to similar conclusions as those in the present study. Remmer (1998) finds that, apart from the role of financial need (as expressed by economic crisis and the importance of foreign aid) in triggering reform, ideology (share of vote for left-wing parties) and export-related interests affect the extent of pro-market reform. A qualitative assessment by Armijo and Faucher (2002) concludes that economic crisis is 'necessary but not sufficient for the initiation of reform' (p. 4), that ideological shifts are also necessary, but that the lack of political constraints (in the form of the political insulation of the executive office) is not.[3] These findings are relevant because the analytical framework presented in the book should also be applicable to restructuring experiences in other countries and in industries of similar technology, such as water, telecommunications, or natural gas production and delivery.

Within Latin America, there are several other experiences of ESI reform that merit a brief contrast with the model. Peru undertook reform of its ESI from 1992 on, with the process still incomplete. In the Peruvian reform, generation, transmission and distribution utilities were privatized or awarded under long-term concessions, and a wholesale electricity market along the lines of Chile's was created, together with an antitrust agency. Peru has a long history of militant unionism and left-wing contestation. Its governmental institutions, including the judiciary, have been weakened over the last decade and a half by economic crisis, corruption, terrorism and counterterrorism, and finally by the 'neo-populist' politics of President Alberto Fujimori, who pursued economic reform under a highly personalistic rule (Roberts 1995). These conditions are fully reflected in the ESI reform, in which shares of the privatized utilities have been set aside for employees and for Peruvian citizens, foreign utility ownership has been restricted, and the regulatory commission is not fully independent from political control. In fact, special 'legal stability' agreements with a ten-year term had to be executed between the government and foreign investors to allay the latter's fears of direct or indirect expropriation in the future (*IPPQ* 1998). Despite all these measures to deal with opposition to privatization and the attending uncertainty for private investors in privatized entities, recent attempts to sell two generation companies in the country's second largest city, Arequipa, were derailed by violent riots in this city that required the temporary imposition of martial law.

In Colombia, straight privatizations have been combined with Bolivian-style capitalizations and the permanence of several public entities owned by different levels of government; a wholesale market exists as well, but vertical integration is allowed, so long as separate accounts are kept for different activities. Although Colombia does not have a history of militant unionism as found in Bolivia or Argentina, it has been, and continues to be, scarred by violent conflict between competing parties and guerrilla movements. Violence has also had a deep impact on the judiciary, most egregiously when many members of the Supreme Court were killed during a guerrilla takeover of the Supreme Court's building some years ago. Although the primary motivator for ESI restructuring was a supply shortage in the 1990s caused by low rainfall, the outcome of the reform process reflects fierce ideological disputes in the country, including the opposition to foreign investment in key industries by the various guerrilla groups active in Colombia. Interparty competition encourages public sector patronage, while the desire to end guerrilla warfare through peaceful means may put pressure on successive governments to keep a maximum of the ESI in public hands and to resist vertical separation. These pressures have led to the sale of special share packages to the employees of privatized or capitalized utilities, and to the resistance to the capitalization of the distribution utilities in parts of the country where they play an important patronage role through employment opportunities (ibid.). In fact, even where these utilities have been privatized, as along the Caribbean coast, the utilities are on the brink of bankruptcy due to resistance to rate increases and massive theft of electricity. Meanwhile, guerrilla attacks against the transmission infrastructure have derailed the privatization of the government-owned generator ISAGen and wreaked havoc on the wholesale electricity market by creating opportunities for the abuse of market power by generators in areas isolated by the attacks (Ayala and Millán 2002).

As a test of the predictive power of the theoretical framework developed in this book, the next section offers an analysis of the prospects for reform in the one major Latin American country where ESI restructuring has advanced the least, Mexico.

## PROSPECTS FOR REFORM IN THE MEXICAN ESI

After a minor reform that allowed the public electricity monopoly to buy from private producers, recent Mexican governments have attempted to deepen reforms to create a wholesale market and possibly privatize generation and distribution units. Having reviewed four cases where ESI restructuring has already taken place, or is well under way, it may be of interest to put the model of institutional change through a further test, the test of forecasting the outcome of restructuring efforts in Mexico, where they have made limited progress so far. In the Mexican case, resistance to reform – delayed far beyond similar reforms in other infrastructure sectors – has come from all of the three explanatory factors discussed in this book, reinforced by the problems experienced in the privatization of telecoms, banks and toll expressways. The previous administration explicitly acknowledged in its restructuring proposals that reform of the ESI has to be preceded by the full development of a credible and competent regulatory system, thus acknowledging the limitations of judicial independence in what was for many years a one-party state. Together with the oil sector, the ESI was one of the pillars of the former ruling party's ideology of nationalism and state leadership in economic affairs. Finally, the vast state electricity monopoly has been an abundant source of patronage for politicians throughout the country, especially through generous employment conditions provided to its heavily unionized workforce.

**Reform Proposals**

Since the nationalization of the remaining privately-owned electric utilities in 1960, the Mexican ESI has been entirely in public hands, separated into two vertically-integrated utilities operating as government departments: Luz y Fuerza del Centro (LFC) in the Federal District area, and the Comisión Federal de Electricidad (CFE) in the rest of the country. There is no separate regulatory authority and rates are set by the government. The exclusive role of the public sector in the ESI is enshrined in Articles 27 and 28 of the Mexican constitution. At present, the CFE has 90 percent of generation capacity and 90 percent of distribution assets; LFC has 2.3 percent of generation and 10 percent of distribution assets, while the remainder of generation capacity is held by Pemex (4.4 percent) and private owners (3.3 percent), including the new independent producers allowed since the 1992 reform. The CFE serves about 16.5 million customers, and LFC some five and a half million. Agricultural and residential rates are highly subsidized: the difference between average residential rates and cost of service exceeds 50 percent (Mexico, National Government n.d.: 20–21).

In 1992, existing laws were changed to allow the development of private generation plants, for self-generation, sale to industrial consumers from a dedicated facility, or sale to the CFE under build–operate–transfer (BOT) arrangements.[4] These limited measures did not prove sufficient, however, to supplement the CFE's limited financial resources in meeting the rapidly growing demand for electricity in Mexico, and saddled the CFE with contract payments for many years into the future. The selection of developers under competitive and transparent procurement procedures, the negotiation of long-term BOT contracts, and the cost of the guarantees required by the developers and their lenders, have made this approach cumbersome and excessively slow, putting pressure on the need to implement a more comprehensive restructuring proposal.

Another important initiative was the creation of the Comisión Reguladora de Energía (CRE) in 1993, which is described below. So far, the CRE has mainly been regulating the natural gas industry,[5] with still limited intervention in the ESI, but it has already gained a reputation for technical competence, openness, and impartiality. In contrast to the experience of Brazil, Argentina and Bolivia, a well-developed regulatory framework is in place in Mexico prior to ESI restructuring.

In February 1999, the Mexican government unveiled a proposal for a profound restructuring of the Mexican ESI. Although the long-standing hold on power of the Partido Revolucionario Institucional (PRI) was broken in the 2000 presidential election, the ambitious 1999 blueprint set the goalposts for ESI restructuring in Mexico, as evidenced in the latest reform proposal (summarized below). For this reason, it is worth summarizing in terms of competition and ownership as in the comparative chapter:

1. *Ownership*

- *distribution of ESI property rights after reform*: transmission (including grid expansion), dispatch and nuclear generation (only 2 percent of total installed capacity) to remain in the public sector, although as separate entities; hydroelectric plants to be awarded through concessions; private capital attracted to distribution through non-exclusive, renewable 30-year concession agreements rather than through outright privatization;
- *restrictions on rights of private owners*: foreign investment will be allowed; distribution concessionaires will have the obligation to provide service;
- *ownership composition of privatized or capitalized electric utilities*: ownership stakes for employees and pension funds to be 'encouraged'; the government would guarantee the rights of current and retired utility employees;
- *protection of investors from adverse regulatory decisions:* sector regulation to be entrusted to the CRE, an independent entity which is led by commissioners appointed for staggered terms and protected from arbitrary removal; whose government-approved budget is funded through a unit charge on energy transactions; whose decisions can be appealed to the courts; and which is allowed to conduct hearings as part of its decisionmaking process; existing BOT contract obligations to remain with the public sector, backed by contracts with distribution utilities.

2. *Competition*

- *ESI market structure:* full vertical separation; introduction of competition in generation and supply; single transmission provider, barred from owning other ESI assets; distributors and generators not allowed to hold controlling stakes in the other segment open to private ownership (respectively, generation and distribution);
- *barriers to entry and exit:* distributors not allowed to be suppliers in their own service territories;
- *antitrust enforcement:* in addition to the CRE, an independent antitrust agency was created in 1992 to monitor and penalize abuses of dominant position, and has already advised the government in

many privatization auctions (Rowat 1997); this agency would monitor and penalize the abuse of horizontal market power;

- *ISO governance:* a new, independent public sector entity would be created under the oversight of the regulator (CRE) and market participants (generators, transmission company, distributors, and users active in the market);
- *regulation of generator spot market bids:* establishment of a wholesale electricity market; generators, including hydroelectric operators in the southern part of Mexico, would be allowed to bid into the market without restrictions; northern hydro plants would remain under public sector control due to their multiple functions (generation, irrigation, and flood control);
- *wholesale market access thresholds:* set initially at 5.0 GWh consumption per annum;
- *distributor purchasing regulations:* not specified;
- *use of performance-based regulation:* creation of several distribution concessions to facilitate yardstick competition; price-cap tariff regime;
- *franchise bidding:* expected to be used for distribution concessions, as already done for generation BOT contracts and for gas distribution concessions.

Overall, then, the 1999 restructuring plan for Mexico sought to emulate the Argentine restructuring scheme, although with a greater component of public ownership envisaged (the transmission company); the system operator would be indistinguishable in practice from the non-profit organizations emerging in the US or from CAMMESA in Argentina. On the competition side, the plan introduced all the competitive mechanisms available to policymakers in the ESI.[6] The threshold of 5 GWh for access to the wholesale market, for instance, is – for a reasonable range of large-user electricity consumption patterns – lower than any of the four cases previously compared with the exception of Argentina.[7]

The 1999 plan was not implemented. Due to the constitutional rank of public monopoly in the ESI, the plan required a constitutional amendment. For the reasons discussed below, exacerbated by the pressure of elections in 2000, the Mexican legislature refused to consider the 1999 proposals.

Lacking a legislative majority, and aware of congressional opposition to reform, the current administration of President Vicente Fox has undertaken several restructuring initiatives. Initially, the government attempted to introduce incremental reforms by decree, thus bypassing the legislature. However, the constitutionality of these measures was successfully challenged by opposition deputies. In fact, the Supreme Court made it very clear that ESI restructuring would require a constitutional amendment. As a result, the government recently submitted a new plan which, by curtailing the role of private ownership, may stand a chance of being supported by enough PRI deputies to make the constitutional amendment possible (which entails a two-thirds supermajority of favorable votes in the legislature). Since opposition to ESI restructuring is, for reasons discussed below, concentrated on the privatization side, the new proposal keeps most of the formal competition aspects of the previous plan but maintains the CFE entirely under public ownership. The private sector role is limited to the development of new generation capacity, which can be used to supply large consumers (industrial, commercial, or service users above a 2.5 GWh annual consumption threshold) through freely negotiated contracts, to participate in the spot market (where large users can also buy electricity), or to sell to the public entities.[8] With the CFE's dominant status untouched by the proposal, and given the experience of dominant players in Mexico's gas and telecommunications sectors, and in Brazil's generation sector, the new proposal is very likely to introduce a marginal amount of competition in the Mexican ESI, although the infusion of private capital may be sufficient to avert capacity bottlenecks that could choke economic growth.

As in the case studies in the preceding chapters, we now turn to an evaluation of the hypothesized explanatory variables before examining how well they account for the unfolding of current reform efforts and what prospects for reform they offer.

## Judicial Independence

With regard to the rankings reported in Table 5.1 of the comparative chapter, Mexico's position is as follows:

- Johnson's (1976a, b) measure of judicial independence for the 1945–75 period is 240 for Mexico, ahead of Argentina, Brazil and Bolivia (Verner 1984);
- the median tenure of Supreme Court justices was 3.26 years for the short period of observation between 1986 and 1996 (Henisz 2000) (this figure is lower than for the three cases where data was reported, Chile, Argentina and Brazil, although the limited set of observations for Mexico may skew the data.);
- the index of perceived judicial independence (from World Economic Forum 1997) was 3.72 in 1997, again below the other three reported data points (Chile, Argentina and Brazil);
- the index of perceived judicial quality (IMD 1997) is 2.19, also lower than in those three other cases (Bolivia's is not reported);

- the relative security of property rights in 1995–96 (Messick and Kimura 1996) was rated at the middle level, like those of Argentina and Chile;
- an alternative measure, the relative protection of property rights in 1998 (Johnson et al. 1998) took a value of 3 out of a maximum of 4, below Chile but equal to Argentina and above Brazil and Bolivia.

Verner's (1984) classification of Latin American Supreme Courts lists the Mexican Supreme Court as Latin America's only 'stable-reactive' judiciary, meaning that while 'it has not experienced direct assaults on its integrity or autonomy' (ibid.: 484), it only reacts to events to set limits to governmental institutions, and 'restricts itself to 'non-political' questions' (ibid.: 485). In this sense, it is regarded by this author as less independent than the Chilean Supreme Court, but more independent than the Supreme Courts of Argentina, Brazil and Bolivia. A constitutional reform in 1994 increased judicial independence by reducing the power of the executive in the appointment of judges and increasing the scope of judicial review (Domingo 1999).

The conclusion from the available evidence is that in terms of judicial independence, Mexico lies certainly below Chile, but above Bolivia and Argentina. The Mexican judiciary has not experienced the widespread corruption and turnover of the Argentine judiciary under the Menem administrations and currently in the disputes about convertibility of bank deposits. Although both narrative and numerical assessments indicate that the Mexican courts were careful not to meddle with the political primacy of the PRI by challenging the actions of its governments, under the last PRI administration and the current one of the Partido de Acción Nacional (PAN), independence has been on the rise, bolstered by the creation a few years ago of an independent council to oversee the selection and appointment of judges.

**Ideology**

Mexican politics have been dominated for most of the twentieth century by the PRI, which as the self-styled heir of the Mexican Revolution, has traditionally positioned itself at 'center left', mediating between the aspirations of workers and peasants, and the interests of private business and state enterprises. Traditionally, the main electoral competition to the PRI has come from the PAN, which has overt links to the conservative industrialists of Monterrey, Mexico's second largest economic concentration, and to the Catholic Church. Beginning in the 1980s, however, the PRI drifted to the right, pushed by major economic crises that undermined the previous mixed-economy model and the concomitant rise to the top of technocrats trained in top US universities. As a result, some of the more left-oriented members of the party left to form the Party of the Democratic Revolution (PRD) in 1992 and have ever since challenged the PRI on the left.

As in the other cases previously reviewed, populism and clientelism have been very important axes of political activity in Mexico – in fact, arguably more important in Mexico than in some of the other cases, because the domination of politics by a single party within a formally democratic system was to a large extent achieved by means of a populist rhetoric (for example, in support of land reform) and the exchange of votes for concrete favors, such as infrastructure or social services expenditure by the government in a particular village or area.[9]

The increasing presence of US-trained technocrats – or technopols – in Mexico's administrations since the early 1980s had probably turned Mexico into the country with the strongest influence of orthodox economics by the end of the century, since Chile's 'Chicago boys' were displaced from the government with the advent of democracy and the electoral dominance of the Concertación coalition of Christian Democrats and Socialists.[10] The signal event was the selection of Carlos Salinas, a Harvard-trained PhD in public policy, as presidential candidate in 1988 after a rapid rise through senior government positions. Salinas's minister of finance, and hence the second most influential person on economic affairs in the administration, was Pedro Aspe, an MIT economics PhD. The previous president, Ernesto Zedillo, holds a PhD in economics from Yale. Finally, Zedillo's energy minister and author of the ESI restructuring blueprint, Luis Téllez, was yet another PhD economist, from MIT. The channels of ideological influence on the 1999 restructuring plan are thus as clear in Mexico as they were in Pinochet's Chile or in Argentina when Cavallo was in the government. In fact, Aspe regularly met with Argentina's key reformer, Domingo Cavallo, when they were both doctoral students in Cambridge, Massachusetts.

In addition to the importance of policymakers from technocratic backgrounds, the ideological role of the business community cannot be neglected, particularly after the victory of the PAN and its candidate, Vicente Fox. The main Mexican business groups such as the Business Coordinating Council (Consejo Coordinador Empresarial, CEE) favor private property and individual initiative; business groups more generally displayed 'a doctrinal commitment to free market ideology and a firm belief in the unproductive nature of statist policies' (Teichman 1995: 100–101). Although business strongly opposed trade liberalization (ibid.: 105), this must be seen as an attempt to continue to enjoy protectionist rents rather than as a sign of support for economic heterodoxy. Business influence has come to the fore with the historical victory of the PAN presidential candidate Fox in July 2000. Not only is Fox a former Coca-Cola executive, but as already mentioned, the PAN's electoral basis and cadres hail mostly from the northern states, where the importance and influence of private initiative have historically been stronger than in the rest of the country.

As regards public opinion, Mexicans regard themselves on average as slightly left of center, and this position has barely moved between 1996 and 2002. This is confirmed by attitudes about the role of the state in economic affairs (*The Economist*, 2002). The main ideological manifestation outside the established political channels has been the armed rebellion started in Chiapas in January 1994, although the rebellion is a response to a multitude of factors – many of them of an ethnic and geographic nature – rather than to 'neoliberalism' alone. What is equally significant is that the rebellion triggered a wave of protests against orthodox reform, organized by the PRD and other opposition left-wing parties, and by the unions[11] as well as some elements within the PRI (Teichman 1995: 182). The brutal macroeconomic retrenchment that followed the 1994–95 financial crisis added further ammunition to the opponents of orthodoxy. In this regard, the PAN victory in the presidential election did not signify a shift to the right among voters. The PAN and PRI platforms were very similar. Voters appear to have been moved more by the desire to end PRI hegemony than by ideological preference for the PAN; in the concurrent congressional elections, votes shifted slightly in favor of the PRD. Lastly, the PRI defeat was also caused by low turnout among traditional PRI constituencies (Klesner 2002). Election data thus confirm the poll data mentioned above.

Overall ideological positions within the Mexican polity can be ascertained by looking at the indicators used in Table 5.3 of the comparative chapter:

- the index for the scope of government involvement in Mexican society (1946–86 average, ranging from 1 for highest to 10 for lowest) is 4.24, substantially below the figures for Argentina, Bolivia, Brazil, and Chile (which, with the lowest value for the four, has a score of 5.25);
- the activity of state-owned enterprise in Mexico during 1985–90 (World Bank 1998) was 6.7 percent of GDP, only higher than the level for Argentina among the four cases previously compared (although most of this is probable accounted for by the state oil monopoly Pemex);
- the index of freedom for foreign investment in 1998 (Johnson et al. 1998, ranging from 1 for highest to 4 for lowest) was 2, like Argentina and Bolivia and showing less freedom than in Chile;

- the extent of price controls in 1995 (Gwartney 1997; inverted scale) was 5 (out of a maximum of 10), indicating more extensive controls than in any of the other cases but Bolivia;
- lastly, the degree of labor market regulation in 1997 (IMD 1997; inverted scale) was 5.48 out of a maximum of 10, almost the same as Brazil's, higher than Chile's and lower than Argentina's (no data were reported for Bolivia).

According to these indicators, Mexico's overall rank would be in the middle of the reference group (Argentina, Bolivia, Brazil, and Chile) in terms of the prevalence of economic orthodoxy. Such a mixed picture of ideology in Mexico is consistent with the impression that emerged from the preceding discussion of political forces in the country: there appears to be an uneasy coexistence of two very strong currents: on one side, a firmly orthodox, US-educated elite with firm business backing, and on the other, a populist tradition favoring state intervention and a commitment to social justice that represents the continuity with the ideals of the Revolution. For more than a decade, the former have had the upper hand, but at the cost of increasing political and social antagonism (Teichman 1995: 25).

**Distributional Conflict**

After the great upheaval of the Mexican Revolution early in the twentieth century, distributional conflict was muted in Mexico by the singular ability of the PRI to mediate between the conflicting interests of workers (and peasants) and employers (including landowners). Traditionally, the mediation process took two complementary aspects: on one hand, cooperation was fostered through a system of cooptation that delivered land reform for the peasants, certain social services and workplace benefits for workers (but especially substantial economic and political rewards for union leaders), and trade protection and financial support for businesses; on the other hand, repression was not spared for those who refused to accept the terms of the deal, ranging from removal from powerful positions to outright military action.

In comparative terms, we can examine Mexico's position as measured by the indicators of Table 5.4 in the comparative chapter:

- the first indicator is the Gini coefficient, which was 50.3 for Mexico in 1992, lower than Chile's and Brazil's (World Bank 1998);
- during the 1993–95 period, Mexico had an annual average of 16.18 lost workdays per 1,000 population, lower than Argentina and Chile and higher than Brazil (IMD 1997; there are no data for Bolivia);

- the average number of strikes or lockouts per annum for the 1987–91 period (ILO, various years) was 142, very similar to Chile (130), Bolivia (138), and substantially lower than for Argentina (543) and Brazil (1890);
- during 1985–90, SOEs experienced losses equivalent to 2.4 percent of GDP (World Bank 1998), versus 7.6 percent for Bolivian SOEs, 8.6 percent for Chilean ones and only 0.6 percent for those in Brazil (no data for Argentina);
- as for the average decentralization level during the post-war era (1946–94), Mexico ranked as more decentralized than the other four cases except for Brazil (Jaggers and Gurr 1996);
- Mexico's public sector deficit was 6 percent of GDP on average between 1972 and 1990, like Argentina's, lower than Brazil's and Bolivia's, and higher than Chile's;
- finally, the perceived degree of labor disputes in 1997, as measured by the *Global Competitiveness Report* (World Economic Forum 1997; inverted scale) was only 1.9 out of a highest conflict rating of 7, below the figures reported for Argentina (2.55), Chile (2.45) and Brazil (2.76).

These different measures of distributional conflict confirm the previously explained moderation of this phenomenon in contemporary Mexico. Only in decentralization was Mexico placed at the maximum level. This may explain why territorial issues have generally been less salient in Mexico than in Argentina or Brazil – Chiapas excepted.

The inclusive nature of the PRI and the political system that emerged in the aftermath of the Revolution naturally made cooptation and, as a consequence, clientelism, the most systematic manifestations of distributional conflict in Mexico during the post-war era. Cooptation and clientelism were, in turn, most evident in labor relations and agriculture.[12] In the latter, farming cooperatives known as *ejidos,* which arose from the collectivist aspirations of peasants during the Revolution, were supported by the PRI governments with financial and other benefits in exchange for political support. Outside the rural areas, the PRI sought to privilege supportive unions and union leaders with a variety of measures, a system known as *charrismo* after the nickname of a PRI-linked union leader. Favored unions would be awarded closed-shop representation in their industry, and union leaders would receive material rewards (such as privileged supply contracts in the case of SOEs) and even access to PRI and elected office, in exchange for delivering worker support. In turn, the leaders could use their material wealth to privilege cooperative workers and to hire thugs to discipline uncooperative members, along the lines of a classic clientelistic pyramid.

In recent years, the relation between government and labor unions has increasingly turned from cooptation to confrontation, becoming in fact the focus of distributional conflict in the country. As mentioned, territorial issues have not had the relevance of other countries due to the centralized and, until recently, homogeneous political structure of the Mexican Federation.[13] Business interests have accepted dramatic economic reform and especially trade liberalization with protests but no serious attempts at reversing these reforms. By contrast, on the labor side the reorientation of economic policy towards greater orthodoxy has been accompanied on occasion by serious confrontation with unions in SOEs, although at the macroeconomic level Mexico did achieve one of the few successful cases of incomes policy in the world as a response to economic crisis.[14] Teichman (1995) has convincingly shown that the implementation of economic orthodoxy required SOE unions to accept painful measures such as layoffs and decreases in traditionally generous benefits. Some unions resisted these changes and were faced with the repressive response that the PRI reserves for the recalcitrant: military occupation of SOE facilities, forced removal of union leadership from union and SOE positions, and closure of SOEs with the attendant liquidation of their unions. The most famous and exemplary case was the use of military means in 1989 to remove and indict the president of the oil workers' union, probably the most powerful union in the country and in the most important SOE, Pemex (ibid.: 116–17; 121–7). With the accession to power of a government lacking corporate or ideological affinities with the union movement, the latter has even fewer reasons to avoid confrontation with the government over issues such as privatization and deregulation.

### Restructuring the Mexican ESI: What Can We Expect?

The review of the explanatory variables for Mexico suggests that the main axes on which restructuring outcomes will turn are ideology and especially distributional conflict. At present, Mexico's courts are, in all likelihood, more independent than those of Argentina, which accomplished a highly orthodox reform of the ESI. In fact, a remarkable display of judicial independence followed from the recent ESI restructuring attempts undertaken by the Fox administration. When congressional leaders challenged the constitutionality of the ESI reform decrees before the Supreme Court, the Court not only agreed that the degrees were unconstitutional, but went so far as to question the constitutionality of the 1992 reforms that allowed private participation through BOT projects

(Silver 2002b). Equally important, Mexico has already established a regulatory agency with mechanisms to protect its independence and which is already demonstrating considerable technical capacity. In addition to the CRE, the creation of the independent Federal Competition Commission (Comisión Federal de Competencia, CFC) under antitrust legislation passed in 1992 has already been mentioned, offering participants in the ESI further separation of political considerations from decisions affecting the ESI.[15] As a result, even with the possibility that ESI restructuring may force the renegotiation of long-term BOT contracts, the auctions of these contracts since the announcement of the reform initiative have continued to attract bidders (Power Finance & Risk 2001).

On the ideological side, the dominance of economic policymaking by US-trained economists and business interests would indicate that privatization and deregulation have excellent prospects, but there are important caveats to this view. As already shown, populist and state-centric ideology is still alive and well in the left-oriented opposition parties, not only in the PRD but in the PRI itself now more than in the recent past, as the main opposition party to a conservative or center-right government. Proponents of orthodoxy face both electoral and internal threats in trying to apply their ideas to the ESI. Reinforcing the electoral threat, public opinion appears to be highly skeptical, if not downright hostile, to ESI restructuring initiatives. Poll data show a marked deterioration of support for privatization between 1998 and 2002 (*The Economist*, 2002). Whereas a majority of respondents regarded privatization as beneficial in 1998, in 2001 and 2002 a large majority took a negative view. A public opinion poll taken shortly after the announcement of the original ESI restructuring plan under the previous administration, showed that 55 percent of respondents favored keeping the ESI in the public sector (Friedland 1999a). A petition against the restructuring plan was reported to have received 2.4 million signatures in a matter of weeks (Friedland 1999b). The public does not see an urgent need for restructuring because distribution consumers currently get cheap power at acceptable levels of quality, while there is a widespread perception that privatization in other infrastructure sectors has resulted in price increases without worthwhile quality improvements.[16] The PRI deputies that would be needed to pass a pro-restructuring constitutional amendment have clearly realized the electoral appeal of opposing ESI privatization, and thus regaining the party's mantle of defender of the Revolution's achievements.

The benefits offered to the public under the current system are mainly a distributional issue and thus are discussed below. The temporal sequence of privatizations, however, has had an impact on voter perceptions about the practical problems of privatization and deregulation, and thus belongs appropriately in the discussion of ideology. In this sense, the way privatization has unfolded in Mexico fundamentally differentiates the country from the previously analyzed cases, where restructuring has occurred in parallel across a variety of sectors such as telecoms, natural gas, or pensions. In Mexico, privatization and deregulation have been taking place for more than a decade now,[17] with negative repercussions and high concentrations of ownership in some very visible cases (Teichman 1995: 152–6):

> [T]he massive privatization program of the Salinas government is perceived as a failure, both from a financial and a microeconomic perspective. The cumulative 8 percent of GDP earned in privatization revenues is dwarfed by the 21 percent of GDP cost of the banking sector alone. With the exception of telephones, most of the industries privatized ... later required substantial cash injections from the government and failed to deliver better service. (Standard & Poor's 1999).

And even TELMEX was sold as a monopoly without a proper regulatory framework and to an inexperienced Mexican investor group, thereby negating the benefits of competition to telephone users. Quality levels have substantially increased, but so have basic service rates (Friedland 1999a).

On the distributional side, the most formidable problems faced by the government are, on one hand, the radical opposition to restructuring by one of the most militant unions in the country, the Mexican Electricians' Union (Sindicato Mexicano de Electricistas, SME), and on the other, the importance of electricity within the overall architecture of clientelism in the PRI machine. The SME, the union of the LFC workers, is one of the oldest in Mexico and remarkably has preserved its independence from the PRI and *charrismo*. To avoid amalgamation with the CFE workers' union (the Sindicato Unificado de Trabajadores Electricistas de la República Mexicana, SUTERM), which was from its inception a thoroughly *charrista* union (Teichman 1995: 54), the SME managed to keep LFC as a separate company from the CFE since the former's nationalization in 1960.[18]

The SME has assumed a position of fierce opposition to the government's ESI restructuring proposal, in contrast to SUTERM which, in keeping with its tradition of subservience, was willing to agree on an acceptable package before the plan was unveiled – in fact, it was SUTERM's president who announced the plan. In taking its current position, the SME appears to differ from its previous strategy of 'negotiating modernization, rather than opposing it outright' and its past support for Salinas (ibid.: 120), perhaps as a result of increasing rank-and-file resistance to 'deteriorating working conditions, measures to increase productivity, and layoffs' (ibid.: 169). SME members certainly have a lot at stake with the potential privatization of LFC, particularly in employment benefits such as generous overtime pay and allowances for travel and meals within LFC's service territory, and in massive overemployment, including the existence of stable keepers in a company that 'hasn't used a dray horse in decades' (Friedland 1999b: A1). While the CFE has 236 customers per employee, LFC has 143, although this comparison is distorted by the fact that LFC is mainly a distribution company, and distribution is the most labor-intensive part of the ESI. Yet in dealing with the SME, repressive action is probably not a viable alternative as it had been in the Salinas government with the Pemex union. Public anger with the bank privatization fiasco and other botched privatizations means that repression of the SME could generate a backlash against the government.

The patronage benefits of public ownership of the ESI are substantial. The CFE employs around 70,000 workers throughout the country, with another 35,000 at LFC. The greatest overemployment, by international standards, is concentrated in distribution, where employees come into closest contact with the public. The high level of subsidies in electricity rates, particularly to residential and farming customers, has already been noted. In the Federal District, many government entities and as many as 625,000 customers apparently do not pay their electricity bills without adverse consequences (Friedland 1999b). Unlike other countries, however, high subsidies are not accompanied in Mexico by a breakdown in the quality of service, at least to date, so subsidies are very likely to yield net electoral benefits to the government. Electricity reaches about 95 percent of the population of Mexico – amounting in 1998 to about 22 million users. The levels of availability and efficiency of generation plants are well within the typical levels in economically advanced countries. Total energy losses hover around 11 percent of total energy generated, only slightly above the level in advanced countries and far below the levels in excess of 20 percent encountered in Argentina and other countries prior to restructuring. Management reforms undertaken during the 1990s in the CFE reduced the average wait for new connections from 13 days in 1991 to 1.7 days in 1997, and the total time of service interruptions experienced by the average user in a year from 405 minutes to 178 minutes during the same period[19] (Rodríguez Padilla 1999; Téllez Kuenzler 1999).

Another, albeit less prominent, question concerning the effect of distributional conflict on ESI restructuring is the pressure on the government by large domestic business groups to award ownership of the privatized activities or assets to these groups rather than to foreign firms or smaller Mexican and foreign investors. As already mentioned, past privatizations led to a significant concentration of ownership in a few large groups, which negated the benefits of competition to consumers. Teichman

(1995: 188) has documented the very close links between the major Mexican business associations, which are dominated by large domestic groups, and the PRI through campaign contributions and personal contact. Two factors, however, may mitigate this type of pressure. First, the very high capital intensity of the ESI may limit the purchasing power of even large Mexican groups; and second, the perils of ownership concentration as dramatically revealed in the current banking crisis may be becoming apparent to the government, and now foreign banks are being allowed to buy some of the failed banks. In this regard, it is instructive that all BOT contracts to date have been awarded to foreign groups.[20]

## Conclusion

Successive Mexican governments of different party backgrounds have proposed reforms of the Mexican ESI that would bring competition and more private ownership into the industry. The analysis of the hypothesized explanatory variables for the outcomes of ESI restructuring would indicate that there are good possibilities for implementation of the proposed restructuring blueprint. Mexico has reasonably independent courts, relative to earlier Latin American reformers, and a very strong bent towards orthodox economic policy at top executive levels in the government. On the other hand, reform faces strong opposition by a powerful union, the SME, and by a hard core of economic populists in the PRI, the party whose votes would be needed for a constitutional amendment, backed by substantial voter opposition to privatization. The combination of these factors has so far halted ESI restructuring beyond the BOT and regulatory measures taken by previous administrations. Whether any further progress towards privatization and deregulation of the Mexican ESI occurs will thus depend fundamentally on:

- the ability of proponents of orthodoxy to convince voters that it is the only viable alternative, leading to the electoral victory of pro-reform deputies in the next legislative elections; or,
- by outright cooptation of enough deputies from opposing parties to muster the required congressional votes for a constitutional amendment; or,
- through a successful negotiation with the SME of a compensation package generous enough to make the union accept meaningful restructuring measures.

## REFORMS IN OTHER SECTORS

The applicability of the model of institutional change presented in this book extends beyond the ESI. The logic of the model is equally appropriate for any institutional transformation processes that involve a loss of control by the government over policy domains providing important political benefits. Policy domains of this nature comprise not just the ESI, but other infrastructure industries as well, such as water and sanitation, transport, and telecommunications; even judicial autonomy may be subject to a similar calculus. In many countries, the executive power exerts de facto control over the courts. This gives the government greater freedom of action and is thus politically very valuable. As a result, the outcome of reforms intended to increase judicial independence may also depend on ideology, distributional conflict, and the existence of political constraints that make policy reversals less likely.

This suggests that other infrastructure industries in the four countries studied above should have been subject to similar reforms, and have experienced similar outcomes. To some extent, the differences in outcomes observed across industries have to do with the nature and extent of technological change in each industry. Over the last decade, technological change has eroded natural monopoly to the greatest extent in electricity generation and in telecommunications. Combined-cycle technology broke a century-old trend towards economies of scale in power generation. Microwave and cellular technologies have drastically reduced the need for fixed-line telephone networks. By contrast, no such breakthroughs have occurred in transport or in water and sanitation. Hence, reforms in infrastructure sectors the world over have been most common in electricity supply and in telecommunications.

Yet even with these limitations, the ESI reform initiatives and outcomes in Argentina, Bolivia, Brazil, and Chile have been, as a rule, paralleled by those undertaken in other infrastructure sectors. [21] Thus, the Chilean government privatized the telephone company industry around the same time as the ESI, but as in the ESI, it failed to introduce competition until after the transition to democracy. [22] Instead, two minimally regulated private monopolies were created, one in long distance (Entel) and one in fixed lines (CTC). Competition (through entry of cellular and other long-distance operators) did not come until the advent of democracy in 1990 brought a new government critical of private monopolies (Murillo 2001).

In contrast, Argentina's radical reform program under Cavallo's tenure as minister of economic affairs was not limited to electricity, but included hydrocarbons (oil and natural gas), water and sanitation, roads and railroads, and the mail, whereas the pre-Cavallo privatization of telecoms was plagued by regulatory instability and limited competition among the private operators.[23] Wherever it was feasible, Cavallo's reforms introduced competition. Thus, the gas sector was split both vertically and horizontally to maximize competition;[24] multiple franchises were created for harbors, railroads, the Buenos Aires subway, and toll expressways. Free entry into postal services was allowed upon privatization of the mail.

In Bolivia, capitalization involved not only the ESI but also many other government-owned assets: oil and gas, telecoms, railroads, and the national airline. Finally, the record of reform in Brazil has been as uneven outside the ESI as in this sector. The federal government privatized and introduced substantial competition in the telecoms sector alone. The various regional rail networks were privatized (there is no national rail network in Brazil). By contrast, very limited change took place in hydrocarbons (oil and natural gas), which continue to be under the control of the public monopoly Petrobrás through its lock on the production and importation of natural gas.[25] And the privatization of water companies stalled after the first experience in Rio de Janeiro state. It is clear that the commitment to private ownership has been weaker in Brazil than in Chile or Argentina, telecoms being the sole (although important) exception.[26]

## LIMITATIONS

The perspective followed in this book is certainly limited in important ways that should be borne in mind. At a general level, the analysis is limited to how new institutions are created, not to the actual impact of these institutions on economic performance, which is a question that in the area of public versus private ownership has already received enormous attention, and which in any case would excessively extend the scope of the research. Second, the forces identified and evaluated here may be of greater applicability in developing countries than in developed ones, where judicial independence is generally high, ideological consensus more prevalent, and the distribution of resources more egalitarian. Not surprisingly, institutional stability appears, at least to the casual observer, to be greater in developed countries than in developing nations. Third, although the analysis takes historical factors very much into account, it does not delve into the complex issue of the interaction between past and present. Institutional change is obviously not a one-way process, since institutions influence the distribution of resources, the ideological map of policymakers, and the independence of the judicial system. But analytical tractability requires the imposition of limits on the scope of research questions, and the low frequency of major institutional transformations, such as the one now being experienced by the ESI on a worldwide scale, justifies treating ESI institutions as dependent variables.

Although the theoretical model demonstrates the political sustainability of public enterprise, it might be of interest to consider not only the determinants of the output of services (represented by $Q$, which also acts as a proxy for the three institutional arrangements available), but also of the cost of public funds ($\sigma$) and the tax shares ($k$). In this regard, the financially deficitary nature of public enterprise as modeled may, over time, result in increasing public indebtedness or higher tax burdens, altering the cost of public funds. In turn, this suggests that over a longer time span than that considered in the model, public enterprise may be a politically unstable arrangement, leading to cycles in institutional organization of infrastructure sectors. In Latin America, for instance, many infrastructure supply firms (in energy, transport, telecoms, and other sectors) were nationalized in the post-Second World War era for ideological and patronage reasons as predicted by the model (Gómez-Ibáñez 1999); however, the growing deficits and debts of many public enterprises led to a wave of privatization and, in some cases, deregulation during the 1990s, which now appears to be coming to an end.

The theoretical model glosses over agency problems in the consideration of various institutional arrangements. This contrasts with much of the debate on public versus private ownership, in which the analysis of managerial incentives under different ownership types is the focus of the analysis. For instance, if agency problems were more severe for public enterprise than for either private monopoly or competition, thereby increasing the cost of public enterprise, we could expect, other things being equal, that public enterprise would be less likely to be chosen than in the absence of agency problems. On the other hand, the political economy considerations that the model has attempted to capture should not be ignored. If there is a class of professional managers whose utility is higher under public enterprise because they can 'shirk' more in that setting, then we can expect this class to add to the pressure in favor of public enterprise. In former socialist economies, where this professional group played a highly influential role, these considerations may play no small role in explaining the slow pace of economic and institutional transformation. In many developing countries in Africa and Asia, this factor should not be discounted either. Thus viewed as another type of 'supplier rents' under public enterprise, managerial interests can be readily subsumed in the model along with other supplier interests, so the model accounts at least partially (although not explicitly) for the role of agency problems in institutional change.

The other side of the issue of agency in the theoretical model is the existence of uncertainty or informational limitations among voters regarding the relationship between policy choices and consumption outcomes, which can complicate the electoral calculus of voters as principals and politicians as agents. As argued above, the modeling of institutional constraints presented in Chapter 2 can also be interpreted in terms of uncertainty or informational deficiencies among voters.

With regard to the statistical tests, an important refinement would involve improving the quality of the dependent variable data. Self-coding of narrative accounts is certainly not the most desirable or objective method for obtaining dependent variable data. In the interest of minimizing bias, it would be much better to rely on a data set open to review by other researchers and to improvement on the basis of such feedback. The ESMAP reform dataset achieves this objective, providing additional support for the hypotheses being tested, but it only covers developing countries. Another possibility is to develop other measures of competition and property rights institutions that are easier to compile and less subject to coding bias. For instance, I created the variable ISOGOV after the rest of the data set, when I realized that the governance of ISOs also indicated ownership choices emanating from the political system. A third possible improvement of the dependent variable data set is to add more data points, since testing is substantially constrained by the relatively small number of data points available at present. This possibility, however, is clearly limited by the number of political jurisdictions undertaking reform of the ESI. In some cases, such as the US or the UK, disaggregation into states and 'kingdoms', respectively, is hampered by the lack of explanatory variable data at the subnational level.

## IDEAS AND RENT-SEEKING IN MICROECONOMIC REFORMS

The book emphasizes the power of ideas, which it finds to be a powerful determinant of outcomes. That this is the case in developing countries with weakly institutionalized party structures may seem counterintuitive, but in fact in these situations policymakers may face fewer pressures to bow to party consensus and fewer institutional limitations, such as constitutional doctrine and precedent. Additionally, ideology may be particularly important as a road map in instances of major institutional changes, when prior circumstances may offer little guidance. Put in a slightly different way, ideological concepts can act as focal points for institutional change, inducing actors to narrow the range of choices under consideration and making bargaining over institutional change easier.

Another powerful source of institutional structures is found in social conflicts over the distribution of resources, because institutions can powerfully limit the possibilities for resource redistribution once they have acquired enough of a momentum of their own to shape perceptions and preferences. While inequality in the distribution of political and economic power is an integral part of structuralist or dependence theories, it is only in recent years that it has begun to figure in positive political economy models, where it has generally been found to play an important role in many processes such as economic growth. In this regard, a contribution of the book lies in examining the broad variety of channels through which distributional pressures affect market institutions, applying the insights of sophisticated analyses such as those of Bates (1981), Ames (1987) or Geddes (1994). As this literature shows, the scramble for public resources can occur under the cooperative solution of an exchange for political support, or under the noncooperative solution of political competition with the incumbents in the government.

The answers suggested above can take us one step beyond the 'crisis' literature that has analyzed mainly macroeconomic reforms, to look at the determinants of longer-term 'structural' reforms. This explains why the crisis framework has been largely left aside for the issues addressed here. While crises may convince politicians of the need to undertake reform (and even then, as Dani Rodrik (1993) has pointed out, we know little about what degree of crisis is needed to accomplish it), the final outcome of the reform process may be determined by other factors: for instance, a shortage of capital may not necessarily lead to straight privatization but to capitalization or the award of concessions to private operators without permanent property rights.

## NOTES

1. A multi-industry study of deregulation in the US (Kearney and Merrill 1998) also found strong support for the role of ideology.
2. The evidence reviewed by Messick (1999) shows that a weak judiciary has no adverse economic impact.
3. 'Our most startling conclusion in this regard is that rather large differences among the countries in the amount of political insulation enjoyed by presidents resulted in fairly small differences in economic reform outcomes' (Armijo and Faucher 2002: 19).
4. Under BOT contracts, a private developer builds the facility, operates it under a sales contract for a pre-specified number of years, and then transfers ownership to the buyer, generally the public sector.
5. The natural gas industry, dominated by Pemex Gas y Petroquímica Básica (the petrochemicals and gas production and transport arm of the public hydrocarbons monopoly), was opened to foreign and private investment in 1992.

6. Of course, the actual degree of competition would depend on the degree to which generation assets are sold in a highly concentrated fashion, as in Chile, or in a very fragmented way, as in Argentina.
7. Large users typically consume a constant amount of electricity for most hours of the year. If we assume, for instance, a uniform pattern for the entire year except for 10 percent of the hours (when due to maintenance, holidays or other reasons there is no consumption at all), the 5 GWh minimum is equivalent to 634 kW.
8. The public entities are allowed to purchase electricity from private generators if it results in cost reductions for regulated users. Residential users will continue to be supplied exclusively by the public entities under regulated rates and a public service regime (obligation to serve). Current BOT contracts will continue to be honored by the CFE. I am grateful to Prof. Juan Rosellón of the Centro de Investigación y Docencia Económicas in Mexico City for the full text of the government's proposal.
9. The most recent documented instance of this phenomenon occurred under the 'National Solidarity Program' (Programa Nacional de Solidaridad, PRONASOL), created and implemented by Carlos Salinas de Gortari as President of Mexico.
10. This does not mean that US-trained economists no longer play a significant role in Chile – they do – but that since the advent of democracy they have had to share power with the professional politicians coming from the Christian Democrat and Socialist organizations.
11. Union issues are discussed in regard to distributional conflict.
12. '[T]he consensus is that the state in no way controls the private sector to the extent it controls labor, peasants, and other popular groups' (Teichman 1995: 21).
13. In the post-war era, a state gubernatorial election was won by a non-PRI candidate only in 1989, when the PAN captured Baja California Norte (Teichman 1995: 180).
14. Incomes policy seeks to reduce inflation and macroeconomic imbalances by having business, labor and the government agree, respectively, on reduced price increases, salary adjustments, and expenditure levels. In Mexico, the debt crisis that began in 1982 led eventually to the brokering of a tri-partite pact to facilitate macroeconomic adjustment; the pact held and produced the desired result of restoring macroeconomic balance to the Mexican economy.
15. A point about causality is necessary here. The establishment of the CRE and the CFC are *outcomes* to be explained by the framework proposed in this book. At the same time, these commissions were created before ESI restructuring and with regard, respectively, to other sectors (natural gas) or more general concerns (competition in the economy as a whole). In this sense, they are also part of the *explanation*, because they constitute a precedent of the political will to delegate important aspects of policy to independent entities, as proposed by the hypothesis about judicial independence.
16. A recent government announcement to cut residential electricity rate subsidies was quickly withdrawn after street protests and calls from the PRI for a campaign of civil disobedience (Silver, 2002a).
17. According to Teichman (1995: 131), the first wave of privatizations took place in 1983–84. The first privatization of utilities took place in 1990 with the sale of TELMEX, the telecoms monopoly.
18. By contrast, the union that represented the utilities nationalized from American and Foreign Power also in 1960, was forcibly incorporated into SUTERM and its attempts at preserving its independence ruthlessly crushed (Teichman 1995: 60-61).
19. A similar reform attempt at LFC, however, did not result in similar service quality levels, which remained substantially above the CFE's.
20. Of course, from a distributional perspective, business influence on ESI restructuring could also come from the desire to obtain price subsidies – in fact, industry associations representing small and medium-sized businesses gave vocal support to ESI nationalization during the 1950s in the belief it would make power cheaper (Wionczek 1964). But there is no evidence that business groups believe any longer in this possibility; in practice, as of 1995 there was no subsidy element in electricity rates for non-industrial business customers.

21. In a study of the ESI and the telecoms industry in Argentina, Chile and Mexico, Murillo (2001) finds evidence of the role of ideology ('partisanship') in the outcomes of each restructuring process.
22. Electricity and telecoms were the main targets of privatization under the Pinochet regime. As already noted, the copper industry remained in public hands; there was no natural gas until the construction of trans-Andean pipelines during the late 1990s, and there was no significant rail network. Some water distribution utilities did undergo privatization, however, even though competition is not feasible in this sector.
23. Competition was limited to the creation of two vertically-integrated monopoly franchises (for the northern and southern halves of the country, respectively) to facilitate 'benchmark regulation' (regulation by comparison with each other). Both franchisees were given a seven-year period of protection from new entry into their franchise territories.
24. The gas operations of the former gas and oil monopoly Yacimientos Petrolíferos Fiscales (State Oil Fields, YPF) were split into exploration and production (fully deregulated), long-distance transport (regulated), and distribution (regulated). Several regional franchises were created for the regulated segments to make benchmark regulation, direct competition not being feasible due to natural monopoly conditions in these activities.
25. Although the Bolivia–Brazil gas pipeline was developed by private initiative, and serves the privatized gas distribution company of São Paulo, most of the gas coming from Bolivia is imported by Petrobrás under long-term contracts.
26. The analysis of such differences across sectors must remain as a topic for future research since it exceeds the scope of this book.

Appendix 1    Major variables used in the regression tests and correlation coefficients for dependent and explanatory variables

## Table A1.1 Summary of major variables used in the analysis

### (a) Dependent variables

| Variable | Obs | Mean | Std. Dev. | Min. | Max. | Description | Year | Source |
|---|---|---|---|---|---|---|---|---|
| *Ownership Indicators* | | | | | | | | |
| GENPROP | 87 | 1.138 | 0.574 | 0 | 2 | generation asset ownership | 1990s | IPPQ |
| NUCPROP | 24 | 1.583 | 0.654 | 0 | 2 | nuclear asset ownership | 1990s | IPPQ |
| TRANSPRP | 86 | 1.663 | 0.625 | 0 | 2 | transmission asset ownership | 1990s | IPPQ |
| DISTPROP | 87 | 1.310 | 0.752 | 0 | 2 | distribution asset ownership | 1990s | IPPQ |
| PROPT | 78 | 0.423 | 0.497 | 0 | 1 | full ownership vs concession | 1990s | IPPQ |
| ESOP | 79 | 0.190 | 0.395 | 0 | 1 | employee stock option distributions | 1990s | IPPQ |
| FDI | 85 | 0.224 | 0.419 | 0 | 1 | allowance of foreign ownership | 1990s | IPPQ |
| INDEP | 77 | 0.688 | 0.466 | 0 | 1 | independence of regulator | 1990s | IPPQ |
| JUDREC | 32 | 0.094 | 0.296 | 0 | 1 | recourse to the courts | 1990s | IPPQ |
| ISOGOV | 79 | 2.709 | 0.770 | 0 | 3 | system governance | 1990s | IPPQ |
| *Competition Indicators* | | | | | | | | |
| COMPG | 84 | 0.583 | 0.496 | 0 | 1 | competition in generation | 1990s | IPPQ |
| COMPR | 76 | 0.816 | 0.390 | 0 | 1 | competition in retailing | 1990s | IPPQ |
| VERT | 86 | 0.709 | 0.457 | 0 | 1 | vertical integration | 1990s | IPPQ |
| OPENL | 78 | 0.936 | 0.247 | 0 | 1 | limitations on market access | 1990s | IPPQ |
| YARDSTK | 60 | 0.867 | 0.343 | 0 | 1 | use of yardstick regulation | 1990s | IPPQ |
| COMPST | 81 | 0.704 | 0.459 | 0 | 1 | competitive market structure | 1990s | IPPQ |
| *Summary Variables* | | | | | | | | |
| LPSCORE | 87 | 0.389 | 1.074 | -2.197 | 2.442 | ownership score | see components | |
| LCSCORE | 87 | 3.215 | 3.315 | -1.586 | 6.907 | competition score | see components | |
| LREFORM | 59 | -0.054 | 4.165 | -6.907 | 6.907 | ESI reform score | 1990s | ESMAP |

*(b) Explanatory variables*

| Variable | Obs | Mean | Std. Dev. | Min. | Max. | Description | Year | Source |
|---|---|---|---|---|---|---|---|---|
| *Judicial Independence Measures* | | | | | | | | |
| JUDFAC | 81 | 0.000 | 0.986 | -1.611 | 1.756 | judicial independence factor | see components | |
| RCTTEN | 44 | 0.617 | 0.262 | 0.000 | 1.000 | tenure of supreme court justices | 1940s-90s | Henisz |
| *Ideology Measures* | | | | | | | | |
| IDFACEC1 | 83 | 0.000 | 0.858 | -2.083 | 2.927 | economic ideology factor 1 | see components | |
| IDFACEC2 | 84 | 0.000 | 0.839 | -2.074 | 2.730 | economic ideology factor 2 | see components | |
| IDFACSO | 60 | 0.000 | 0.879 | -2.202 | 1.371 | social ideology factor | see components | |
| IDCL | 48 | 0.333 | 0.476 | 0.000 | 1.000 | center-left government indicator | 1990s | various |
| *Distributional Conflict Measures* | | | | | | | | |
| DISTFAC1 | 59 | 0.000 | 0.811 | -0.889 | 2.376 | distributional conflict indicator 1 | see components | |
| DISTFAC2 | 70 | 0.000 | 0.819 | -0.928 | 2.285 | distributional conflict indicator 2 | see components | |
| DISTFAC3 | 80 | 0.000 | 0.686 | -0.955 | 2.227 | distributional conflict indicator 3 | see components | |
| RETHNOL | 83 | 0.342 | 0.321 | 0.000 | 0.041 | ethno-linguistic fractionalization | 1990s | LP |
| DEFPCY | 79 | -0.042 | 0.040 | -0.141 | 0.041 | government budget deficit, % GDP | 1970-91 | IBRD |
| RSUBSY | 75 | 0.309 | 0.273 | 0.000 | 1.000 | transfers and subsidies as % GDP | 1985 | IMF/EFW |
| SOET8590 | 32 | -0.322 | 2.947 | -8.600 | 7.600 | transfers to SOEs, % GDP | 1985-90 | IMF |
| SOED7075 | 30 | 0.687 | 0.845 | -0.130 | 4.670 | transfers to SOEs, % deficit | 1970-75 | IMF |
| SOEB7075 | 33 | -2.255 | 1.598 | -5.400 | 2.200 | SOE balances, % GDP | 1970-75 | IMF |
| SOEB8590 | 32 | -0.056 | 3.075 | -7.400 | 8.700 | SOE balances, % GDP | 1985-90 | IMF |
| *Interactive Terms* | | | | | | | | |
| DISTDEM | 80 | -0.091 | 0.280 | -0.584 | 0.748 | distributional conflict and democracy | 1946-94 | PIII/other |
| JUDDEM | 79 | -0.298 | 0.681 | -1.611 | 0.573 | judicial independence and democracy) | 1946-94 | PIII/other |
| *Control Variables* | | | | | | | | |
| INSTAB | 56 | 0.000 | 0.975 | -1.158 | 3.010 | political instability factor | 1946-94 | PIII/other |
| PARL | 83 | 1.289 | 1.205 | 0.000 | 3.000 | parliamentary control over gov't | 1946-86 | PII |
| EXRESTR | 88 | 4.547 | 2.054 | 1.156 | 7.000 | restraints on chief exec | 1946-94 | PIII |
| FORKPCI | 83 | 0.120 | 0.134 | -0.290 | 0.485 | foreign investment as % total | 1970-91 | IBRD |
| LYC85 | 81 | 7.505 | 1.300 | 5.011 | 9.733 | log of real per cap income | 1985 | IBRD |
| LYC94PP | 88 | 8.595 | 1.004 | 6.430 | 10.487 | log of real per cap income, PPP | 1994 | WDI |

## (c) Variables included in causal factors

| Variable | Obs | Mean | Std. Dev. | Min. | Max. | Description | Year | Source |
|---|---|---|---|---|---|---|---|---|
| *Judicial Independence Indicators* | | | | | | | | |
| PROPRTS | 88 | 2.432 | 1.048 | 1.0 | 5.0 | respect for property rights | 1998 | IEF |
| REPUD | 86 | 6.804 | 1.853 | 3.6 | 10.0 | contract repudiation | 1982-95 | IRIS |
| LORDER | 86 | 3.683 | 1.564 | 1.1 | 6.0 | level of law and order | 1982-95 | IRIS |
| CORRUPT | 86 | 3.759 | 1.370 | 0.6 | 6.0 | degree of corruption | 1982-95 | IRIS |
| BURQUAL | 86 | 3.621 | 1.555 | 1.1 | 6.0 | civil service quality | 1982-95 | IRIS |
| CIVILFR | 90 | 3.067 | 1.564 | 1.0 | 7.0 | respect for civil liberties | 1990 | Gastil |
| POLRTS | 90 | 3.056 | 1.939 | 1.0 | 7.0 | respect for political rights | 1990 | Gastil |
| LEGACC | 88 | 4.318 | 3.277 | 1.0 | 10.0 | access to legal redress | 1995 | EFW |
| EXTFR | 88 | 2.477 | 0.478 | 1.5 | 3.0 | formality of exec power transfer | 1946-94 | PII |
| JUDIND | 81 | 1.938 | 1.088 | 0.0 | 3.0 | judicial independence | 1986 | Sull |
| *Ideology Indicators* | | | | | | | | |
| SCOPE | 84 | 5.123 | 1.796 | 1.0 | 8.34 | scope of gov't | 1946-86 | PII |
| SOE75 | 82 | 4.000 | 2.455 | 0.0 | 10.0 | importance of SOEs, 1975 | 1975 | EFW |
| COMPFR | 86 | 6.948 | 2.023 | 2.0 | 10.0 | freedom for competition | 1995 | EFW |
| PRCONT | 88 | 2.432 | 0.691 | 1.0 | 4.0 | importance of price controls | 1998 | IEF |
| INTERV | 88 | 2.568 | 0.894 | 1.0 | 5.0 | gov't interventionism | 1998 | IEF |
| FDIFREE | 88 | 2.375 | 0.666 | 1.0 | 4.0 | foreign investment freedom | 1998 | IEF |
| MFILLIT | 87 | 11.609 | 11.857 | -8.0 | 38.0 | male-female illiteracy gap | 1970 | WDI |
| BIRTHC | 84 | 49.231 | 25.130 | 0.0 | 84.0 | married women's contraceptive use | 1990 | Sull |
| ABORTP | 78 | 1.231 | 1.031 | 0.0 | 3.0 | abortion policy | 1981 | Sull |
| DIVR | 71 | 1.492 | 1.295 | 0.0 | 5.6 | divorce rate | 1980-88 | Econ |
| PROTAR | 84 | 6.538 | 6.297 | 0.1 | 38.4 | % protected national land | 1990 | Sull |
| ENVTR | 83 | 6.337 | 2.451 | 1.0 | 11.0 | no. ratified environmental treaties | 1990 | Sull |
| DEATHP | 85 | 1.435 | 1.401 | 0.0 | 3.0 | policy on death penalty | 1980-90 | Sull |
| IDCL | 48 | 0.333 | 0.476 | 0.0 | 1.0 | center-left government indicator | 1990s | various |
| *Distributional Conflict Indicators* | | | | | | | | |
| FSCH7591 | 85 | 96.453 | 16.628 | 25.3 | 123.0 | female primary school enrollment | 1975-91 | IBRD |
| CENTR | 88 | 1.357 | 0.686 | 1.0 | 3.0 | degree of centralization | 1946-94 | PII |
| ETHNOL | 83 | 0.304 | 0.286 | 0.0 | 0.9 | ethno-linguistic fractionalization | 1990s | LP |
| PARTIES | 89 | 18.281 | 12.140 | 1.0 | 71.0 | no. of major political parties | 1996 | PSW |
| STRKAVG | 72 | 316.642 | 499.878 | 0.0 | 1890.0 | no. of strikes and lockouts | 1988-91 | YLS |
| SEPAR | 75 | 3.350 | 10.139 | 0.0 | 45.0 | % pop in separatist areas | 1975 | T&J |
| DEFPCY | 79 | -0.042 | 0.040 | -0.1 | 0.0 | government deficit as % GDP | 1970-91 | IBRD |

*Key to sources (full references in Bibliography):*

| | |
|---|---|
| Econ | The Economist Books Ltd (1990). |
| *EFW* | *Economic Freedom in the World* (Gwartney 1997). |
| ESMAP | Energy Sector Management Assistance Program (1999). |
| Gastil | *Freedom in the World* (Freedom House, various years). |
| Henisz | Henisz (2000). |
| IBRD | World Tables of Social and Economic Indicators (World Bank 1993c). |
| *IEF* | *Index of Economic Freedom* (Johnson et al. 1998). |
| *IPPQ* | *International Private Power Quarterly* (1998). |
| IRIS | Institute for Reform and the Informal Sector (n.d.). |
| IMF | International Monetary Fund (Floyd et al. 1984). |
| LP | La Porta et al. (1998). |
| PII | Polity II data set (Gurr 1989/1990). |
| PIII | Polity III dataset (Jaggers and Gurr 1995/1996). |
| *PSW* | *Political Systems of the World* (Derbyshire and Derbyshire 1996). |
| Sull | Sullivan (1991). |
| T&J | Taylor and Jodice (1982/1983). |
| *WDI* | *World Development Indicators* (World Bank 1998). |
| *YLS* | *Yearbook of Labour Statistics* (ILO various years). |

*Table A1.2  Explanatory variable correlation matrix*

| | JUDFAC | IDFACEC1 | IDFACEC2 | IDFACSO | IDCL | DISTFAC1 | DISTFAC2 | DISTFAC3 | RETHNOL | DEFPCY |
|---|---|---|---|---|---|---|---|---|---|---|
| JUDFAC | 1 | | | | | | | | | |
| pr = 0 | | | | | | | | | | |
| N | 81 | | | | | | | | | |
| IDFACEC1 | 0.3663 | 1 | | | | | | | | |
| pr = 0 | 0% | | | | | | | | | |
| N | 79 | 83 | | | | | | | | |
| IDFACEC2 | 0.4938 | 0.9361 | 1 | | | | | | | |
| pr = 0 | 0% | 0% | | | | | | | | |
| N | 80 | 83 | 84 | | | | | | | |
| IDFACSO | -0.8317 | -0.0964 | -0.3134 | 1 | | | | | | |
| pr = 0 | 0% | 46% | 1% | | | | | | | |
| N | 59 | 60 | 60 | 60 | | | | | | |
| IDCL | -0.1406 | 0.0813 | -0.0071 | 0.2365 | 1 | | | | | |
| pr = 0 | 34% | 58% | 96% | 14% | | | | | | |
| N | 48 | 48 | 48 | 41 | 48 | | | | | |
| DISTFAC1 | 0.3571 | 0.1925 | 0.3237 | -0.2842 | -0.0722 | 1 | | | | |
| pr = 0 | 1% | 15% | 1% | 6% | 66% | | | | | |
| N | 59 | 58 | 58 | 46 | 39 | 59 | | | | |
| DISTFAC2 | 0.4164 | 0.2108 | 0.3481 | -0.3853 | -0.1088 | 0.996 | 1 | | | |
| pr = 0 | 0% | 8% | 0% | 0% | 49% | 0% | | | | |
| N | 69 | 69 | 69 | 53 | 42 | 59 | 70 | | | |
| DISTFAC3 | 0.4164 | 0.1911 | 0.3494 | -0.5158 | -0.0535 | 0.8156 | 0.8773 | 1 | | |
| pr = 0 | 0% | 10% | 0% | 0% | 73% | 0% | 0% | | | |
| N | 74 | 77 | 77 | 56 | 44 | 59 | 70 | 80 | | |
| RETHNOL | 0.4092 | 0.135 | 0.2605 | -0.4824 | -0.1238 | 0.8723 | 0.9012 | 0.8636 | 1 | |
| pr = 0 | 0% | 24% | 2% | 0% | 42% | 0% | 0% | 0% | | |
| N | 77 | 79 | 80 | 56 | 45 | 59 | 70 | 80 | 83 | |
| DEFPCY | -0.1698 | -0.3205 | -0.2638 | 0.2 | -0.2872 | -0.1205 | -0.1367 | -0.0927 | -0.089 | 1 |
| pr = 0 | 15% | 0% | 0% | 14% | 6% | 37% | 26% | 42% | 44% | |
| N | 73 | 76 | 76 | 55 | 43 | 58 | 69 | 77 | 78 | 79 |

| | | | | | | | | | | |
|---|---|---|---|---|---|---|---|---|---|---|
| SOED7075 | -0.0048 | 0.2546 | 0.2537 | 0.0206 | -0.0699 | 0.0124 | -0.0659 | -0.1499 | -0.1513 | 0.0874 |
| pr = 0 | 98% | 17% | 18% | 92% | 77% | 95% | 73% | 43% | 42% | 65% |
| N | 29 | 30 | 30 | 25 | 20 | 25 | 29 | 30 | 30 | 29 |
| SOEB7075 | -0.0772 | -0.2743 | -0.2108 | 0.1225 | -0.2386 | -0.1188 | -0.1601 | 0.0442 | -0.0335 | 0.1905 |
| pr = 0 | 68% | 12% | 24% | 57% | 30% | 57% | 42% | 81% | 85% | 30% |
| N | 31 | 33 | 33 | 24 | 21 | 25 | 28 | 32 | 33 | 32 |
| SOEB8590 | -0.2774 | -0.426 | -0.4696 | 0.4411 | 0.1836 | -0.1722 | -0.3161 | -0.2994 | -0.2834 | -0.0646 |
| pr = 0 | 15% | 2% | 1% | 4% | 45% | 43% | 12% | 10% | 12% | 73% |
| N | 29 | 31 | 31 | 23 | 19 | 23 | 26 | 32 | 32 | 32 |
| SOET8590 | 0.3038 | 0.3446 | 0.4094 | -0.3524 | -0.1539 | 0.0742 | 0.1574 | 0.2445 | 0.2214 | 0.1271 |
| pr = 0 | 11% | 6% | 2% | 11% | 53% | 74% | 44% | 18% | 22% | 49% |
| N | 29 | 30 | 30 | 22 | 19 | 22 | 26 | 32 | 32 | 32 |
| DISTDEM | 0.5749 | 0.2506 | 0.3734 | -0.5856 | -0.0255 | 0.7533 | 0.732 | 0.6919 | 0.6997 | -0.0646 |
| pr = 0 | 0% | 3% | 0% | 0% | 87% | 0% | 0% | 0% | 0% | 58% |
| N | 74 | 77 | 78 | 56 | 44 | 59 | 70 | 80 | 80 | 77 |
| JUDDEM | 0.9033 | 0.27 | 0.3778 | -0.7673 | -0.0635 | 0.2551 | 0.2823 | 0.3145 | 0.3337 | -0.1973 |
| pr = 0 | 0% | 2% | 0% | 0% | 67% | 5% | 2% | 1% | 0% | 9% |
| N | 79 | 78 | 78 | 58 | 48 | 59 | 69 | 74 | 76 | 73 |
| INSTAB | 0.4138 | -0.2304 | -0.1317 | -0.4188 | -0.0145 | 0.024 | -0.0115 | 0.0166 | -0.048 | -0.0851 |
| pr = 0 | 0% | 9% | 33% | 1% | 94% | 88% | 94% | 90% | 73% | 53% |
| N | 53 | 56 | 56 | 39 | 33 | 43 | 49 | 55 | 56 | 56 |
| PARL | -0.6278 | 0.0496 | -0.0684 | 0.5011 | 0.0849 | -0.1108 | -0.1579 | -0.2959 | -0.22 | -0.1348 |
| pr = 0 | 0% | 66% | 54% | 0% | 57% | 41% | 20% | 1% | 5% | 24% |
| N | 78 | 81 | 81 | 58 | 46 | 58 | 69 | 78 | 80 | 77 |
| FORKPCI | 0.3524 | -0.0356 | 0.1164 | -0.4753 | 0.1664 | -0.1064 | -0.0156 | 0.2959 | 0.1844 | -0.1405 |
| pr = 0 | 0% | 76% | 30% | 0% | 27% | 42% | 90% | 1% | 10% | 22% |
| N | 77 | 79 | 80 | 57 | 45 | 59 | 70 | 80 | 82 | 79 |
| LYC85 | -0.8961 | -0.3693 | -0.5347 | 0.8167 | 0.1025 | -0.3475 | -0.4768 | -0.5887 | -0.5405 | 0.2257 |
| pr = 0 | 0% | 0% | 0% | 0% | 51% | 1% | 0% | 0% | 0% | 5% |
| N | 75 | 77 | 78 | 56 | 44 | 59 | 69 | 78 | 80 | 78 |
| LYC94PP | -0.8697 | -0.4281 | -0.594 | 0.7794 | 0.0691 | -0.407 | -0.5264 | -0.6447 | -0.5688 | 0.2075 |
| pr = 0 | 0% | 0% | 0% | 0% | 65% | 0% | 0% | 0% | 0% | 7% |
| N | 79 | 81 | 82 | 60 | 46 | 59 | 70 | 79 | 81 | 79 |

| | SOED7075 | SOEB7075 | SOEB8590 | SOET8590 | DISTDEM | JUDDEM | INSTAB | PARL | FORKPCI | LYC85 | LYC94PP |
|---|---|---|---|---|---|---|---|---|---|---|---|
| SOED7075 | 1 | | | | | | | | | | |
| pr = 0 | | | | | | | | | | | |
| N | 30 | | | | | | | | | | |
| SOEB7075 | -0.4249 | 1 | | | | | | | | | |
| pr = 0 | 5% | | | | | | | | | | |
| N | 22 | 33 | | | | | | | | | |
| SOEB8590 | 0.1211 | 0.0799 | 1 | | | | | | | | |
| pr = 0 | 66% | 76% | | | | | | | | | |
| N | 16 | 17 | 32 | | | | | | | | |
| SOET8590 | -0.1045 | 0.1706 | -0.8706 | 1 | | | | | | | |
| pr = 0 | 69% | 53% | 0% | | | | | | | | |
| N | 17 | 16 | 26 | 32 | | | | | | | |
| DISTDEM | -0.1364 | -0.0408 | -0.2143 | 0.2477 | 1 | | | | | | |
| pr = 0 | 47% | 82% | 24% | 17% | | | | | | | |
| N | 30 | 32 | 32 | 32 | 80 | | | | | | |
| JUDDEM | 0.0716 | -0.1371 | -0.0986 | 0.1184 | 0.5326 | 1 | | | | | |
| pr = 0 | 71% | 46% | 61% | 54% | 0% | | | | | | |
| N | 29 | 31 | 29 | 29 | 74 | 79 | | | | | |
| INSTAB | -0.0572 | 0.1465 | 0.2172 | -0.31 | 0.1417 | 0.4532 | 1 | | | | |
| pr = 0 | 79% | 47% | 29% | 14% | 30% | 0% | | | | | |
| N | 24 | 27 | 26 | 24 | 55 | 53 | 56 | | | | |
| PARL | -0.0689 | -0.0288 | -0.3518 | 0.2741 | -0.3663 | -0.5992 | -0.3481 | 1 | | | |
| pr = 0 | 72% | 87% | 5% | 14% | 0% | 0% | 1% | | | | |
| N | 30 | 33 | 31 | 31 | 78 | 77 | 56 | 83 | | | |
| FORKPCI | -0.3463 | 0.0357 | -0.2259 | 0.0551 | 0.1218 | 0.3779 | 0.0995 | -0.3503 | 1 | | |
| pr = 0 | 6% | 85% | 21% | 76% | 28% | 0% | 47% | 0% | | | |
| N | 30 | 32 | 32 | 32 | 80 | 76 | 56 | 83 | 83 | | |
| LYC85 | 0.1842 | 0.0806 | 0.411 | -0.2342 | -0.5816 | -0.8573 | -0.2793 | 0.5633 | -0.5306 | 1 | |
| pr = 0 | 33% | 66% | 2% | 20% | 0% | 0% | 4% | 0% | 0% | | |
| N | 30 | 32 | 32 | 32 | 78 | 74 | 56 | 80 | 83 | 81 | |
| LYC94PP | 0.0457 | 0.1316 | 0.4631 | -0.2446 | -0.5368 | -0.7932 | -0.1666 | 0.5808 | -0.4791 | 0.9183 | 1 |
| pr = 0 | 0.8105 | 0.4728 | 0.0076 | 0.1774 | 0% | 0% | 22% | 0% | 0% | 0% | |
| N | 30 | 32 | 32 | 32 | 79 | 77 | 56 | 81 | 82 | 81 | 88 |

# Appendix 2 Operationalization of dependent and explanatory variables

## PROPERTY

The logic of the theory and hypotheses is certainly neutral about the unit of measurement of property allocation, as property rights can be allocated at various levels of government. In general, the unit of measurement for ownership allocation is the country, since property laws are generally common within a single country. Where some legal decisions also made at the subnational level (such as the federal cases of Argentina and Brazil), or even at the supranational level (Mercosur, for these two countries too), care must be taken to specify the relevant unit of measurement and measure property rights at the proper level, although one can expect federal actions to carry a greater weight and therefore be taken as representative of a country as a whole.

The major estimators of property rights comprise:

- the percentage of assets (in monetary value) fully owned by private actors, that is, with rights of operation, modification, disposition, exchange, and control over output in the hands of non-governmental entities or individuals;
- the existence of restrictions on any of these dimensions, such as limits on repatriation of profits or on ownership by foreign entities;
- the nature of the owners themselves, which may be a mixture of private and public;
- the use of subsidies or giveaways for particular groups, like employees;
- the existence of mechanisms for the protection of claims from arbitrary encroachment by the government or other parties (particularly the availability of judicial recourse against regulatory decisions and the independence of regulatory commissions from political control through staggered commissioner terms, restrictions on the appointment and removal of commissioners, the sources of commission funding and the process of commission budget approval);

- use of concession contracts instead of unrestricted property (although concessions can be an instrument to deal with the incentive problems of monopoly).

Estimator reliability: most of the estimators listed above are either contained in legal texts or reported by industry and financial information services, and they can be observed with little ambiguity.

## COMPETITION

Unit of measurement: in the ESI, competition decisions must be taken at the level of each interconnected transmission system, since decisions at lower levels are unfeasible in the presence of strong interdependence among the components of such a system. The scope of an interconnected system may or may not match national boundaries: for instance, both Chile and Brazil have two separate subnational systems of significant size, and many countries have small isolated systems. On the other hand, because in most countries there is a single domestic market (that is, internal barriers to trade are prohibited) competition policy is a national-level decision.[1]

The major estimators of competition are:

- degree of horizontal and vertical concentration;
- barriers to entry and exit, which in the ESI refer to access to technology, to fuel (including water rights), and to capital (barriers to capital mobility, nonmarket sources of capital like government programs), and for exit, concern mainly the liquidity of financial markets (which allows the resale of interests) and public service obligations;
- the scope of legal instruments available to government to punish anticompetitive behavior, and the means of enforcement of such instruments (particularly the existence and capabilities of regulatory and antitrust commissions);
- the governance structure of the interconnected system operator, since the ESI necessarily relies on such a network to deliver its output, and nonstorability of electrical energy requires the continuous coordination of demand and supply, while the system operator can favor some participants over others;
- the degree of mandatory separation of the different components of distribution service, since certain of these components, like meter reading and billing, can be provided competitively;

- the degree to which small users can directly contract for supply (metering and other costs limit but do not impede access to direct contracting by small users);
- use of mechanisms to stimulate competitive behavior in monopolistic segments, or to capture monopoly rents away from monopoly suppliers to use them in socially more efficient ways:

  a. yardstick competition, or explicit comparison among similar domestic or foreign firms to determine regulated prices; the decision to break a nationwide monopoly into several distributors and transmitters can be taken as an implicit intent to use yardstick competition, since otherwise the existence of economies of scale in these activities would lead to higher privatization prices if a single company structure was preserved;
  b. competition 'for the market' through franchise bidding (particularly if supplemented by refinements such as the periodic rebidding of concessions to mitigate incentive problems at the end of the concession term).

Estimator reliability: most of these estimators are also embodied in regulations and statutes, with the exception of market concentration, because there is no clear standard on what constitutes a competitive market structure, and in the ESI system operating rules can be an additional complicating factor. A possible solution to this problem is to break this indicator into further variables which can hopefully be more readily observed, such as the number of firms, their relative sizes, and the competitiveness of the assets they control (according to production cost, flexibility of production levels, and so forth).

## JUDICIAL INDEPENDENCE

The unit of measurement for judicial independence is in most cases the country, as the relation of judiciary with the other powers is a basic element of the constitutional framework in a modern democracy, the enforcement of major judicial decisions is a prerogative of national governments (as opposed to international law or subnational units, whose courts may be unable to enforce their decisions or have only limited powers), and judicial systems tend to follow a pyramidal structure with a nationwide supreme court at the top.

At the same time, the centralized structure of the court system, in which courts examine cases involving a variety of matters, makes it necessary to consider more than just measures of direct importance for the ESI, such as the property rights regime. Actors look at overall judicial independence for clues to the reliability of property rights and competition in ESI, as corruption or bias in judges will affect all of their decisions. In this regard, even a wider measure like the independence of SOEs is a valid estimator insofar as it is also indicative of the restraint among politicians that underlies the explanatory power of judicial independence.[2]

The reliability of the indicators of judicial independence is only high for the formal mechanisms, which can be evaluated from laws and other codifications of norms; other indicators can take many intermediate values and may be difficult to observe, particularly the legitimacy or prestige of courts as a means of enforcing their decisions.


## IDEOLOGY

Ideology cannot be directly observed, but it can be inferred from the following indicators:

- poll and interview responses, and the public pronouncements and writings of decisionmakers (although biases are introduced in the interpretation such material, and public messages may diverge significantly from private views);
- actual behavior, using interpretive research: electoral records (for voter ideologies), party affiliation, legislative voting record, policy initiatives and decisions, and the choice of ministers and collaborators (interpretive caveat also applies);
- policymakers' background: education, professional experience (in this case, there is a tradeoff between lower validity, since the relation between backgrounds and ideas is not automatic, and higher reliability, since backgrounds can be more objectively assessed).

There are three major units of measurement of ideology:

- the policymakers involved in the ESI restructuring process: the politicians in power and if relevant, senior civil servants, as well as actors external to the government and state agencies, but who are involved in policy design or implementation (from multilateral institutions, from foreign governments with influence due to size,

security, or origin of foreign investment, and from foreign financial and consulting firms, as providers of capital and practical know-how);
* party structure (relative positioning of parties along the major issue areas of a polity);
* the electorate (in democratic regimes) and influential lobbies (especially business associations and labor unions).

The abstract nature of the concept of ideology, and the interpretive requirement it imposes on the researcher, makes the reliability of ideological measures poor. Ideological beliefs have to be separated from political convenience, or meaning given to words in terms of preferences for ESI outcomes. The possibility of biasing interpretations in favor of one's own hypotheses is significant.

Like judicial independence, ideology is a multidimensional variable, since we expect that individuals hold more or less internally consistent beliefs, and since political socialization results in the ascription of individuals to ideological programs that cover many different issues. We can therefore examine not only the ideas held by groups and individuals about the ESI, but broader views on social values (for example, on the importance of group solidarity versus individual incentives) and on allocative arrangements (statism, competition, private property, regulation, the effectiveness of state intervention, and so forth).

An important aspect of the validity of ideological estimators is the extent to which, as more or less coherent sets, they can be reduced to a manageable number of dimensions in order to simplify analytical tasks. More specifically, in Latin America the European or North American left–right classification of ideologies is problematic because of the historical importance of populism and nationalism. The key question is whether these ideologies form coherent wholes, or are only dimensions of broader ideological sets.

In this regard, recent literature on Latin American populism has challenged a necessary association with progressive or conservative ideologies, and redefined populism instead as political style rather than as a concrete ideology (Roberts 1995). As such, we can ignore populism as an ideological alternative to the left–right divide in contemporary Latin America. On the other hand, the recent historical record of nationalist regimes (particularly military ones) in the region indicates that nationalism results in a consistent pattern of preferences regardless of the official left/right positioning of the regimes:

* restrictions on foreign investment and control over productive assets;

- promotion of domestic production.

These policies have clear implications for the dependent variables:

- market size is constrained so competition decreases (even when multinational corporations are allowed, their financial resources relative to domestic financial markets tend to increase market concentration);
- public ownership is often expanded to increase domestic production and technology absorption.

Hence, it is important to identify nationalist ideology, through the use of those estimators listed above that register concern about foreign control or the desire to assert independence from foreign powers in domestic or international affairs.


## DISTRIBUTIONAL CONFLICT

Inequality in the distribution of a society's resources is not sufficient for distributional conflict to arise, although it is necessary in the sense that all other things equal, a higher level of inequality is likely to produce higher levels of distributional conflict. Political mobilization is a key intervening variable between inequality and conflict, so estimators of distributional conflict must consider both inequality and the level of political or labor mobilization. With this caveat, possible estimators of distributional conflict are:

- the level of industrial conflict (strikes, lockouts);
- political infighting over tax allocation and tax revenues (for example, states versus federal government disputes);
- political infighting and logrolling over expenditure allocation (pork-barrel issues);
- explicit patronage promises in political campaigns;
- outputs of the political system: subsidy and cross-subsidy schemes, special tariff regimes, privatization subsidies, tolerance for theft of electricity and other public services, and the existence of differential access to public services that is not justified by differences in supply costs.

The unit of measurement of distributional conflict is necessarily the unit at the level where political decisions are made, since the logic of the argument is that distributional conflict acts through pressure on policymakers to harness economic resources. This means that in some cases subnational-level observations may be appropriate. As with measures of property outcomes, a possible strategy is to measure initially at the national level, then use the subnational level as a source of further observations.

The reliability of estimators of distributional conflict is in general poor, because the concept is broad, covering a variety of activities and behaviors, and because interpretation is required for most estimators to separate true distributional conflict from behavior that corresponds to other political motivations, such as ideology. Output estimators can be more easily documented, but they are only indirect measures.

The logic of the hypotheses indicates that valid estimators of distributional conflict need to look beyond the ESI, as in a unitary political system conflicts in a particular area of economic regulation and intervention have a direct impact on all other areas through the public budget, as well as being indicative of general pressure on society's resources.

## NOTES

1. An important exception, but irrelevant for the cases at hand, are trade-related competition rules, which are increasingly delegated to supranational entities like Mercosur.
2. As Stephenson (n.d.) notes, measuring judicial independence is not straightforward because there are many manifestations of judicial independence, and formal measures are generally insufficient because they are often manipulated.

# Bibliography

*Author's Note:* in addition to the references below, both the theory and the analysis of the case studies presented in this book have been extensively informed by a large number of consulting assignments in the ESI over a period of 15 years in the Americas and Europe. Clients included international and domestic energy firms of various sizes, governmental agencies, multilateral institutions, and financial firms, among others.

Abdala, M.A., 'The Regulation of Newly Privatized Firms: An Illustration from Argentina', ch. 3 in W. Baer and M.H. Birch (eds), *Privatization in Latin America: New Roles for the Public and Private Sectors* (Westport, CT: Praeger, 1994).

Acuña, C.H., 'Business Interests, Dictatorship, and Democracy in Argentina', ch.1 in L.A. Payne and E. Bartell (eds), *Business and Democracy in Latin America* (Pittsburgh: University of Pittsburgh Press, 1995).

Aharoni, Y., *The Evolution and Management of State-Owned Enterprises* (Cambridge, MA: Ballinger, 1986).

Aizenman, J., 'Fiscal Discipline in a Union', ch. 9 in F. Sturzenegger and M. Tommasi (eds), *The Political Economy of Policy Reform* (Cambridge, MA: MIT Press, 1998).

Allende, J.A., 'Historical Constraints to Privatization: The Case of the Nationalized Chilean Copper Industry', *Studies in Comparative International Development* (Spring 1988): 55–81.

Alquerés, J.L., 'IPPs in Brazil', *Independent Energy*, January 1995: 38, 40.

Ames, B., *Political Survival: Politicians and Public Policy in Latin America* (Berkeley: University of California Press, 1987).

Ames, B., 'Electoral Rules, Constituency Pressures, and Pork Barrel: Bases of Voting in the Brazilian Congress', *Journal of Politics* 57(2) (May 1995): 324–43.

Aoki, M., *Toward a Comparative Institutional Analysis* (Cambridge, MA: MIT Press, 2001).

Argentina, National Congress, Law No. 23,696 of 18 August 1989, on Administrative Emergency and Reform of the State ('Emergency Act').

Argentina, National Congress, Law No. 24,065 of 19 December 1991, on Electrical Energy ('Electricity Act').

Argentina, National Government, Decree No. 1398/92 of 1992, with implementing regulations for Electricity Act.

Armijo, L.E., and P. Faucher, '"We Have Consensus": Explaining Political Support for Market Reforms in Latin America', *Latin American Politics and Society* 44(2) (2002): 1–40.

Armstrong, M., S. Cowan and J. Vickers, *Regulatory Reform: Economic Analysis and British Experience* (Cambridge, MA: MIT Press, 1994).

Ayala, U., and J. Millán, 'Sustainability of Power Sector Reform in Latin America: The Reform in Colombia', Working Paper, Inter-American Development Bank, May 2002.

Bacon, R.W., and J. Besant-Jones, 'Global Electric Power Reform, Privatization and Liberalization of the Electric Power Industry in Developing Countries', *Annual Review of Energy and the Environment* 26 (2001): 331–59.

Baer, W., and C. McDonald, 'A Return to the Past? Brazil's Privatization of Public Utilities: The Case of the Electric Power Sector', *Quarterly Review of Economics and Finance* 38(3) (1998): 503–23.

Baer, W., and A.V. Villela, 'Privatization and the Changing Role of the State in Brazil', ch. 1 in W. Baer and M.H. Birch (eds), *Privatization in Latin America: New Roles for the Public and Private Sectors* (Westport, CT: Praeger, 1994).

Baron, D.P., 'Regulation and Legislative Choice', *Journal of Economics* 19(3) (Autumn 1988): 467–77.

Baron, D.P., 'Electoral Competition with Informed and Uninformed Voters', *American Political Science Review* 88(1) (March 1994): 33–47.

Bartell, E., 'Privatization: The Role of Domestic Business Elites', ch. 4 in W. Baer and M.H. Birch (eds), *Privatization in Latin America: New Roles for the Public and Private Sectors* (Westport. CT: Praeger, 1994).

Bartell, E., 'Perceptions by Business Leaders and the Transition to Democracy in Chile', ch. 2 in L.A. Payne and E. Bartell (eds), *Business and Democracy in Latin America* (Pittsburgh: University of Pittsburgh Press, 1995).

Bastos, C.M., and M.A. Abdala, *Transformación del sector eléctrico argentino* [Transformation of the Argentine Electricity Sector] (Santiago de Chile: Antártica, 1993).

Bates, R.H., *Markets and States in Tropical Africa: The Political Basis of Agricultural Policies* (Berkeley: University of California Press, 1981).

Becker, G.S., 'A Theory of Competition Among Pressure Groups for Political Influence', *Quarterly Journal of Economics* 98(3) (August 1983): 371–400.

Becker, G.S., 'Public Policies, Pressure Groups, and Dead Weight Costs', *Journal of Public Economics* 28 (1985): 329–47.

Bergara, M.E., W.J. Henisz and P.T. Spiller, 'Political Institutions and Electric Utility Investment: A Cross-Nation Analysis', *California Management Review* 40(2) (Winter 1998): 18–35.

Bernstein, S., 'Pragmatic Privatization', *Independent Energy*, October 1995: 30–36.

Bitrán, E., and E. Saavedra, 'Algunas reflexiones en torno al rol regulador y empresarial del estado' [Some reflections on the regulatory and business role of the state], pp. 249–80 in O. Muñoz (ed.), *Después de la privatización: Hacia el estado regulador* (Santiago de Chile: CIEPLAN, 1993).

Bitrán, E., and R.E. Sáez, 'Privatization and Regulation in Chile', ch. 7 in B.P. Bosworth, R. Dornbusch and R. Labán (eds), *The Chilean Economy: Policy Lessons and Challenges* (Washington, DC: Brookings Institution, 1994).

Bitrán, E., and P. Serra, 'Regulation of Privatized Utilities: Lessons from the Chilean Experience', mimeo, 4 October 1995.

Bitrán, E., and P. Serra, 'Regulatory Issues in the Privatisation of Public Utilities: The Chilean Experience', pp. 141–50 in OECD, *Privatisation in Asia, Europe, and Latin America* (Paris: Organization for Economic Cooperation and Development, 1996).

Blanlot, V., 'La regulación del sector eléctrico: la experiencia chilena' [Electricity Regulation: The Chilean Experience], pp. 281–321 in O. Muñoz (ed.), *Después de la privatización: Hacia el estado regulador* (Santiago de Chile: CIEPLAN, 1993).

Bolivia, National Congress, Law No. 1600 of 28 October 1994, of Sectoral Regulation.

Bolivia, National Congress, Law No. 1604 of 21 December 1994, on Electricity ('Electricity Act').

Bolivia, National Government, Capitalization Program Brochure, n.d.

Bolivia, National Government, Decree No. 24,043 of 28 June 1995, with implementing regulations for Electricity Act rate provisions.

Bowen, S., 'Bolivian Watchdog Proud of Its Teeth', *Financial Times*, 30 July 1997: 7.

Brazil, National Congress, Law No. 8,897 of 13 February 1995, on Concessions and Permits for the Provision of Public Services.

Brazil, National Congress, Law No. 9,074 of 7 July 1995, on Concession Awards.

Brazil, National Congress, Law No. 9,427 of 26 December 1996, Instituting the National Electric Energy Agency (ANEEL).

Brazil, National Government, 'States Are Speeding Up Their Privatization Programs', *The Wall Street Journal* (Special Advertising Section), 18 June 1996: A14.

Brazil, National Government, Decree No. 2,335 of 6 October 1997, with implementing regulations for the creation of ANEEL.

Brazil, National Government, 'Privatization Program Moves Forward', *The Wall Street Journal* (Special Advertising Section), 3 April 1998a: A16.

Brazil, National Government, 'Creating Energy Entities', *The Wall Street Journal* (Special Advertising Section), 3 April 1998b: A16.

Brazil, National Government, 'Legal Framework', *The Wall Street Journal* (Special Advertising Section), 3 April 1998c: A17.

Brazil, National Government, 'Ventures Poised to Meet Demand', *The Wall Street Journal* (Special Advertising Section), 3 April 1998d: A17.

Brazil, National Government, 'Program for Energy Sector Reform', *The Wall Street Journal* (Special Advertising Section), 14 April 1998e: B14.

Brazil, National Government, 'Management Changes Preceded Sell-Off', *The Wall Street Journal* (Special Advertising Section), 14 April 1998f: B14.

Bresser Pereira, L., 'Brazil', pp. 333–54 in J. Williamson (ed.), *The Political Economy of Policy Reform* (Washington, DC: Institute for International Economics, 1993).

Bronstein, B.. (Coordinator of the privatization of SEGBAs distribution area), 'Privatization of SEGBA', Published in Bureau de Investigaciones Empresariales, *Privatizaciones en Argentina* (Buenos Aires: BIE, 1991).

Brown, A., 'Brazilian ESI restructuring', seminar presentation, Kennedy School of Government, Harvard University, Cambridge, MA, April 1998.

Burr, M.T., 'Attracting IPPs', *Independent Energy*, October 1995: 42, 44.

Cavallo, D.F., 'Lessons from Argentina's Privatization Experience', *Journal of International Affairs* 50(2) (Winter 1997): 459–74.

Chile, National Government, Decree-Law No. 1 of the Ministry of Mines, 13 September 1982.

Chisari, O., A. Estache, and C. Romero, 'The Distribution of Gains from Utility Privatization and Regulation in Argentina', *Public Policy for the Private Sector* (January 1997): 41–4.

Clague, C., P. Keefer, S. Knack, and M. Olson, 'Democracy, Autocracy and, the Institutions Supportive of Economic Growth', ch. 5 in C. Clague (ed.), *Institutions and Economic Development: Growth and Governance in Less-Developed and Post-Socialist Countries* (Baltimore, MD: Johns Hopkins University Press, 1997).

Collier, R.B., and D. Collier, *Shaping the Political Arena: Critical Junctures, the Labor Movement, and Regime Dynamics in Latin America* (Princeton, NJ: Princeton University Press, 1991).

Collis, D.J., and C.A. Montgomery, *Corporate Strategy: A Resource-Based Approach* (New York: Irwin/McGraw-Hill, 1998).

Conaghan, C.M., 'The Private Sector and the Public Transcript: The Political Mobilization of Business in Bolivia', ch. 3 in L.A. Payne and E. Bartell (eds), *Business and Democracy in Latin America* (Pittsburgh: University of Pittsburgh Press, 1995).

Conaghan, C.M., and J.M. Malloy, *Unsettling Statecraft: Democracy and Neoliberalism in the Central Andes* (Pittsburgh: University of Pittsburgh Press, 1994).

Conaghan, C.M., J.M. Malloy, and L.A. Abugattas, 'Business and the "Boys": The Politics of Neoliberalism in the Central Andes', *Latin American Research Review* 25 (Spring 1990): 3–30.

Contente, S., and S. Callou, 'The Brazilian Electricity Market', presentation to Harvard Electricity Policy Group, Cambridge, MA, 16 November 1998.

Coopers & Lybrand, Brazil Electricity Sector Restructuring Study, Draft Report IV-1, n.d.

Corrales, J., 'From Market-Correctors to Market-Creators: Executive-Ruling Party Relations in the Economic Reforms of Argentina and Venezuela 1989–1993', PhD dissertation, Department of Government, Harvard University, Cambridge, MA, 1996.

Council on Foreign Relations and Center for Comparative Political Research of the State University of New York at Binghamton, *Political Handbook of the World* (New York: Published for the Center for Comparative Political Research of the State University of New York at Binghamton and for the Council on Foreign Relations by McGraw-Hill Book Co., various dates).

Cukierman, A. and M. Tommasi, 'When Does It Take a Nixon to Go to China?', *American Economic Review* 88(1) (March 1998): 180–97.

Daland, R.T., *Explaining Brazilian Bureaucracy: Performance and Pathology* (Washington, DC: University Press of America, 1981).

Demsetz, H., 'Why Regulate Utilities?', *Journal of Law and Economics* 11 (April 1968): 59ff.

Derbyshire, J.D., and I. Derbyshire, *Political Systems of the World* (London: Helicon Publishing, 1996).

Dewatripont, M., and G. Roland, 'Economic Reform and Dynamic Political Constraints', *Review of Economic Studies* 59 (1992): 703–30.

Dias Leite, A., *A energia do Brasil* [Brazil's energy], (Rio de Janeiro: Nova Fronteira 1997).

Dixit, A.K., *The Making of Economic Policy: A Transaction-Cost Politics Perspective* (Cambridge, MA: MIT Press, 1996).

Domingo, P., 'Judicial Independence and Judicial Reform in Latin America', ch. 10 in A. Schedler, L.J. Diamond and M.F. Plattner (eds),

*The Self-restraining State: Power and Accountability in New Democracies* (Boulder, CO: Lynne Rienner, 1999): 151–75.

Domínguez, J.I., 'Technopols: Ideas and Leaders in Freeing Politics and Markets in Latin America in the 1990s', ch. 1 in J.I. Domínguez (ed.), *Technopols: Freeing Politics and Markets in Latin America in the 1990s* (State College, PA: Pennsylvania State University Press, 1997).

Domínguez, J.I., and J.K. Giraldo, 'Conclusion: Parties, Institutions, and Market Reforms in Constructing Democracies', ch. 7 in J.I. Domínguez and A.F. Lowenthal (eds), *Constructing Democratic Governance: Latin America and the Caribbean in the 1990s – Themes and Issues* (Baltimore, MD: Johns Hopkins University Press, 1996).

Drazen, A., *Political Economy in Macroeconomics* (Princeton, NJ: Princeton University Press, 2000).

Dyer, G., '"Big Bang" Approach to State Sell-Offs', *Financial Times*, 29 April 1997a: 20.

Dyer, G., 'Brazil Pushes Energy Plans to Keep Lights Burning', *Financial Times*, 2 October 1997b: 5.

Dyer, G., 'Hearts Have Yet to Follow', *Financial Times* (US edn), Survey of Brazilian Privatization (special supplement), 26 May 1998.

*Economist, The*, 'Privatisation, It's Fairly Wonderful', 5 January 1994: 42.

*Economist, The*, 'Slimming the State', Brazil Survey, 29 April 29 1995: 16, 21.

*Economist, The*, 'Privatisation Trundles Ahead', 15 June 1996: 42.

*Economist, The*, 'An Example in the Andes', 9 August 1997: 29–30.

*Economist, The*, 'An Overdue Reform of Justice', 10 April 1999: 34.

*Economist, The*, 'Democracy Clings on in a Cold Economic Climate', 15 August 2002.

Economist Books Ltd, The, *The Economist Book of Vital World Statistics* (London: The Economist Books, 1990).

Energy Sector Management Assistance Programme (ESMAP), 'Bolivia: Private Power Generation and Transmission', (Report 137/91, January 1992).

Energy Sector Management Assistance Programme [ESMAP], 'Global Energy Sector Reform in Developing Countries: A Scorecard' (Report 219/99, July 1999).

Epstein, D., and S. O'Halloran, *Delegating Powers: A Transaction Cost Politics Approach to Policy Making Under Separate Powers* (New York: Cambridge University Press, 1999).

Estache, A., and M. Rodríguez-Pardina, 'Regulatory Lessons from Argentina's Power Concessions', *Public Policy for the Private Sector* (September 1996): 81–4.

Estache, A., and M. Rodríguez-Pardina, 'The Real Possibility of Competitive Generation Markets in Hydro Systems – The Case of Brazil', *Public Policy for the Private Sector* (February 1997): 85–8.

Ewing, A., and S. Goldmark, 'Privatization by Capitalization: The Case of Bolivia. A Popular Participation Recipe for Cash-Starved SOEs', *Public Policy for the Private Sector* (November 1994): 1–4.

Fairfield, R.P. (ed.), *The Federalist Papers* (Garden City, NY: Anchor Books, 1966).

Fernández, R., and D. Rodrik, 'Resistance to Reform: Status Quo Bias in the Presence of Individual-Specific Uncertainty', ch. 3 in F. Sturzenegger and M. Tommasi (eds), *The Political Economy of Policy Reform* (Cambridge, MA: MIT Press, 1998).

Floyd, R.H., C.S. Gray, and R.P. Short, *Public Enterprise in Mixed Economies: Some Macroeconomic Aspects* (Washington, DC: International Monetary Fund, 1984).

Framework Agreement [for resolution of electricity theft problem in Greater Buenos Aires], Buenos Aires, 10 January 1994.

Freedom House, *Freedom in the World* (New York: Freedom House, various years).

Friedland, J., 'Chile Auction Fails, in Turning Point for Power Sector', *The Wall Street Journal*, 16 October 1996a: A16.

Friedland, J., 'Chile's Enersis Juices Up Latin America', *The Wall Street Journal*, 25 November 1996b: A14.

Friedland, J., 'Brazilian Utility Deals Lose Some Dazzle', *The Wall Street Journal*, 13 May 1997a: A16.

Friedland, J., 'Bolivia's Regulatory System Stumbles: Watchdog Authority Is Challenged by Recent Incidents', *Wall Street Journal*, 2 December 1997b: A18.

Friedland, J., 'Excesses of Old Privatizations Dog Mexico's Latest Efforts at Reform', *The Wall Street Journal*, 17 March 1999a: A22.

Friedland, J., 'Power Play: In This Mexican Union, Changing a Light Bulb Is a Three-Man Job', *The Wall Street Journal*, 3 December 1999b: A1.

Friedland, J., and B.A. Holden, 'Utility Deregulation in Argentina Presages Possible US Upheaval', *The Wall Street Journal*, 19 June 1996: A1, A12.

Galal, A., 'Chile: Regulatory Specificity, Credibility of Commitment, and Distributional Demands', ch. 4 in B. Levy and P.T. Spiller (eds), *Regulations, Institutions and Commitment: Comparative Studies of Telecommunications* (Cambridge: Cambridge University Press, 1996).

Galal, A., L.P. Jones, P. Tandon, and I. Vogelsang (eds), *The Welfare Consequences of Selling Public Enterprises: An Empirical Analysis* (New York: Oxford University Press for the World Bank, 1994).

Gamarra, E.A., 'The Privatization Debate in Bolivia', ch. 13 in D.J. Gayle and J.N. Goodrich (eds), *Privatization and Deregulation in Global Perspective* (New York: Quorum Books, 1990).

Gamarra, E.A., *The System of Justice in Bolivia: An Institutional Analysis* (San José, Costa Rica: Centro para la Administración de Justicia, 1991).

Gamarra, E.A., and J.M. Malloy, 'The Patrimonial Dynamics of Party Politics in Bolivia', ch. 12 in S. Mainwaring and T.R. Scully (eds), *Building Democratic Institutions: Party Systems in Latin America* (Stanford, CA: Stanford University Press, 1995).

Gatica, P., and E. Skoknic, 'Marcos regulatorios en el sector eléctrico sudamericano' [Regulatory frameworks in the South American electric power sector], Comité Chileno de la CIER, Santiago, Chile, June 1996 (accessed 28 August 1998). http://www.int/puc/cl~power/cier.htm.

Geddes, B., *Politician's Dilemma: Building State Capacity in Latin America* (Berkeley: University of California Press, 1994).

Geddes, B., 'The Politics of Economic Liberalization', *Latin American Research Review* 30 (1995): 195–214.

Geddes, B., and A. Ribeiro Neto, 'Institutional Sources of Corruption in Brazil', *Third World Quarterly* 13(4) (1992): 641–61.

Gibson, E.L., 'The Populist Road to Market Reform: Policy and Electoral Coalitions in Mexico and Argentina', *World Politics* 49 (April 1997): 339–70.

*Global Power Report GPR*, formerly *Independent Power Report*, various issues.

Gómez-Ibáñez, J.A., 'The Future of Private Infrastructure: Lessons from the Nationalization of Electric Utilities in Latin America 1943–79', John F. Kennedy School of Government, Harvard University, Cambridge, MA, January 1999.

Gómez-Ibáñez, J.A., and J.R. Meyer, *The Political Economy of Transport Privatization: Successes, Failure and Lessons for Developed and Developing Countries* (Cambridge, MA: Harvard University, John F. Kennedy School of Government, Taubman Center for State and Local Government, 1992).

González Fraga, J.A., 'Argentine Privatization in Retrospect', ch. 5 in W.E. Glade (ed.), *Privatization of Public Enterprises in Latin America* (New York: International Center for Economic Growth, 1991).

Graham, C., *Private Markets for Public Goods: Raising the Stakes in Economic Reform* (Washington, DC: Brookings, 1998).

Grindle, M.S., and J.W. Thomas, *Public Choices and Policy Change: The Political Economy of Reform in Developing Countries* (Baltimore, MD: Johns Hopkins University Press, 1991).

Grossman, G.M., and E. Helpman, 'Electoral Competition and Special Interest Politics', *Review of Economic Studies* 63 (1996): 265–86.

Grossman, G.M, and E. Helpman, 'Intergenerational Redistribution with Short-Lived Governments', *Economic Journal* 108 (September 1998): 1299–329.

Gurr, T.R., Polity II: Political Structures and Regime Change, 1800–1986 [computer file] (Boulder: Center for Comparative Politics 1989, and Inter-university Consortium for Political and Social Research [distributor], 1990).

Gwartney, J.D., *Economic Freedom in the World: 1997 Annual Report* (Vancouver: Fraser Institute, 1997).

Hachette, D., and R. Lüders, *Privatization in Chile: An Economic Appraisal* (New York: International Center for Economic Growth, 1993).

Haggard, S, and R. Kaufman (eds), *The Politics of Economic Adjustment* (Princeton, NJ: Princeton University Press, 1992).

Hagopian, F., *Traditional Politics and Regime Change in Brazil* (Cambridge: Cambridge University Press, 1996).

Harteneck, G., and B. McMahon, 'Privatisation in Argentina', pp. 67–86 in Organization for Economic Cooperation and Development, *Privatisation in Asia, Europe, and Latin America* (Paris: OECD, 1996).

Harvard Electricity Policy Group, 'Survey of ISO Governance Structures', photocopy, July 1996.

Heller, W.B., and M.D. McCubbins, 'Politics, Institutions, and Outcomes: Electricity Regulation in Argentina and Chile', *Policy Reform* 1 (1996): 357–87.

Hendrix, S., 'A Capital Idea in Bolivia', *The Wall Street Journal*, 22 September 1995: A15.

Henisz, W.J., 'The Institutional Environment for International Investment', *Economics and Politics* 12 (2000): 1–31.

Hill, A., and M.A. Abdala, 'Argentina: The Sequencing of Privatization and Regulation', ch. 6 in B. Levy and P.T. Spiller (eds), *Regulations, Institutions and Commitment: Comparative Studies of Telecommunications* (Cambridge: Cambridge University Press, 1996).

Hinchberger, B., 'Privatization Becomes a State Affair', *Institutional Investor*, December 1996: 123–6.

Hinich, M.J., and M.C. Munger, *Ideology and the Theory of Political Choice* (Ann Arbor, MI: University of Michigan Press, 1994).

Hira, A., *Ideas and Economic Policy in Latin America: Regional, National, and Organizational Case Studies* (Westport, CT: Praeger, 1998).

Horn, M., *The Political Economy of Public Administration: Institutional Choice in the Public Sector* (Cambridge: Cambridge University Press, 1995).

Institute for Management Development (IMD), *The World Competitiveness Yearbook 1997* (Lausanne: IMD, 1997).

Institute for Reform and the Informal Sector, University of Maryland, IRIS Data Set [computer file], (College Park, MD: no date; distributed by Political Risk Services, Inc.).

International Labour Organisation (ILO), *Yearbook of Labour Statistics* (Geneva: ILO, various years).

*International Private Power Quarterly* (*IPPQ*), 'Brazil', First Quarter 1998: 2–14.

Jaggers, K., and T.R. Gurr, Polity III: Regime Change and Political Authority, 1800–1994 [computer file] (Boulder: K. Jaggers/College Park, MD: T.R. Gurr, 1995, and Inter-university Consortium for Political and Social Research [distributor], 1996).

Johnson, B.T., K.R. Holmes and M. Kirkpatrick, *1998 Index of Economic Freedom* (Washington, DC: Heritage Foundation and The Wall Street Journal, 1998).

Johnson, K.F., 'Scholarly Images of Latin American Political Democracy in 1975', *Latin American Research Review* 11(2) (Spring 1976a): 129–40.

Johnson, K.F., 'Measuring the Scholarly Image of Latin American Democracy', in J.W. Wilkie (ed.), *Statistical Abstract of Latin America* 17 (1976b): 347–76.

Joskow, P., 'The Evolution of an Independent Power Sector and Competitive Procurement of New Generating Capacity', *Research in Law and Economics* 13 (1991): 63–100.

Kalt, J.P., and M.A. Zupan, 'Capture and Ideology in the Economic Theory of Politics', *American Economic Review* 74(3) (June 1984): 279–300.

Kalt, J.P., and M.A. Zupan, 'The Apparent Ideological Behavior of Legislators: On-the-Job Consumption or Just a Residual?', *Journal of Law and Economics* 33 (April 1990): 103–32.

Kaplan, M., 'Brazil's Energy Restructuring and Privatization: Under the Microscope', *Journal of Project Finance* (Summer 1998): 58–76.

Karp, J., 'AES Suspends Plans in Brazil For Power Plants', *The Wall Street Journal*, 9 May 2001.

Kearney, J.D., and T.W. Merrill, 'The Great Transformation of Regulated Industries Law', *Columbia Law Review* 98(6) (October 1998): 1323–409.

King, G., R.O. Keohane and S. Verba, *Designing Social Inquiry: Scientific Inference in Qualitative Research* (Princeton, NJ: Princeton University Press, 1994).

Kingstone, P.R., *Crafting Coalitions for Reform: Business Preferences, Political Institutions, and Neoliberal Reform in Brazil* (University Park, PA: Pennsylvania State University Press, 1999).

Kirkman, G.S., 'The Privatization of Light – Serviços de Eletricidade, SA', mimeo, John F. Kennedy School of Government, Harvard University, Cambridge, MA, October 1997.

Klesner, J.L., 'Presidential and Congressional Elections in Mexico, July 2000', *Electoral Studies* 21 (2002): 140–47.

Knight, J., *Institutions and Social Conflict* (New York: Cambridge University Press, 1992).

Kurian, G.T., *Fitzroy Dearborn Book of World Rankings* (London: Fitzroy Dearborn Publishers, 1998).

La Porta, R., F. López de Silanes, A. Shleifer, and R. Vishny, 'The Quality of Government', mimeo, Harvard University, Cambridge, MA, August 1998.

Laffont, J.-J., and J. Tirole, *A Theory of Incentives in Procurement and Regulation* (Cambridge, MA: MIT Press, 1993).

Landes, W.M., and R.A. Posner, 'The Independent Judiciary in an Interest-Group Perspective', *Journal of Law and Economics* 18 (1975): 875–901.

Leff, N.H., *Economic Policy-Making and Development in Brazil 1944–1964* (New York: Wiley & Sons, 1968).

Levy, B., and P. Spiller, 'A Framework for Resolving the Regulatory Problem', ch. 1 in B. Levy and P. Spiller (eds), *Regulations, Institutions, and Commitment: Comparative Studies of Telecommunications* (Cambridge: Cambridge University Press, 1996): 1–35.

López de Silanes, F., A. Shleifer, and R.W. Vishny, 'Privatization in the United States', *RAND Journal of Economics* 28(3) (Autumn 1997): 447–71.

Maia, F., 'The Brazilian Electricity Market', presentation to Harvard Electricity Policy Group, Cambridge, MA, 2 November 1998.

Maloney, W.F., 'Privatization with Share Diffusion: Popular Capitalism in Chile 1985–1988', ch. 7 in W. Baer and M.H. Birch (eds), *Privatization in Latin America: New Roles for the Public and Private Sectors* (Westport, CT: Praeger, 1994).

Mankiw, N.G., and M.D. Whinston, 'Free Entry and Social Inefficiency', *Rand Journal of Economics* 14(1): 48–58 (Spring 1986).

Martínez, J., and A. Díaz, *Chile: The Great Transformation* (Washington, DC: Brookings Institution/United Nations Research Institute for Social Development, 1996).

Mas-Colell, A., M.D. Whinston, and J. Green, *Microeconomic Theory* (New York: Oxford University Press, 1995).

Maxfield, S., *Gatekeepers of Growth: The International Political Economy of Central Banking in Developing Countries* (Princeton, NJ: Princeton University Press, 1997).

Maxfield, S., 'Brazilian Politics Brought Down the Real', *The Wall Street Journal*, 1 February 1999: A15.

McGuire, J.W., *Peronism without Perón: Unions, Parties and Democracy in Argentina* (Stanford, CA: Stanford University Press, 1997).

McQuerry, E., 'Private Sector Responses to Economic Liberalization Policies in Brazil: A Look within São Paulo's Capital Goods Sector', *Revista de Economia Política* 16(3) (July–September 1996): 31–53.

Messick, R.E., 'Judicial Reform and Economic Development: A Survey of the Issues', *World Bank Research Review* 14(1) (February 1999): 117–36.

Messick, R.E., and K. Kimura, *World Survey of Economic Freedom 1995–96: A Freedom House Study* (New York: Transaction, 1996).

Mexico, National Government, Secretaría de Energía, 'Policy Proposal for Structural Reform of the Mexican Electricity Industry', Mexico, n.d.

Moffett, M., 'Sour Juice: In Brazil, a Utility Dims Public's Enthusiasm for Privatizations', *The Wall Street Journal*, 27 April 1998: A1, A10.

Moguillansky, G., 'La gestión privada y la inversión en el sector eléctrico chileno' [Private Management and Investment in the Chilean Electricity Sector] United Nations Economic Comisión for Latin America and the Caribbean (ECLAC)/Comisión Económica para América Latina y el Caribe (CEPAL), Serie Reformas Económicas No. 1, 1997 (available at www.eclac.org).

Molano, W.T., *The Logic of Privatization: The Case of Telecommunications in the Southern Cone of Latin America* (Stamford, CT: Greenwood Press, 1997).

Morales, J.A., 'Democracy, Economic Liberalism, and Structural Reform in Bolivia', ch. 5 in W. Baer and M.H. Birch (eds), *Privatization in Latin America: New Roles for the Public and Private Sectors* (Westport, CT: Praeger, 1994).

Morales, J.A., 'Economic Policy in Bolivia after the Transition to Democracy', ch. 2 in J.A. Morales and G. McMahon (eds), *Economic Policy and the Transition to Democracy: the Latin American Experience* (London: Macmillan, 1996).

Moulián, T., and P. Vergara, 'Ideología y políticas económicas en Chile, 1973–1978' [Ideology and economic policies in Chile 1973–1978], *Cuadernos CIEPLAN*, June 1980: 65–119.

Murillo, M.V., 'Union Politics, Market-Oriented Reforms, and the Reshaping of Argentine Corporatism', ch. 3 in D.A. Chalmers (ed.), *The New Politics of Inequality in Latin America: Rethinking Participation and Representation* (Oxford: Oxford University Press, 1997).

Murillo, M.V., 'Conviction versus Necessity: Public Utility Privatization in Argentina, Chile and Mexico', paper presented at the 97th Annual

Meeting of the American Political Science Association, San Francisco, August 30–September 2, 2001.

Newbery, D.M., *Privatization, Restructuring, and Regulation of Network Utilities* (Cambridge, MA: MIT Press, 1999).

Noll, R.G., 'Economic Perspectives on the Politics of Regulation', in R. Schmalensee and R. Willig (eds), *Handbook of Industrial Organization*, vol. II (Amsterdam: North-Holland, 1989): 1253–87.

Noll, R.G., 'Telecommunications Reform in Developing Countries', Working Paper 99-10 (November 1999), AEI–Brookings Joint Center for Regulatory Studies.

North, D., *Institutions, Institutional Change, and Economic Performance* (Cambridge: Cambridge University Press, 1990).

North, D., and R.P. Thomas, *The Rise of the Western World: A New Economic History* (Cambridge: Cambridge University Press, 1973).

Olaya, J., and S. Popik, 'The Political Management of Economic Transitions: Privatizing the Argentine Mail', mimeo, Kennedy School of Government, Harvard University, Cambridge, MA, 1998.

Olson, M., *The Logic of Collective Action: Public Goods and the Theory of Groups* (Cambridge, MA: Harvard University Press, 1965).

Ostrom, E., *Governing the Commons: The Evolution of Institutions for Collective Action* (Cambridge: Cambridge University Press, 1990).

Palermo, V., and M. Novaro, *Política y poder en el gobierno de Menem* [Politics and power in the Menem administration], (Buenos Aires: Grupo Editorial Norma, 1996).

Paredes, R., 'Privatización y regulación: lecciones de la experiencia chilena' [Privatization and regulation: Lessons from the Chilean experience], pp. 217–48 in O. Muñoz (ed.), *Después de la privatización: Hacia el estado regulador* (Santiago de Chile: CIEPLAN, 1993).

Paredes, R.D., 'Evaluating the Cost of Bad Regulation in Newly Privatized Sectors: The Chilean Case', *Revista de Análisis Económico* 10(2) (November 1995): 89–112.

Payne, L.A., 'Brazilian Business and the Democratic Transition: New Attitudes and Influence', ch. 6 in L.A. Payne and E. Bartell (eds), *Business and Democracy in Latin America* (Pittsburgh: University of Pittsburgh Press, 1995).

Pearson, M., 'Capitalization: The Politics of Privatization in Bolivia', mimeo, John F. Kennedy School of Government, Harvard University, Cambridge, MA, October 1997.

Persson, T., and G. Tabellini, 'Is Inequality Harmful for Growth?' *American Economic Review* 84(3) (June 1994): 600–621.

Pires, J.C.L., 'The Reform Process within the Brazilian Electricity Sector', mimeo, BNDES/PNUD, n.d.

Powell, W.W., and P.J. DiMaggio (eds), *The New Institutionalism in Organizational Analysis* (Chicago: University of Chicago Press, 1991).

Power Finance & Risk, 'Mexico's IPP Program', 25 November 2001 (www.iipower.com, downloaded 6 February 2002).

Przeworski, A., and H. Teune, *The Logic of Comparative Social Inquiry* (New York: Wiley-Interscience, 1970).

Rausch, A.E., 'Monitoring and Regulatory Aspects of Privatization in Argentina', in V.V. Ramanadham (ed.), *Privatization and After: Monitoring and Regulation* (London: Routledge, 1994).

Remmer, K., 'The Politics of Neo-liberal Economic Reform in South America 1980–1994', *Studies in Comparative International Development* 33(2) (1998): 3–29.

Revollo, A.C., 'Reflections on the Politics of Reform', *ESMAP Annual Report 1998* (Washington, DC: The World Bank, 1998).

Roberts, K.M., 'Neoliberalism and the Transformation of Populism in Latin America: The Peruvian Case', *Word Politics* 48(1) (October 1995): 82–116.

Roca, J.L., *Fisonomía del regionalismo boliviano* [Physiognomy of Bolivian regionalism], (La Paz: Editorial Los Amigos del Libro, 1980).

Rodríguez Padilla, V., 'Impacto de la reforma económica sobre las inversiones de la industria eléctrica en México: el regreso del capital privado como palanca de desarrollo' [The impact of economic reform on investment in the electricity industry in Mexico: The return of private capital as lever to development], United Nations Economic Commission for Latin America and the Caribbean (ECLAC)/Comisión Económica para América Latina y el Caribe (CEPAL), Serie Reformas Económicas, No.18, February 18, 1999.

Rodrik, D., 'The Positive Economics of Policy Reform', *American Economic Review (AEA Papers and Proceedings)*, 83(2) (May 1993): 356–61.

Rodrik, D., 'The Rush to Free Trade in the Developing World: Why So Late? Why Now? Will It Last?', ch. 10 in F. Sturzenegger and M. Tommasi (eds), *The Political Economy of Policy Reform* (Cambridge, MA: MIT Press, 1998).

Rowat, M.D., 'Competition Policy in Latin America: Legal and Institutional Issues', ch.8 in J. Faundez (ed.), *Good Government: Legal and Institutional Reform in Developing Countries* (London: St. Martin's Press, 1997).

Rufin, C., 'Institutional Change in the Electricity Industry: A Comparison of Four Latin American Cases', Discussion Paper, Belfer Center for Science and International Affairs, John F. Kennedy School of Government, Harvard University, Cambridge, MA, December 1999.

Sánchez, C.E. (Under-Secretary of Economy and Public Works and Services, Argentine Federal Government), Speech to Argentine Privatization Convention 1991. In: Bureau de Investigaciones Empresariales, *Privatizaciones en Argentina* [Privatization in Argentina] (Buenos Aires: BIE, 1991).

Schneider, B.R., 'The Politics of Privatization in Brazil and Mexico: Variations on a Statist Theme', ch. 14 in E. Suleiman and J. Waterbury (eds), *The Political Economy of Public Sector Reform and Privatization* (Princeton, NJ: Princeton University Press, 1990).

Schneider, B.R., 'The Career Connection: A Comparative Analysis of Bureaucratic Preferences and Insulation', *Comparative Politics* (April 1993): 331–50.

Schneider, B.R., 'Big Business and the Politics of Economic Reform: Confidence and Concertation in Brazil and Mexico', ch. 7 in S. Maxfield and B.R. Schneider (eds), *Business and the State in Developing Countries* (Ithaca, NY: Cornell University Press, 1997).

Scott, W.R., and J.W. Meyer (eds), *Institutional Environments and Organizations: Structural Complexity and Individualism* (Thousand Oaks, CA: Sage, 1994).

Shapiro, C., and R.D. Willig, 'Economic Rationales for the Scope of Privatization', ch. 3 in E.N. Suleiman and J. Waterbury (eds), *The Political Economy of Public Sector Reform and Privatization* (Boulder, CO: Westview, 1990).

Shleifer, A., and R.W. Vishny, 'Politicians and Firms', *Quarterly Journal of Economics* (1994): 995–1025.

Shleifer, A., and R.W. Vishny, *The Grabbing Hand: Government Pathologies and Their Cures* (Cambridge, MA: Harvard University Press, 1998).

Shugart, M.S., and J.M. Carey, *Presidents and Assemblies: Constitutional Design and Electoral Dynamics* (Cambridge: Cambridge University Press, 1992).

Sigmund, P., 'Chile: Privatization, Reprivatization, Hyperprivatization', ch. 15 in E.N. Suleiman and J. Waterbury (eds), *The Political Economy of Public Sector Reform and Privatization* (Boulder, CO: Westview, 1990).

Silva, E., 'From Dictatorship to Democracy: The Business-State Nexus in Chile's Economic Transformation 1975–1994', *Comparative Politics* (1996a): 299–319.

Silva, E., *The State and Capital in Chile: Business Elites, Technocrats, and Market Economics* (Boulder, CO: Westview, 1996b).

Silva, P., 'Technocrats and Politics in Chile: From the Chicago Boys to the CIEPLAN Monks', *Journal of Latin American Studies* 23(2) (1991): 385–410.

Silver, S., 'Mexico Reneges on Plans to Cut Electricity Subsidy', *Financial Times*, 7 February 2002a.

Silver, S., 'Mexico Stops Power Sell-off', *Financial Times*, 27 April 2002b.

Sims, C., 'To Argentines, Judges Are Often Biggest Lawbreakers', *New York Times*, 19 August 1997: A8.

Sims, C., 'Workers Bitter at Pay and Privatization Tie Up Bolivian Capital', *New York Times*, 28 March 1998: A7.

Sola, L., 'The State, Structural Reform, and Democratization in Brazil', ch. 6 in W. Baer and M.H. Birch (eds), *Privatization in Latin America: New Roles for the Public and Private Sectors* (Westport, CT: Praeger, 1994).

Spiller, P., 'Institutions and Regulatory Commitment in Utilities' Privatization', *Industrial and Corporate Change* 2(3) (1993): 387–450.

Spiller, P., 'Institutions and Commitment', *Industrial and Corporate Change* 5(2) (1996): 421–52.

Spiller, P.T., and L. Viana Martorell, 'How Should It Be Done? Electricity Regulation in Argentina, Brazil, Uruguay, and Chile', ch. 3 in R. Gilbert and E.P. Kahn (eds), *International Comparisons of Electricity Regulation* (Cambridge: Cambridge University Press, 1996).

Stephenson, M., 'Judicial Independence: What It Is, How It Can Be Measured, Why It Occurs', World Bank, n.d. (www1.worldbank.org/publicsector/legal/judicialindependence.htm, accessed on 19 August 2002).

Standard & Poor's, 'United Mexican States', Sovereign Ratings Service, November 1999.

Stigler, G., 'The Theory of Economic Regulation', *Bell Journal of Economics* 2 (1971): 3–21.

Stokes, S., 'Public Opinion and Market Reforms: The Limits of Economic Voting', *Comparative Political Studies* 29(5) (1996): 499–519.

Stokes, S.C., *Mandates and Democracy: Neoliberalism by Surprise in Latin America* (New York: Cambridge University Press, 2001).

Suleiman, E.N., and J. Waterbury (eds), *The Political Economy of Public Sector Reform and Privatization* (Boulder, CO: Westview, 1990)

Sullivan, M.J., *Measuring Global Values: The Ranking of 162 Countries* (Stamford, CT: Greenwood Press, 1991).

Taylor, C.L., and D.A. Jodice, *The World Handbook of Political and Social Indicators III: 1948–1977* (Köln: Zentralarchiv für Empirische Sozialforschung 1982, in conjunction with Wissenschaftszentrum-Berlin, and Inter-university Consortium for Political and Social Research [distributor], 1983).

Teichman, J.A., *Privatization and Political Change in Mexico* (Pittsburgh: University of Pittsburgh Press, 1995).

Teichman, J.A., 'Mexico and Argentina: Economic Reform and Technocratic Decision Making', *Studies in Comparative International Development* 32(1) (Spring 1997): 31–55.

Téllez Kuenzler, L., 'The Mexican Electricity Industry', *World Energy* 2(2) (1999).

Tendler, J., *Electric Power in Brazil: Entrepreneurship in the Public Sector* (Cambridge, MA: Harvard University Press, 1968).

Thomas, S., and M. Tiomno Tolmasquim, 'Privatise and Be Damned', *FT Energy Economist*, December 1997: 3–7.

Tornell, A., 'Economic Growth and Decline with Endogenous Property Rights', *Journal of Economic Growth* 2 (September 1997): 219–50.

Torres, C., 'Regulatory Schemes and Investment Behavior in Transmission of Electricity: The Case of Argentina', *Revista de Análisis Económico* 10(2) (November 1995): 203–35.

Transparency International, '1998 Corruption Perceptions Index' (accessed on 4 October 1998) (www.transparency.de/documents/cpi).

Tsebelis, G., *Nested Games: Rational Choice in Comparative Politics* (Berkeley: University of California Press, 1990).

United Nations, Department for Economic and Social Information and Policy Analysis, Statistics Division 19*95 Energy Statistics Yearbook* (New York: United Nations, 1997).

Verbitsky, H., 'Argentines Tire of Menem's Politicized Justice', *The Wall Street Journal*, 13 March 1998: A17.

Verma, S.K., 'Competitive Markets for Electricity in Brazil', Policy Analysis Exercise, John F. Kennedy School of Government, Harvard University, Cambridge, MA, 1997.

Verner, J.G., 'The Independence of Supreme Courts in Latin America: A Review of the Literature', *Journal of Latin American Studies* 16: 463–506 (1984).

Vickers, J., and G. Yarrow, *Privatization: An Economic Analysis* (Cambridge, MA: MIT Press, 1988).

Vispo, A., *Los entes de regulación: problemas de diseño y contexto. Aportes para un urgente debate en la Argentina* [Regulatory entities: Design and context problems. Contributions to an urgent debate in Argentina], (Buenos Aires: Grupo Editorial Norma, 1999).

Warn, K., 'Argentina Tries to Do Justice to Demands for Legal Reform', *Financial Times*, 16 January 1997: 4.

Waterbury, J., *Exposed to Innumerable Delusions: Public Enterprise and State Power in Egypt, India, Mexico, and Turkey* (Cambridge: Cambridge University Press, 1993).

Weingast, B.R., K.A. Shepsle, and C. Johnsen, 'The Political Economy of Benefits and Costs: A Neoclassical Approach to Distributive Politics', *Journal of Political Economy* 89(5) (1981): 642–64.

Werneck, R.L.F., 'The Uneasy Steps Toward Privatization in Brazil', ch. 4 in W.E. Glade, *Privatization of Public Enterprises in Latin America* (New York: International Center for Economic Growth, 1991).

White, M.W., 'Power Struggles: Explaining Deregulatory Reforms in Electricity Markets', *Brookings Papers on Economic Activity, Microeconomics* 1996: 201–67.

Williamson, O.E., *The Economic Institutions of Capitalism* (New York: Free Press, 1985).

Wionczek, M.S., 'Electric Power: The Uneasy Partnership', ch. 1 in R. Vernon (ed.), *Public Policy and Public Enterprise in Mexico* (Cambridge, MA: Harvard University Press, 1964).

World Bank, 'Bolivia: Private Power Generation and Transmission', Report No. 137/91, Energy Sector Management Assistance Programme, January 1992.

World Bank, 'The World Bank's Role in the Electric Power Sector: Policies for Effective Institutional, Regulatory, and Financial Reform', World Bank Policy Paper, Washington, DC, 1993a.

World Bank, *Argentina's Privatization Program: Experience, Issues, and Lessons* (Washington, DC: Development in Practice Series, World Bank, 1993b).

World Bank, World Tables of Economic and Social Indicators 1950–1992 [computer file], (World Bank, International Economics Department, 1993, and Inter-university Consortium for Political and Social Research [distributor], 1993c).

World Bank, 'Argentina – Reforming Provincial Utilities: Issues, Challenges and Best Practice', Report No. 15063-AR, Infrastructure Division, Country Department I, Latin America and the Caribbean Region, 6 June 1996a.

World Bank, *From Plan To Market* (New York: Oxford University Press for the World Bank, 1996b).

World Bank, *1998 World Development Indicators* (Washington, DC: World Bank, 1998).

World Economic Forum, *The Global Competitiveness Report 1997* (Geneva: World Economic Forum, 1997).

Yajima, M., *Deregulatory Reforms of the Electricity Supply Industry* (New York: Quorum Books, 1997).

Yergin, D., and J. Stanislaw, *The Commanding Heights: The Battle between Government and the Marketplace That Is Remaking the Modern World* (New York: Simon & Schuster, 1998).

Zelner, B.A., and W.J. Henisz, 'Politics and Infrastructure Investment', mimeo, Georgetown University and University of Pennsylvania, September 2000.

# Index